ON YOUR OWN

ON YOUR OWN

A Woman's Guide to Building a Business

Second Edition

Laurie B. Zuckerman

UPSTART PUBLISHING COMPANY, INC.
The Small Business Publishing Company

Published by Upstart Publishing Company, Inc.
a division of Dearborn Publishing Group, Inc.
155 North Wacker Drive
Chicago, Illinois 60606-1719
(800)235-8866 or (312)836-4400

Library of Congress Cataloging-in-Publication Data

Zuckerman, Laurie
        On your own : a woman's guide to building a business / Laurie B.
    Zuckerman. — 2nd ed.
              p.   cm.
        Includes index.
        ISBN 0-936894-52-0
        1. New business enterprises. Women in business. I. Title.
    HD62.5.Z83   1993
    658.1'141'082—dc20   93-26395
                                                                 CIP

Printed in the United States of America
10 9 8 7 6 5 4

For a complete catalog of Upstart's small business publications, call (800) 235-8866.

This book is dedicated to my daughters, Jennifer and Leslie.

Table of Contents

Introduction to the Second Edition

Much has changed in the four years since I wrote *On Your Own.*

In 1989 I had one infant and had never actually run a business and cared for a child at the same time. I now have two children and have been actively attempting to balance the care of my business, my children, my husband, my household and myself.

Caring for two children is very different from caring for one and has significantly influenced my ideas about balancing work and family. For those of us who cannot afford a full-time housekeeper and who value having a significant role in raising our children, this balancing act can be tenuous at best and soul-searing at worst. What do you do when you have a sick child, no immediate family to support you, have called every possible backup babysitter (including neighbors you haven't spoken to all year—I was desperate!), and have a critical client meeting you must attend?! The original version of *On Your Own* addressed questions like this in very simple terms; this edition addresses them in all their complexity.

In 1989 I believed business planning was primarily done with the logical left brain. I have now learned for myself that logic and rationality are only part of successful planning. The other parts—equally as important—are our creativity and intuition, and *On Your Own* has been adjusted to reflect this.

In 1989 I did not yet recognize the powerful role our unconscious mind plays in the success of our businesses. As women, we often find this in the negative self-talk that plagues our businesses and our lives. (You know, that little voice inside us that is forever saying: "He disagrees so I must be wrong" or "It's not feminine to build a big business or to care about money" or "I don't know what he's talking about so maybe I shouldn't be a business owner.") I have updated *On Your Own* in a few appropriate places to help you become more aware of these self-defeating behaviors so you can stop them and begin to make choices that are more beneficial for you.

In 1989 the Decade for Women had not yet begun; Anita Hill had not yet raised our collective anger or frustration about the plight of women in a man's world; Deborah Tannen had not yet published her bestselling book *You Just Don't Understand,* which acknowledged and popularized the notion that men and women speak and behave differently *and that that's OK;* Joline Godfrey had not yet expounded on the special qualities women bring to a business in her outstanding book *Our Wildest Dreams;* empowerment was discussed in but a few closed circles, if at all; the Mommytrack was being disparaged. In short, most of us were still not willing to even whisper that there might be differences between men and women business owners.

I still vividly remember comments I received from angry male and female colleagues as I was writing *On Your Own*. Some literally screamed at me: "Why are you writing a book for women?" "How can you say there are differences in how men and women should run their businesses?" (Which was not what I was saying at all). I discovered that even raising the idea that men and women might be different was frightening to both men (they expected us to use these differences to get special treatment) and women (they were appropriately fearful that men would cite differences as reasons for unequal treatment of women).

In four short years the world has changed, and I have updated *On Your Own* to reflect these changes and to address comments from readers. Some of the differences include:

- An expanded section on "The Realities of Owning a Business"

- A new section entitled "Validating Your Intuition"

- An update on banking and credit discrimination against women (surprisingly different from four years ago)

- The latest programs offered by the Small Business Administration and ways to access them

- A new appendix which details contacts, technical assistance programs and *financing sources* (yes, financing sources!) available for women from federal and state agencies. This data is listed on a state-by-state basis, making it easy for you to find the pertinent information.

- A new appendix with two complete business plans, one for a retail business and one for a consulting business.

Prior readers have made the following comments and suggestions for you:

"I wish I would have taken 'The Realities of Owning a Business' more seriously. Please highlight it in the new edition."

"I learned so much from the section on 'Networking'; it greatly impacted how I marketed my business."

"Please, please stress the importance of keeping good sales tax records, right from the start. I wish I'd done it."

"If they need money, have them read Section Three first so they can immediately start developing a relationship with their banker."

"I found Section Two overwhelming, but necessary. Tell them how important it is. Also emphasize Section Three."

"Add more examples about self-deprecating comments we make to ourselves. We all do it, and we need to see it more clearly so we can finally STOP."

I used to believe everyone could benefit from having their own business. I now believe it's right for some, not for others. I hope this book will help you make the right choices for yourself and then **plan accordingly**. Good luck!

Preface

On Your Own: A Woman's Guide to Building a Business is a resource for women who want to start, improve or expand their businesses but who aren't sure how to do it or, perhaps, even where to begin. It describes how to get started, how to plan a business, how to successfully implement the plan and how to get financing.

Other business planning guides identify the questions that need to be answered in order to build a business. *On Your Own: A Woman's Guide to Building a Business* provides the tools necessary for you to *understand and answer* those questions.

I've addressed such typical business issues as:

- Your definition of success

- Developing your product or service

- Researching your market and competition

- How to manage your business

- Financial management

- How to get money

In addition, this book highlights the special needs of women in business.

- It is written in clear, concise language which you will understand even if you have no business background.

- It discusses some of the trade-offs you will face in business as you deal with your responsibilities as primary caregiver to children or elderly parents and as you balance your home life with your business life.

- It deals straightforwardly with prejudices against women in the male-dominated business world.

- It encourages you to take action.

Building a business is not easy. It takes perseverance, resourcefulness, hard work, energy, independence, perseverance, perseverance and perseverance.

And it takes knowledge.

Many of us have the traits required to build a business, but we lack the knowledge. If you are seeking the know-how to build your business, this book is for you.

How to Use This Book

This book is divided into three parts, some or all of which may be useful to you depending upon your specific needs. The first part, Getting Started, gives you guidance on how to get the information you need for going into business and writing a business plan and how to get motivated when the going gets tough. Read it before you begin your plan. Then re-read it when you get stuck in the planning process and frustrated with your business.

The second part, The Business Plan, describes the business plan itself. It defines the concepts you need to understand to be in business and provides instructions and worksheets on how to think through your business and prepare your plan. When you have finished this section, you will have a complete coherent document which serves your needs and the needs of others who may require information about your business. You may also want to refer to the sample business plans in Appendix II as you prepare your own plan.

The section entitled Using Your Business Plan provides specific action steps for using your business plan to manage your business. In addition, I've offered guidance on how to use your business plan to prepare your financing proposal.

Lastly, there is valuable resource information in the appendices. In particular, Appendix III lists the agencies within your state which can help you find technical assistance and financing for your business.

This book is written primarily for businesses just getting started; however, the business principles are the same whether you're starting a new business or improving an existing one.

A Brief Note on Funding Sources

Throughout this book the term "funding sources" is used to describe those people who could provide the money you need to finance your business. These funding sources might include yourself, your relatives, your friends and other acquaintances. These are the most often used funding sources for small businesses.

However, you may be hoping a third party will be willing to finance your business, such as a bank or an outside investor. You may have heard the term "venture capitalist" and be hoping to find one of them to help you take your great idea and turn it into a profitable business.

Unfortunately, getting money is not that easy, and myths for finding "easy start-up money" abound. These myths are discussed in the chapter on Using Your Business Plan to Get Financing. If you need money quickly, I suggest you read Chapter Eight first and get a clear understanding of what's involved in financing your business. Also, the chapter describes ways to get to know your banker—you would be wise to start this process now.

## PART 1

Getting Started

* Business idea - first aid kits specifically assembled for CEA providers/centers

* My business vision - to ensure that teach parent the peace of mind of being knowing that their children are being well cared for.

## CHAPTER ONE

The Realities
of Owning a Business

"I wish I had read this chapter more thoroughly and taken it more seriously." This is by far the most frequent comment I received about the first edition of *On Your Own*. As with any job, owning a business can be both wonderful and difficult, but it is generally different from what most people expect. I hope you will read this chapter and take it seriously as you start or build your business.

A study of women entrepreneurs is a study of contrasts. Stories range from Liz Claiborne, who started a multibillion dollar clothing business, to Julie Rosso and Sheila Lukins, who started the Silver Palate gourmet food business in their kitchen and turned it into an eight million dollar business in 11 years, to the many, many women who start small, part-time businesses that provide them with a modest income and flexible working hours.

One thing is certain: Owning your own business will have an impact on your personal life. The nature of that impact depends very strongly on the nature of your business and on how you choose to manage your life. Here are three examples:

• Dolores Pento is trying to get her children's accessories manufacturing business off the ground. Since she is the sole employee of the business, she is responsible for developing her products, making sales calls, preparing financial projections, writing letters to prospective customers, typing the letters and buying the stamps, having her logo designed and printed, working with business counselors, buying the fabric, cutting, sewing, packing and mailing the product, and more.

Dolores has three pre-school children and has primary responsibility for their care. In addition, she cleans the house and puts dinner on the table, and she must bring in income for the family to meet its monthly budget.

Dolores had no idea when she started her business that it would take up so much of her time. In fact, she started it so she would have *more* time to spend with her children. Nothing could be further from reality.

Dolores believes in her business, but she is overcommitted, overtaxed and overstressed.

• Louise Tucker used to spend 50 plus hours a week at her job with a large corporation. She was required to be at the office from 7:30 A.M. to 4:00 P.M. and was usually there much longer. On this schedule Louise was very concerned about successfully combining childrearing and work.

One thing is certain: Owning your own business will have an impact on your personal life.

Two years ago, Louise started her own consulting business. She worked very long hours the first year getting it going and then had a baby. Louise took two full months off from work and started back to work slowly—first two half days a week, then two full days a week, and so on until she worked her way up to five days a week four months after the baby was born.

Louise now works long hours again, but on her own schedule. She picks up her daughter from the babysitter at 4:15 P.M. every day and occasionally takes an unexpected day off when her daughter is sick. If she needs to, she works in the evening after the baby is sleeping.

Louise has had to turn down some jobs because of her schedule—in fact, she now earns roughly half the income she received as a full-time employee. Most of the time, her time with her daughter is worth more to her than extra money, though sometimes she feels frustrated at her business' lack of progress. Most importantly to Louise, she knows that turning down work won't hinder her own promotion possibilities, though it will definitely affect the growth rate of her company.

• Lynn Darien was a critical care nurse when her father asked if she wanted to take over his almost-bankrupt manufacturing business. In three years Lynn has turned the business around: it is now profitable and growing. Her management style is very different from her father's. In fact, many long-time employees say "this is the best feeling the company has ever had." Lynn is very proud of her role in the business and is committed to seeing the company grow.

Lynn's older daughter is 11 and is a latchkey child. Every day she comes home on the school bus, lets herself into the house and takes care of herself for the three hours until Mom or Dad arrives home.

Lynn's younger daughter is three years old and goes daily to a babysitter. When the separation from her young child became especially painful, Lynn tried bringing her to the office, but that was simply not workable: the toddler was too distracting, both for herself and her employees, and many of her customers thought less of her business when they heard a child crying in the background. Lynn now finds the daily separation times (dropping off her daughter and picking her up) very difficult, but during the workday she is consumed with business and rarely thinks of her.

When Lynn meets new people outside of work, she typically does not tell them about her business. Most people—both men and women—find it too threatening or intimidating. Consequently, Lynn has no one to commiserate with during the hard times. Lynn loves her business, but deep inside she is often lonely.

These three situations highlight some of the realities—*and the tradeoffs*—of owning your own business.

Owning a business is a time-consuming and stressful occupation. Many people think of business ownership as a way to get paid for doing what they love. This is true if what you love to do is run a business. Think of business ownership as taking on a new job—the job of running your business. Included in your job description might be some or all of the following:

• If a customer imposes a tough deadline, you must see to it that the work is done on time.

- If an employee calls in sick, you must make sure her work is performed by someone else (usually you).

- If your clients will only work with you during the evenings or on weekends, you must be available at those times.

- If you're just getting started and can't afford employees, you must do all the work of the business yourself.

- If you do have employees, you carry the responsibility not only for your own paycheck but for theirs as well.

Rarely do business owners leave their problems at the office. When your paycheck, your savings and the livelihoods of the people who work for you are on the line, you learn a whole new meaning for words like "hard work" and "commitment."

There are some businesses, like consulting or other freelance service businesses, that are conducive to more flexible working hours. But you usually trade off in income and business growth what you gain in flexibility.

What makes all this more difficult is that as women, unlike our male counterparts, *we don't have wives.* We are the ones with primary responsibility for child care, home care, putting dinner on the table, doing the laundry, arranging for holiday meals, getting the kids to wherever they need to be, dealing with sick children, caring for aging parents and even for keeping the lines of communication open in our marriages.

Some of us want these multiple roles. We want to spend time with our children or our parents without having to worry that it will hurt our careers. We want the self-fulfillment and we need the money that a job or business brings, but we also want to lead balanced lives.

It is not easy to deal effectively with the changes in our lives that are brought about by owning our own businesses. Here are some suggestions for managing despite them:

- *Accept that change will occur.* Owning a business will alter not only your available time but also the way you see yourself and the way others see you. Family and friendship dynamics will change. It may be a while (if ever) before your kids, your husband and your friends take your business seriously, and this can cause extra stress for everyone and self-doubt for you. You may have to negotiate with your family to get chores done that were traditionally your bailiwick. You may have to let some chores go entirely. These choices are not always pleasant, and you should give serious thought to whether you even want to deal with them before you start your business.

- *Learn how to manage your time.* There will always be far more to be done than time to do it. Prioritizing activities is important for every business owner, and it's especially critical if you want to lead a balanced life. There are entire books and training courses on how to manage your time, and you may want to avail yourself of them. In addition, I recommend the following: 1) Use a time management system. There are many available, and most can be purchased at your local office supply store. I use a combination of Day-Timer® and Planner

We want the self-fulfillment and we need the money that a job or business brings, but we also want to lead balanced lives.

Pads®. 2) Learn to say no. People will make multiple demands on your time, and they may all sound like reasonable, important requests, but you cannot do everything, and you are *not* a bad person if you occasionally take care of yourself instead of someone else.

• *Know in your heart that Superwoman does not exist.* As women, many of us believe that if we were only smart enough or organized enough or efficient enough, we could make this "balance thing" work out perfectly. I used to believe this, and it often left me feeling frustrated and anxious—like every time I had a business meeting scheduled and my young daughter unexpectedly got sick. With the birth of my second child, I finally faced the fact that life is filled with a continuous stream of difficult choices, and the best any of us can do is evaluate our options, make decisions that fit with our values and live with these decisions. Sometimes my decisions are wise, sometimes not. Often, knowing I've made a "right" choice doesn't take away my sadness or frustration about what I've given up. But for me, accepting that these choices are a part of life makes it easier to relax and cope *because I can't do everything.* (Of course, it *really* helps to have backup childcare alternatives *and* friends who support you through your choices.)

• *Find support people who can identify with your multiple roles.* Many women find that their old friends simply do not understand—or, worse, are intimidated by—their new role as business owner. For some, as soon as they begin raising a problem, these "friends" actually try to talk them out of being in business! During difficult times you need people who are understanding of your business issues, who can relate to your difficulty balancing business with home and who can give you fresh ideas for coping. Most of these people will likely be other women business owners with a family situation similar to yours. There is a whole section in this book dedicated to finding support people. I hope you will make the opportunity to find some because they add energy to you and your business when you most need it.

• *Get very clear about your goals and your priorities and structure your time to match.* For most of us there are trade-offs between business success and spending time with family and friends. For some, the balance tips toward the business and they strive to fulfill the American Dream of growing a multimillion dollar company out of a $500 investment. For others, the balance tips toward family and friends and they start a small, part-time service business in their home. For still others, the balance is just that—an even balance—and they start full-time businesses which do reasonably well and which they plan to build at a faster rate after their children leave the nest. Whatever your reason for starting a business, remember and re-commit to it when times get tough.

Ultimately, you will be happy with your life if you develop your own personal vision of success and plan for it. That's what this book is all about.

Owning a business can be difficult and time-consuming, but there are pay-offs. It is extremely gratifying to be responsible for the future of something larger than yourself. It's exhilarating to watch your business grow, knowing you did it. It's exciting to land that new contract or finish a job on time. It feels great to get that letter from the customer telling you what a wonderful job you did.

Owning a business can be pretty nerve-wracking at times, but much of the time it's very satisfying and downright fun.

Ultimately, you will be happy with your life if you develop your own personal vision of success and plan for it. That's what this book is all about.

SUPPORT PEOPLE

Most of us have had people in our lives who have provided the personal or moral support we needed to get through a difficult situation. We may have needed someone to talk to or to help us sort through our problems objectively or to provide advice and guidance. This kind of support is also appropriate in business. In fact, men do it all the time through the "Old Boy Network" or by having a mentor (i.e., a trusted advisor) or by hiring business advisors.

The value of having good support people cannot be overstated. In the business world support people can save you time and money and alleviate stress by:

- Providing guidance in areas of business with which you are unfamiliar—including answering the question "This is what he said—can you please explain it to me in English?"

- Telling you how they solved the problems you're experiencing now.

- Serving as an objective sounding board for your business ideas.

- Helping you stick to your plans and schedules. Nothing forces you to make that phone call you've been dreading like the knowledge that you'll be meeting with someone to discuss it.

- Providing moral support when things don't go as planned.

- Giving your business name out as a referral.

It is sometimes more difficult for women to find support people. Many men don't take our businesses seriously or they can't identify with some of our unique problems. Many women are intimidated by us, especially if we have even modestly successful businesses or are in non-traditional industries. Those of us who combine the roles of business owner and homemaker have precious little time for cultivating new relationships. And, since we are so used to the role of caregiver, many of us have difficulty asking for help.

Yet in many ways it can be easier for us to find support people because as children we were taught the value of connecting with people and we were trained to do it effectively and naturally. There are no magic formulas, only this knowledge: All outstanding businesspeople realize that the success of their business is dependent on sound, supportive relationships with others.

There are innumerable ways in which business people can support you.

Moral Support

They can provide you with moral support that will keep you going when the going gets tough (and it will). They are the people who encourage you when your best customer sues you for breach of contract or when the third bank turns down your loan application. They cheer for you when you get that huge new contract, and they'll drop everything to meet you for lunch when you're feeling unbearably lonely. If you are happily married and your spouse is supportive of your business, he is probably your most powerful moral supporter. Other moral supporters are likely to be other women entrepreneurs—and some male entrepreneurs—who know what it's like to be in your shoes.

One excellent way of getting moral support is by starting a Business Owner Success Team as outlined in *Teamworks*, by Barbara Sher and Annie Gottlieb (Part 2, Chapters Seven through Thirteen). Three years ago, I followed their "cookbook" instructions and created my own Success Team. We met every other week for two years, and all participants agreed that it was the most powerful business support we had during that time.

Technical Support

Technical support people can answer specific business questions based on their expertise and knowledge. For example:

- He quoted me $25 a page for typesetting. Is he ripping me off?

- Who is the best person at XYZ Bank to talk to about getting a loan?

- That prospective customer said she'd call me last Friday with her decision, and she hasn't called. What should I do now?

- He told me my inventory turnover is terrible and I need to closely monitor my receivables. What is he talking about?

- Any day now I know one of my best customers' kids is going to knock over a $200 vase. How would *you* handle that situation?

The best technical support people have first-hand knowledge of whatever problem you're struggling with.

The best technical support people have first-hand knowledge in whatever problem you're struggling with and can tell you what worked and didn't work for them and others. These people are invaluable. They keep you from tripping over the same landmines they did. They save you an enormous amount of time and money by keeping you from reinventing the wheel.

People in your industry make great technical support people. For example, if you can find someone in the same business who lives in a distant city, keep in contact by phone and support each other. People in similar but different businesses make great technical support people, and you don't have to worry that you're competing directly with them. For example, if you own a florist shop, you may get sound advice from someone who owns a gift shop or card store.

Some businesses create a Board of Advisors to provide them with technical support. Unlike a Board of Directors, a Board of Advisors has no legal liability for your business, rather its sole purpose is to help guide you through the mire and muck of building a business. Typically it is comprised of four to five people who meet once a quarter to review all aspects of your business that you are willing to share. Fees vary—some people will serve on these boards for free, some require modest payment and others may want a stake in your business. You select board members by evaluating your technical needs and bringing in people to plug any knowledge gaps in your business.

If you choose to create a Board of Advisors, make your request clear by stating the objectives, functions and time commitment of board members. Some of you may be wondering how you could possibly ask busy business owners to serve on your Board of Advisors. Rest assured that they will take your request as a compliment and will say no if they do not have the time.

There are several excellent organizations which have been specifically set up to provide free technical support to small business owners, including the Service Corps of Retired Executives (SCORE), your local Small Business Development Center (SBDC) or Small Business Institute (SBI) and the Small Business Administration (SBA). The end of this chapter provides additional information on what these organizations do and how you can contact them.

Believe it or not, bank loan officers are top-notch technical support people—and so are people who have gotten bank loans.

Mentors

Mentors are experienced businesspeople who take you under their wing and enthusiastically support you. More than answering a specific technical question, mentors help you solve problems. You can go to them even if you don't know what questions to ask, and they'll help you sift through the problem until you come up with a solution. In most cases, you don't find mentors—they find you. They see in you someone worthy of their respect, their time, and their support. These relationships are very hard to come by and very precious when you have them.

Many women in business have learned to use support people effectively. In my consulting business, I have a coach who guides me through the sales process, from making the initial sales presentations to preparing proposals to closing the sale. I also meet regularly with a goal-setting partner who helps me stick to my goals even when the going gets tough. And at different times I create other support systems that I call on for business guidance and moral support. Consider these other examples:

- Dee Burns writes newsletters. She has a group of people she can call on to help her effectively deal with suppliers and customers. Her supporters help her determine when she is getting incorrect information, when she is overpaying for supplies and so on.

- Before Donna Skoder started her business selling original artwork, she met one-on-one with more than 25 people to find out what she could expect once she opened her doors. For her first few months in business, she met weekly with her mentor who helped her deal with such issues as the mechanics of customer relations, business etiquette when attending meetings and how to get a loan.

- Jane Walks opened her women's clothing business two years ago. She still meets weekly with her mentor, who supports her in following her business plan, evaluating results and making changes when appropriate.

- Gina Poleo doesn't have support people, but is starting to wish she did. Her toy store is doing phenomenally well after only one year, but she resents the amount of time it takes to manage it; she wants to spend more time with her two young daughters. She wishes someone had told her what it takes to run a business before she started. Her friends don't understand what she's going through. Gina is beginning to recognize that she needs to talk to other businesswomen to ease her loneliness and to get fresh ideas for making time for her business *and* finding time for her kids.

The key to finding

support people is to

get out and meet

businesspeople.

The key to finding support people is to get out and meet businesspeople. Join service clubs, like Rotary or Kiwanis. Get involved with your local Chamber of Commerce or Regional Development Board. Serve on committees for business women's groups. Attend trade association meetings or business planning workshops. Call on your local SCORE chapter, SBDC or SBI.

This is called networking. The idea is:

• The more people you meet, the more likely you are to find people with whom you feel rapport.

• The larger your support network, the more likely you are to know someone who can help (or someone who knows someone who can help you) when you run into a specific problem. Or, conversely, since you can never predict what your problems will be, the more potential solutions you have on hand, the better.

The most effective networking is to serve on committees of business organizations or non-profit agencies where other people can see your leadership ability, your creativity, your ability to get things done, your reliability in meeting commitments and your talent in your field of endeavor—and where you can find other people doing the same thing.

Realistically, you can't spend all your time networking because you won't have enough time left over for your business. But it's vital that you set aside some time for networking—it will be a significant savings in the long run.

Some Guidelines for Effective Networking

1. *Relax.* The purpose of networking is to expand your circle of acquaintances, not to make a sales pitch. People often feel resentful when they're pushed to exchange business cards with someone they hardly know. Most of us connect better when we're being ourselves, rather than trying to be our image of the perfect businessperson, and the better we connect with people, the more likely they are to want to support us.

2. *Prepare, prepare, prepare.* The more prepared you are, the more confident and relaxed you will be. Decide on what you want to say about your business and rehearse it with a trusted friend or in front of the mirror. Think of some opening lines and practice them. "What business are you in?" usually works pretty well. Then think of at least five more questions you can ask to get the conversation going, such as: "How long have you been in business?" "How did you get into that business?" "I'm not familiar with your business. Tell me about it." "That sounds similar to what I'm doing. I'd like to discuss it further. Can we meet for lunch next week?" "I'm looking for organizations where I can meet other consultants (or retailers or manufacturers or customers). Has this one been valuable for you in that regard? How about other organizations?" By preparing in advance, you'll never be at a loss for conversation *and* you'll develop important new contacts.

   You may also want to set goals for each networking event as long as this does not deter you from relaxing and being yourself. Examples include:

- To learn how three new businesses operate.

- To find a woman in a similar business to yours.

- To meet and get business cards from five prospective customers.

- To spend at least five minutes talking to someone you've wanted to meet so that she or he knows who you are and what you do.

3. *Be professional.* As a business owner or a prospective business owner, you *are* a professional and you have as much to offer as anyone else in the room (even if you don't feel that way).

   - Introduce yourself. A simple "Hello, I'm Mary Smith" and a handshake will get the conversation going. If you're not used to shaking hands, practice.

   - Dress professionally. Wear a suit, a skirt and sweater outfit, or a professional-looking dress. If you're unsure what looks professional, look in current issues of women's business magazines or observe what other professional women are wearing. It may be a cliche, but the more professionally you dress, the more likely people are to take you seriously. Never wear anything even remotely sexy. You may get a lot of attention, but probably not the kind of attention you want.

   - There is often alcohol served at these functions. Don't overdo it. While you want to relax and enjoy the function, remember you are representing your business.

   - This is not the time to spill your guts about your business problems. Talk about your successes and your goals.

4. *Follow up appropriately.* This is the step that most people forget, and they lose the value of having attended the networking function in the first place. For example, if someone gives you a valuable piece of information, write a brief note thanking them for helping you. Or if someone seems like a potential client, call them and ask if you can make a formal sales presentation. Or if you meet someone with whom you just click, invite them out to lunch and get to know them better. Or send them newspaper and magazine articles which you believe would be of interest to them. You will find out soon enough if they would like to further the relationship.

   As a woman you must be careful that your overtures aren't misinterpreted when establishing a business relationship with a man. This is unfortunate, but it's true—just about any businesswoman will be able to tell you a few horror stories. Make sure that all your conversations are professional and clear as to your purpose.

5. *Nurture the relationships.* Supportive relationships don't just happen—they are nurtured. You've begun the process by meeting people and doing some initial follow up. Now you need to keep them informed of what you're doing so they can feel good about having helped you. For people who develop into good friends, treat them as you would any other good friends. For people whom you just don't have the time to get to know better, call them quarterly or semiannually. You're really just

maintaining the relationship so you can feel comfortable calling them if you need support.

A good rule is: always close the loop. If someone helps you, send them a note acknowledging their support. If someone gives you names of prospective clients, call them back and tell them whether or not it worked out for you. If someone suggests a solution to your problem, let them know how you resolved it. People love to help other people, but they want to know their help made a difference to you. Help them feel good about helping you.

People love to help other people, but they want to know their help made a difference to you.

Most people find it difficult to attend networking functions and even more difficult to do the follow-up that good networking requires, but they also find it gets easier with practice. And they know that it is a very effective way of meeting people who can support them with their business. Some people may call on you for support—networking is a two-way street. The important thing is that when you do encounter a problem, you'll be glad you already know people who can help you rather than trying to find help during a crisis.

There may be some of you who, even after you read all the benefits of seeking support, think "I don't need help." Or "It sounds like a great idea, but who would want to help me?" Or "I've met people I'd like to call for help, but I'm nervous about calling them."

If you find yourself thinking along these lines, I'd like to stress two things:

1. We *all* need help. We need it in ways and at times we can't predict. Every established businessperson knows that. Even if you don't believe it yet, force yourself to try it.

2. People love to help. They want to be needed, to feel useful. Truly making a difference in someone else's life is one of the biggest contributions anyone can make in this world. Let people help you. Then let them know they helped you by acknowledging their support.

Others of you may be thinking: "Where can I find the time to network when I have to run a business *and* care for a family?" My networking time was cut dramatically with the birth of my second child, but I still make time for it several times a month. Typically I combine networking with volunteer work for non-profit agencies so I can support my community while I expand my circle of acquaintances. I simply cannot afford to stop building my network.

Go to the meetings, follow up with the people you meet, and develop the relationships. Then call people and ask for help. You will be amazed at how much of a difference it will make in your business and in your life.

Hiring Support People

In addition to informal (unpaid) supporters, at some point every small business needs the advice of paid experts. These might include an accountant, an attorney, an insurance advisor, a bookkeeping service, an advertising agent, a marketing consultant and so on. I also include bankers in this category, not because you pay them (you don't—at least not directly), but because it is their job to help you by providing financial expertise and because you interview for and find your banker in much the same way you find other types of experts.

Of the paid support people, the big four are your accountant, your attorney, your insurance advisor and your banker. Some examples of areas in which they can help you are:

ACCOUNTANT:

Preparing tax returns

Keeping you informed of how the tax laws affect your business and your profits

Helping you set up record-keeping systems

Supporting you in developing your financial statements

Assisting you in complying with your tax-related obligations as an employer (e.g., Social Security tax, unemployment taxes, pension plans, etc.)

Helping you plan for retirement

ATTORNEY:

Helping you decide on the legal form of your business (i.e., sole proprietorship, partnership, corporation, etc.)

Registering your company name with the state or federal government, registering trademarks, assisting with patents and copyrights, etc.

Filing for incorporation

Doing a patent search

Assessing customer and supplier contracts for liability

Preparing non-disclosure agreements (i.e., agreements between you and other people or companies which require each of you to keep certain information confidential)

Advising you of any potential liability issues

INSURANCE ADVISOR:

Advising you and arranging for insurance coverage for:
- Liability on your premises
- Workers compensation
- Medical, disability and life insurance plans for you and your employees
- Errors and omissions, especially if you are in a consulting-type business

BANKER:

Reviewing your financial statements

Recommending how best to finance your business

Helping you through the loan process

Providing additional money management services

Depending on your business, you may or may not see a need for any of this help. But your accountant, your attorney, your insurance advisor and your banker can help you determine whether or not you have these or other needs. And if you're like most small business owners, at the time you really need help, you're usually in a crisis, and that's not a good time to start developing relationships with these important advisors.

How do you find good advisors? The best way is to ask other people you know in business. (That's one of the reasons for networking.) Find out who they're satisfied with as well as who has not met their needs. Also, one good advisor leads to another. Ask your accountant, for example, about good bankers or attorneys. As a last resort, try the Yellow Pages.

The big four are your accountant, your attorney, your insurance advisor and your banker.

Don't just hire a friend—hire the right person for your business.

Hiring business advisors should not be taken lightly. Here are some guidelines:

1. Interview at least three people in each category. Don't be intimidated—you are paying them and you should find someone you're satisfied with, someone who can meet your business' needs. Trust your instincts—if something feels wrong, it probably *is* wrong, even if you're not sure what the problem is.

   Here are some questions to ask:

   • *Have you ever worked with a business similar to mine?* Have them describe the business and how they helped it. See if the situation is really similar to yours.

   • *How long have you been in business?* Use your judgment here. People who've been in business for a long time have more experience but often cost more.

   • *May I have some references?* Try to get at least three. Then call them.

   • *Do you have any brochures or printed information about your company?* Printed material will help you compare options.

   • *What is your fee structure?* Price is one consideration in making your decision. (Remember, for your banker you're asking about loan or service fees. Bankers don't charge for their personal time.)

   • *When do you charge?* Most accountants and attorneys charge in 10- or 15-minute increments, and they start charging as soon as you walk in the door, even if you're only exchanging pleasantries. Many of them also charge for telephone time. Make sure you know what you'll be billed for before you enter into a relationship.

      When you set up the initial interview, state clearly that you are interviewing them—not looking for advice—and make sure there's no charge for the appointment.

2. Make your hiring decision based on who you feel could best meet your needs. You want someone who has worked with small businesses and someone who has dealt with situations similar to yours. You also want to hire someone with whom you have some rapport, since you will be seeking their guidance. But don't just hire a friend—hire the right person for your business.

   You may find an excellent attorney or accountant who has the right experience, but is biased against women in business. Chances are they will not give you the level of support you need. Steer clear of people like that—they are bad for your business and your morale.

3. Once you've made your decision, send a note to the other people you interviewed. Thank them for their time and explain you've selected someone else who you believe is the best match for your business. This is the professional thing to do.

4. After you've hired these specialists, meet with them at least twice a year. Keep them abreast of how your business is doing and how they can better support you.

Utilizing "Free" Support People

The federal government and many state governments have created programs to provide free (sometimes modestly priced) counseling and training to all small business owners and also specifically to women business owners. The contact people for all of these programs are listed by state in Appendix III so you can easily look up the programs that may be applicable to you.

Federal programs for women are administered through the Office of Women's Business Ownership (OWBO), an arm of the Small Business Administration (SBA). Please don't be intimidated by the myriad of acronyms and titles for government agencies; the OWBO people I've spoken with have been wonderfully helpful and supportive. Appendix III of this book lists the OWBO representatives around the country. Their specific programs include:

1. *Demonstration Project for Women Business Owners.* The SBA has set up 38 locations around the country to provide a wide range of assistance for women business owners in such subjects as business planning, employee management, marketing, recordkeeping and financing. While the program is aimed at economically and socially disadvantaged women, anyone can avail themselves of this support. Many of the programs are free and those that aren't often provide scholarships. The sites are listed in Appendix III.

2. *Women's Network for Entrepreneurial Training (WNET).* Available in all 50 states, WNET links established women business owners with entrepreneurs who have been in business for one year or longer and who want free advice and counsel. The "mentors" meet one-on-one with their "proteges" for an average of four hours per month for one year and provide them with moral support along with the knowledge, skills and information they have gleaned in their five or more years of owning a business. There are currently 600 WNET matches around the country, and you can access the program through your OWBO representative (Appendix III).

3. *Access To Capital.* OWBO sponsors conferences throughout the country describing SBA loan programs.

4. *Opportunities in the Global Marketplace.* Together with the SBA's Office of International Trade, OWBO annually sponsors ten conferences around the country to provide training and resources for women entrepreneurs desiring to export products or services.

5. *Selling to the Federal Government.* OWBO representatives provide resources and contacts on how to do business with the federal government.

In addition to the OWBO programs, the SBA provides additional support and resources for all small business owners, including:

1. *The Service Corps of Retired Executives (SCORE).* SCORE is a free counseling service for start-up or ongoing businesses. It is staffed by retired executives, often from large companies, who want to give something back to the community which gave so much to them. They provide assistance in areas such as business planning, marketing, sales and so on.

Contact the nearest

SCORE, SBI, SBDC or

OWBO office.

2. *Small Business Development Centers (SBDC).* SBDCs link small businesses with community resources like accountants, attorneys, other consultants and so on. They help you get the advice you need to start and operate your business. They are sometimes affiliated with your local Chamber of Commerce or university.

3. *Small Business Institutes (SBI).* SBIs provide on-site management assistance to existing small businesses (*not* start-ups). They are staffed by college seniors and graduate students, guided by their faculty advisors, who take on your business problem as a class or individual project for which they eventually receive college credit. There are SBI programs at 500 colleges and universities around the country.

4. *Microloan Demonstration Program.* The SBA has set up 96 non-profit agencies around the U.S. to make very small loans (average of $7,500) to women, minority and low-income entrepreneurs and to entrepreneurs in areas suffering from a lack of credit due to economic downturn. These agencies, which are referred to as "intermediary lenders" also provide intensive (and free) marketing, management and technical assistance to the microloan borrowers. In addition, six other sites have been set up to provide counseling to low-income individuals on how to obtain business financing from banks. All these agencies are listed in Appendix III.

5. *The Small Business Answer Desk* (1-800-827-5722). The Small Business Administration (SBA) provides a toll-free number which you can call to get general information about small business and referrals to SBA services.

You can contact the nearest SCORE, SBI or SBDC office by looking up the Small Business Administration in your phone book or by calling the SBA Answer Desk.

In addition to all this free help from the federal government, many states have special programs for small businesses and for women-owned businesses. The contact people in each state, listed in Appendix III, stay current on programs, organizations, legislation, educational opportunities, and state government procurement opportunities that are available for women business owners within their states, and they can save you a lot of time and energy trying to hunt these down yourself.

As of this writing, in nearly half of the states these contact people also serve as Women's Business Advocates: they work to assure that women have equal access to state-funded small business programs; they recommend legislation to counteract the institutional bias that many of these programs have against the types of businesses women tend to start; they gather data about women business owners in their state; and they continually develop new and innovative programs to support women-owned business.

In addition, these advocates have formed the National Association of Women's Business Advocates (NAWBA), which works to increase support in all states for women business owners and to help other states to adopt programs which have proven successful in supporting women. Since each state's programs are continually changing and expanding, it could be worth your while to routinely stay in touch with the contact person in your state.

There are other non-profit agencies around the country, not affiliated with federal or state government, which provide technical, managerial and/or financial support to women business owners. A directory of micro-enterprise programs can be ordered from Self-Employment Learning Project of the Aspen Institute, Publications Office, PO Box 222, Queenstown, MD 21658 or by calling them at (410) 820-5326. There is a $10 fee for the directory.

Guidelines for Getting this Free Assistance

While all of these state and federal organizations have been set up to assist you in getting into or expanding a business, I have talked with many women who have been very frustrated in trying to get the support they really need from these organizations.

You *can* get the help you need. Follow these two simple guidelines:

1. Understand what these organizations do and don't provide. They do provide advice and counsel. They will assist you in such areas as understanding what it means to be in business, understanding how to do a market survey, understanding how to prepare financial projections, and so on. They do not (and should not) do the work for you. They do not write your business plan for you. They do not do your projections for you. They do not scout your competition for you. (The only possible exception to this is the SBI or university marketing classes which may actually do market surveys or competition analyses for business.) And except for the Microloan Demonstration Program participants, they do not give, lend or grant money for your business.

   In addition, it is unlikely they will understand the intricacies of your business to the tiniest detail, and sometimes this will be where you need help. Allow them to help you by guiding you to other support people with specific experience in your business or industry.

   If you walk in expecting the counselors to tell you exactly what you should do in a step-by-step fashion, you will be disappointed. If you walk in expecting to get some much-needed guidance in specific areas of your business or to guide you to other support people, you will have an excellent chance of getting the help you need.

2. It is 100% your responsibility to get the help you need, and you must be aggressive in asking for it. This is critical. And it translates in a number of ways.

   - Admit when you don't know something and ask for a clarification or explanation. You may have to say things like: "I don't understand what you mean by 'market.' Can you please explain it another way?" "I understand that I need to prepare a business plan, but I don't know where to start. Can you help me?"

   - Get the help you think you need. Consultants, even those who are free, do not always understand how best to help you. It's up to you to make sure they discuss the topics you need to hear about in a way you can understand. You may need to say things like: "The help I need is more basic. What's the first thing I should do to start my business?" "Look, I really think I understand my market. Right now, I need help with financial projections." Of course, be open to the

It is 100% your responsibility to get the help you need, and you must be aggressive in asking for it.

fact that they may have a better understanding than you about what you need to know to build your business.

- If a counselor is not helping you, switch counselors. There can be all kinds of reasons that you're not getting the help you need. The counselor may be biased against the industry or business you've selected, or may be biased against women in business. Or perhaps their expertise is in managing a factory and you need help with a retail store. Especially at SCORE, there are generally a number of counselors at each office. Talk to as many as you need and find the one you feel comfortable with.

- Get clear about which areas you need help with before you talk to a counselor. This is often easier said than done because sometimes you just don't know what you don't know. Try these methods: a) Before you go to the meeting, write down the subjects you'd like to cover and why. Just putting something down on paper often clarifies it. b) Talk to another business person with whom you feel comfortable. Sometimes talking about specific issues with someone else helps you understand what information is missing.

If you follow the five guidelines for effective networking, hire your paid experts and appropriately utilize the free expertise available to you, you will find over time that you have developed what I alternately refer to as your "business advisors" or "support group," a group of people that you can call on when you need help or support. I refer to this group throughout the book—giving you ideas for when it would be appropriate to call them and ask for their guidance. Your business plan will be substantially more sound and your business better managed if you make the time to develop relationships with these special people.

DEALING WITH FEAR

Almost everyone, men and women, has fears about being in business and about writing a business plan. Some common fears include:

- I'm afraid of failing

- I can't do math

- I don't have the right education (or experience or background)

- I don't have enough time

- People won't take me seriously

- If I succeed, I'll lose my friends (or my husband won't love me or I'll be unfeminine)

- Everyone will find out I'm not really good enough (or smart enough or capable enough)

- Everyone will find out I've been faking it all these years

- How will I get employees I can trust?

Figure 1.

Stating Your Fears

List as many fears as you can think of for not starting (or being in) your business.

1._____

2._____

3._____

4._____

5._____

6._____

7._____

List as many fears as you can think of for not writing your business plan.

1._____

2._____

3._____

4._____

5._____

6._____

7._____

Go back through your fears. Put an "R" in the space to the left of your fear if it is based on reality. Put an "I" in the space if it is based on an irrational thought.

• What if I run out of money at a critical time?

• How will I eat while I'm getting the business started?

It can be frightening even to think about fear, yet it needs to be dealt with because so many women allow it to drive their lives, and this impacts how (or even whether) they start or build their businesses.

Some women have said that simply seeing the list of fears above validated their feelings and helped them move forward. Others have found the exercise below ("Rational/Irrational Fears") helpful. There are still other ways of dealing with fear. All of them require that we become aware of our fears and work through them. If you are afraid of starting your business (or of life in general), I hope you will work through the exercise below or take some other kind of action and work through your fears.

Some fears are terrific motivators, causing people to take strong action for their business.

Rational/Irrational Fears

Some fears are terrific motivators, causing people to take strong action for their business. For example, the fear of missing a delivery deadline has caused more than one businesswoman to work day and night to prepare an order for shipment. Motivational fears are based on real circumstances, and they are readily resolved through direct courses of action. For the businesswoman in the above example, the direct course of action was working longer hours. She could also have improved her planning or hired someone to help with the work.

Unfortunately, there is another kind of fear, one which is debilitating. Debilitating fears keep moving over and over through your mind, inhibiting your performance, sapping your motivation and keeping you from taking appropriate action. For example, the fear of failing at business has caused some very talented women and men never even to try.

I know a woman who thought for years about starting a business but kept putting it off because she kept telling herself, "I don't have the right education," "I don't have the right experience" and "I don't know enough." Over the years, she accumulated a bachelor's degree, a master's degree and ten years of experience in her field, and she still felt it wasn't enough.

When she finally faced her fears, she realized they were irrational. The reality was that she had more education, more experience and more common sense than many very successful people in her field. And while there were some specific areas in which she lacked skills for her business, she was able to get the small amount of training she needed to fill the gap without signing up for yet another college degree. I know this story well—it's my story.

You may be saying to yourself, "Well, I can't relate to that example because I only have an associate's degree and four years' experience, so I *really* don't have the right background." You may be right. But you can help move yourself toward your goal of building a business if you open yourself up (as I did) to the possibility that perhaps you have as much education and experience as you need. It may be your fear of failure that's holding you back and not any real deficiencies in your background.

Like me, you will greatly increase your chances of business success by facing your fears and dealing with them realistically.

The first step is to list your fears about starting your business and for writing your business plan. Figure 1 and the list of fears above will help you get started.

Figure 2.

Resolving Your Fears

Restate your rational fears. Then, write down the action(s) you will take to resolve them.

Rational Fear   Action(s) to Resolve

1. _____   _____
                                       _____
                                       _____

2. _____   _____
                                       _____
                                       _____

3. _____   _____
                                       _____
                                       _____

4. _____   _____
                                       _____
                                       _____

Restate your irrational fears. Then, write down a rational starement to counter the fear.

Irrational Fear   Rational Counterstatement

1. _____   _____

2. _____   _____

3. _____   _____

4. _____   _____

5. _____   _____

6. _____   _____

7. _____   _____

If your fear can be readily resolved through a direct course of action, then it is based on reality.

They are taken from my personal, informal survey of women just starting their own businesses and women trying to expand their businesses.

Now, go back through your list of fears. Put an "R" in the blank space to the left of your fear if it is based on reality. Put an "I" in the blank space if your fear is based on irrational thoughts. Many people have a hard time telling the difference. A simple guideline is this: If your fear can be readily resolved through a direct course of action, then it is based on reality. If not, it is probably based on irrational thoughts. If you still cannot identify which fears are which, this is an excellent subject to discuss with your advisors.

The next step is to write a statement about each of your fears. This is done in Figure 2. If your fear is based on reality, write down the action(s) you will take to resolve your fear. For example:

How will I eat while I'm getting my business started?
I will prepare a plan which will indicate how much time it will take before I bring home enough money to live on. Then I will work at my present job until I have enough money to cover my expenses for that length of time.

If your fear is based on irrational thoughts, write down a rational statement which counters your fearful thought. For example:

I'm afraid of math.
There are many aspects of everyday life in which I apply math and don't get anxious about it, such as paying bills, making household purchases or balancing my checkbook. Once I understand the concepts behind the financial information for my business, I will be able to work a solution. And if something is very puzzling to me, I can always get help with it.

People (especially my prospective clients) won't take me seriously.
Some may take me very seriously, some may not. I can't control that. I'll just keep looking for those who do. And if it really gets to be a problem, I can get help from my advisors or from an image consultant to make sure I'm coming across in a professional manner.

Any time you feel a knot in your stomach or a constriction in your throat or you feel as if you're avoiding something that would make sense for your business, go through this process. It can release you to do the things you want to do.

VALIDATING YOUR INTUITION

As women, we bring a wide range of valuable—and some say, necessary—qualities to the business world. Unfortunately, most of us do not yet believe this. For example, studies have shown that if a male and female business owner are both turned down for a bank loan, the man is likely to say: "That banker is a jerk." while the woman is likely to say: "My loan package was terrible. Maybe I shouldn't be a business owner." For most of us, it is unlikely that a bank rejection means we won't cut it as a business owner, yet we tell ourselves just that. And if it's not a bank rejection, there's often something else that generates the expectation within us that we don't have what it takes to succeed.

Part of the fact that we don't feel validated in the business world comes from comments we hear from some men, such as "She's just a one person consultant operating out of her home. That's not a *real* business." or "Oh, that's just a hobby for her. Her husband set her up in business so she'd have something to do." or "Don't you just wish they (women business owners) would all go away?"

But part of it comes from the U.S. perspective of the nature of business. The business world has traditionally been thought of as a harsh, dog-eat-dog environment, where success comes from building hierarchical organizations in which bosses dictate to subordinates what they should do. This model, so successful in war and sports, simply does not match many women's ways of being in the world. I personally spent many years saying "If I could just learn to be like men, I would be successful." That was like saying "The way I am is not good enough to be a successful business owner, so I'd better figure out another way to be."

Recently, articles such as Judy Rosener's *Ways Women Lead* (Harvard Business Review, Nov-Dec, 1990) and books like Joline Godfrey's *Our Wildest Dreams: Women Entrepreneurs Making Money, Having Fun, Doing Good* (HarperBusiness, 1992) have acknowledged that women's ways of being in business are different *and valuable.* In fact, today's management gurus are saying that traditional business management styles will be ineffective in maintaining U.S. predominance in the new global economy (witness the severe downturns of IBM and General Motors), *and it will take a shift toward women's management styles to salvage our economy.* That's pretty powerful stuff.

All this is to say that it is OK—in fact it's preferable—for you to trust your intuition in the business world. If a business meeting seems silly to you, it probably is. If you think it's important to leave work on time so you can be with your kids, it is. If you think your business values should match your personal values, you're right. If you think you're being ignored in a meeting with men, you probably are. If a man's business advice doesn't feel right to you, you don't have to take it. It's not the end of the world nor the downfall of your business if you grow slowly so you have more time for your family.

In addition, many of the things you've learned as wife, mother and woman will serve you well. For example:

- Some of what you learned when raising children—like redirecting anger and letting kids solve their own problems—can help you deal with employee conflict (which is one of the most dreaded management problems).

- Your ability to connect with people can help you develop long-term relationships with suppliers and customers.

- Your willingness to be in touch with your feelings and to let your ethics and morals guide your business decisions can help you create the kind of corporate culture management gurus drool over.

- Your understanding and caring for people, rather than treating them like commodities, can enhance the loyalty and creativity of your employees.

It's not that we're perfect — we're not. And I realize this is a simplistic and generalized discussion of a complex subject. But for so long, we (and others) have behaved as if our way in the world was inconsistent with business, and it's not. We have decided that if we said "A" and a man said "B," then the answer must be "B." This is stressful and an energy drain, and our businesses deserve more.

Listen to what you say to yourself and make the time to validate yourself. When you realize that the men in the room aren't paying attention to you, tell yourself it's nothing personal (because it's not) and that your ideas are just as valuable as theirs. When you hear yourself saying "A real businessman wouldn't do this," look behind that statement. Are you discounting your own judgment because it doesn't fit with traditional business philosophy? Think again, tune into your intuition, and then go with what *you* think is right. Your business will be better for it.

VISUALIZING YOUR DREAMS

Studies have shown that the most successful people set aside time every day for daydreaming! They literally fantasize about the person they would most like to become. And somehow, with a clear vision and a willingness to adapt, they find themselves becoming that person.

Of course, there's no magic to this. Visualizing your dreams is a way to reprogram your unconscious. By repeatedly imagining yourself as successful, you replace negative images of yourself with positive images. As this new, healthy information begins to occupy your unconscious mind, it literally wins over the conscious mind when you make daily decisions. What you put in your mind helps to shape your actions.

Unless you've tried this, it probably sounds hokey. But it has worked for astronauts, athletes, businesspeople and politicians.

The important thing is to get clear on how *you* define "successful." What does it mean to you? How does a successful person behave? How does she speak? What kinds of organizations does she belong to? How does she dress? How does she carry herself? Imagine all these things. Your vision of success may include flexibility, independence, wealth or all of the above. The important thing is to imagine your idea of success.

The list of questions following is designed to help you with the visualization process. Start by setting aside two hours of quiet time. Find a place where no one will bother you (you may even try the library). Read the questions in Figure 3— they will help you think through and clarify your definition of business success. Close your eyes and visualize yourself running your business.

Then write down the answers to the questions. Make sure you write the answers in the present tense—not "I'd like to earn $100,000 per year," but "I *am* earning $100,000 per year." Include other dreams not listed in the figure if they are important to you. Read over again what you have written.

Most women who follow through on this find it energizes them. The more they think about what they would like for their business, the more they believe in the possibilities. And you will too.

Figure 3.

Visualizing Your Dreams

Close your eyes, relax, and see yourself in the future. Answer the following questions:

_____

How much money are you earning?

_____

What kind of lifestyle are you and your family leading? Describe it in detail.

_____

How big is your business?

_____

How does your business reflect you and your values?

_____

What products and services are you offering?

_____

Describe your customers. Who are they? How many?

_____

Where is your business located?

_____

What does your place of business look like?

_____

Describe your employees. How many do you have? What are they doing? How are you treating them?

_____

What are you doing in the business? Do you like it?

## PART 2

The Business Plan

## CHAPTER TWO

Your Business Plan

A business plan serves as a tool to help you run your business successfully. It works like this: First, you prepare your business plan, then you take action—that is, you follow the plan. After a specified period of time you look at your results and compare them to your expectations. You evaluate what worked and what didn't work. Are your costs higher than expected? Is your market smaller than expected? Do you have so many orders that you need more space to fill them?

When you've determined what works, leave it alone! When you've determined what doesn't work, you change the plan. Over time, you improve it by incorporating your valuable new experience. Then you take action again by following the amended plan.

This cycle of taking action, evaluating results, making changes and taking new action is what managing a business is all about. You continue the cycle for as long as you own your business, always improving your business and making it more profitable. And the most effective way to make improvements is with a business plan.

While most people think of using a business plan to get money, that is actually not its most important function. There are three major reasons for preparing a business plan.

1. The business planning process forces you to define your goals and prepare a rational plan for achieving them. You must set the direction for your business based on your own personal vision of success. In this way, you will run your business instead of allowing your business to run you.

2. Your completed business plan is a vehicle for clearly communicating your ideas to others in a consistent and professional manner.

3. Your business plan is an operating tool for helping you run your business efficiently and effectively.

Must a business plan be written? Certainly you have successfully planned things in the past without writing anything down. It is a fact of human nature, however, that we take things more seriously when we write them down. Also, it is difficult to remember your business ideas from three months ago when you're up to your neck in today's business problems. From a practical standpoint, you will not be considered for financing from a banker or from most other funding sources without a written business plan. And why should you expect anything less from yourself than what your banker expects from you?

WHAT IS A BUSINESS PLAN?

A business plan is a written document that describes how you will run your business. It covers the seven basic areas of business:

Business Area	What It Really Means
1. Product Development	Continually refining what you're offering for sale to meet the ever-changing needs of your potential customers.
2. Marketing	Continually taking action to become even more aware of your customers' needs and informing your potential customers that your product or service is meant for them and why.
3. Sales	Talking face-to-face with your potential customers and getting them to say, "Yes, I'll buy from you."
4. Operations	Doing the work of the business. For example, if you're in the secretarial services business, operations might include answering the telephone, typing, filing, etc.
5. Personnel	Managing the people who work for you.
6. Finance	Measuring the financial results of your business and comparing them with your desired results and using this comparison to identify critical business issues.
7. Management	Making sure the above six areas are working in concert to meet your goals for the business.

These areas are discussed in more detail in Chapter Four, Management.

In each of the seven basic business areas, your business plan describes:

- The results you want to achieve.

- The activities that need to be done to achieve them.

- The resources (money, people, time, equipment, etc.) required to perform these activities.

- The criteria you will use to evaluate the results.

- The reasons you believe the plan will succeed.

Your business plan will also help you determine how much money you really need for your business.

Some people decide they need a piece of equipment, such as a $10,000 computer or a $5,000 carpet cleaner, or a $1,000 copy machine, and they believe that if they just had the money all their problems would be solved. However, in business, you need to deal with all of the seven business areas in order to be successful. The only way to know how much money you *really* need is to decide what you're going to do in each of the areas and figure out how much money it will take to do it.

The only way to know how much money you really need is to decide what you're going to do in each of the areas.

You may be surprised to find out that your business will not be profitable if you buy that $10,000 computer. Your business plan may force you to look at cheaper and more creative alternatives.

Through the planning process, you may find that no amount of money will help you to have a profitable business. It is far cheaper not to begin an ill-fated business than to learn by experience what a business plan would have taught you at the cost of several days of concentrated work.

And you may find that you need much less money than you originally thought and that you can start your business more quickly and easily. Your business plan will have saved you from months of hard, painful work trying to obtain unnecessary funding for your business.

Once you are clear on how much money you need, a business plan can help you to get that money because: 1) bankers and other funding sources will only fund businesses that have written business plans and 2) going through the process of clarifying your business ideas will enable you to deal effectively and professionally with your banker.

DOING THE RESEARCH

You will need to do research in order to prepare your business plan. You may need to find out such things as: the number of businesses in your county which have between one and nine employees, the average sales dollars per square foot of retail space in your local mall, the number of children in the U.S. under the age of five, the sales trends in the health care industry, and so on. Other sections of this book will help you clarify the information you need for your business.

Listed below are some suggestions for finding that information. The suggestions may not stick with you on first reading. Just plan to come back to this section anytime you're unsure about how to gather information.

1. Ask your librarian for help. You may not realize it, but your public library is an outstanding source of business information, and librarians are specially trained to help people find the information they need. Many small and medium-sized cities have a librarian who specializes in business-related information. Large cities often have an entire library branch devoted to business. So do universities. Explain to your librarian what you're looking for. Follow their suggestions. If you don't get the information you need, ask again. They expect it and won't think any less of you for asking.

2. Contact your local Chamber of Commerce or regional development board. They often have a great deal of statistical information about the local business and consumer population and about the local business climate and trends. Their reason for existence is to help businesses start up and grow.

3. Contact your local SBDC, SBI and SCORE. Or call the SBA Answer Desk at (800) 827-5722. These organizations, which are discussed in detail on pages 15-18, can be excellent sources of business information. Their services are free.

Call the

SBA Answer Desk

at (800) 827-5722.

The more you think in advance of what you need to know, the easier it will be for other people to help you.

4. Contact the marketing or business department at your local college or university. They are often looking for real-life market studies that their students can do and will charge only their out-of-pocket costs.

5. Talk to other people in the same or similar businesses—they are your best source of information since they face the same problems you do. This may be difficult if they are in competition with you, but often a would-be competitor in another town or city will be happy to talk to someone else in a similar business. After all, they need information too.

6. If possible, visit your competitors. See how their facilities are arranged, what their products look like, what kind of service their salespeople provide. Remember, they will probably visit you to see what you are doing.

7. Almost every industry has an organization or association which does such things as hold regular meetings, sponsor seminars and publish newsletters and magazines for people in that particular industry. Trade associations usually have local, regional or national offices which gather data and respond to questions from people in the industry. If you are not aware of the trade association for your industry, ask your librarian or ask for the current edition of *National Trade and Professional Associations of the United States* or *Encyclopedia of Associations*. Then make the appropriate contact.

8. Ask potential customers. Ask people you know. Ask the people in women's groups or volunteer organizations you belong to. Ask them about their buying habits. Ask them about their personal tastes. Ask them if they would buy your product. Ask them how much they would pay for it. People love to give opinions on things. All you have to do is ask.

Some notes regarding your research efforts:

• The more you think in advance of what you need to know, the easier it will be for other people to help you. In fact, the more work you put into your research, the more people will want to help you. So think about what you're trying to do. If necessary, talk about it with your business advisors. Then ask for help.

• The better documented your research, the more believable it will be to you and your funding sources. So keep track of names, titles, dates and any other pertinent information about your sources of information.

• As you approach people for help, remember that you are a businesswoman. Even if you haven't opened your doors for business, the fact that you are researching your business makes you a businesswoman. And you have just as much right to ask for and receive help as anyone. You don't need to tell the people you're talking to that you're a neophyte. Besides, you probably know a lot more than you think you do. Most women do.

- The above statement notwithstanding, it's possible that you'll encounter skepticism in your ability to run a business or even bias against you as a businesswoman. Some of it may be outright and some of it may be so subtle that you don't realize until you're out the door that they tried to discourage you from getting started. You can choose to let these people get you down or you can choose to move forward despite them. I'd recommend the latter. Meanwhile keep looking—there are plenty of people out there who will gladly help you.

ORGANIZATION OF YOUR PLAN

Below you'll see my suggested outline for your business plan. It may look different from other business plan outlines you've seen. You may even be getting frustrated from seeing so many suggested outlines and may be wondering which one is "right."

They're all correct if they contain the same basic information. Each author presents the information in the way that is most logical to him or her. And, in fact, if you use your business plan to get money, you will find that different funding sources require different outlines and formats. You may have to reorganize your business plan from time to time to suit your purposes; however, the basic content remains the same.

The Cover Sheet

The Cover Sheet should:

- Identify the business and the document
- Identify the business owner(s)
- Identify the location and telephone numbers of the business or where the owners can be reached

The cover sheet should not be elaborate. It should be neat, attractive and short. If the plan is to be used as a financing proposal, use a separate cover sheet for each bank or funding source you submit it to and add a line stating who the plan is for.

The Statement of Purpose

The first page of the plan should briefly and clearly state your objectives for writing the plan. If you are writing the plan for your own use, the statement should be a simple description of how you intend to use the plan once it has been developed. For example: "This plan will be an operating guide for ABC Co. It will also be used as a management tool to regularly evaluate and improve business results."

If the plan is also to be used as a financing proposal, the Statement of Purpose must describe such things as the amount of the requested loan, how you will use the money for your business and how you will repay the loan. In business circles this is known as "the deal."

You'll need to answer these questions:

Statement of Purpose

1. Who is asking for money?

2. What is the business structure (for example: sole proprietorship, partnership, Sub-Chapter S corporation, cooperative)?

3. How much money is needed?

4. How will the funds benefit the business?

5. Why does this loan or investment make business sense?

6. How will the funds be repaid?

Write a paragraph tying all this information together.

You will not be able to complete all the answers until you have finished the rest of your business plan, especially the section on financial data. Answer as many questions as you can right now, and use the answers to write a preliminary statement of purpose. You can come back to this section later and finish your statement of purpose.

Keep the statement short and businesslike. It should have only enough information to whet the reader's appetite, and enable your funding source to make a quick yes or no decision on whether to keep reading. Some funding sources are biased against certain industries or certain sizes of loans or investments, and you don't want to waste your time and theirs with a financing proposal they will eventually turn down. The Statement of Purpose will rarely be longer than half a page. Here's an example:

• Green Consulting Company is a sole proprietorship seeking a $12,000 loan to start a market research and consulting firm. This money will be used to purchase equipment, pay for pre-opening expenses and provide adequate working capital to enable our client base to grow and stabilize. In addition, the owner, Cathy Green, will invest $4,000 of her own money in the business. The loan of $12,000 plus equity investment of $4,000, a total of $16,000, will be sufficient to finance Green's start up. The interest plus principal on the loan will be repaid out of operating profit.

Table of Contents

The Table of Contents follows your Statement of Purpose. It is divided into three main sections:

- The Business
- Financial Data
- Supporting Documents

Some funding sources are biased against certain industries or certain sizes of loans or investments, and you don't want to waste your time and theirs.

Figure 4.

Outline of a Business Plan

- Cover Sheet: Name of business, names of principals, address and phone number
- Statement of Purpose
- Table of Contents

Section One: The Business

A. Description of Business
B. Product/Service Description
C. Market Description
D. Competition
E. Management Plan
    1. Product Development
    2. Marketing
    3. Sales
    4. Operations
    5. Personnel
F. Description of Management Personnel
G. Application and Expected Effect of Loan (if needed)
H. Summary

Section Two: Financial Data

A. Sources and Uses of Cash
B. Capital Equipment List
C. Income Projections (Profit and Loss Statement)
    1. Three-year summary
    2. Detail by month for first year
    3. Detail by quarter for second and third years
    4. Notes of explanation
D. Break-even Analysis
E. Cash Flow Projections
    1. Detail by month for first year
    2. Detail by quarter for second and third years
    3. Notes of explanation
F. Balance Ssheet
G. Historical Financial Reports for Existing Business (if applicable)
    1. Balance sheet for past three years
    2. Income statements for past three years
    3. Tax returns

Section Three: Supporting Documents

    Personal resumes, personal balance sheets, cost of living budget, credit reports, letters of reference, job descriptions, letters of intent, copies of leases, contracts, legal documents and anything else relevant to the plan.

These sections may be broken down even further if necessary as shown below. Since a business plan can run 20 or more pages, you want to help the reader find her or his way to sections or subsections of particular interest. The Statement of Purpose states what your deal is; the Table of Contents makes it easy to find supporting material.

SAMPLE TABLE OF CONTENTS

Contents   *Page*

Description of Business

This section is the introduction to your business plan. It describes your business clearly and concisely and provides the focus for the remainder of the plan. Your ability to briefly describe your business will be invaluable as you communicate your business ideas to prospective customers, suppliers, employees and funding sources.

The Description of the Business is divided into four parts:

- What your business is
- How you will run it
- Historical information about your business (if appropriate)
- Why your business will succeed

WHAT YOUR BUSINESS IS

Deciding what your business is or will be is the most important (and the most difficult) single decision you have to make. You need to answer the following questions:

> What is the primary function of your business? (e.g., manufacturing, service, consulting, retail, distribution)
>
> What are you selling?
>
> What makes it unique?
>
> To whom are you selling?
>
> Why do they buy it?

Many small businesses are tempted to say they'll do anything or provide anything for anyone who wants it. Consultants and other service people are especially prone to fall into this trap.

I know a woman who is starting a one-person computer consulting business selling computer hardware and software to large companies, computer training to small businesses and computerized transmission of income tax returns to small businesses and individuals. She just can't seem to get her business off the ground.

I know another woman who has begun an exciting, nontraditional training company—and, in addition, her company sells bookkeeping services because she used to be a bookkeeper. I find her brochure very confusing.

A company that provides business publications to banks was asked by one bank to produce some nonbusiness publications. With dollar signs in their eyes, they agreed. Before long, they were chasing banks for all kinds of publications, and found themselves competing in a market with which they were unfamiliar. (Their special niche was small business publications.) Their sales became increasingly erratic and their employees were frustrated by the lack of focus.

I had this problem, too. My first business plan for my consulting business listed my products as Business Plans, Market Analyses, Seminars and Defense Industry Proposal Preparation. My markets were small to midsize polymer companies, small, medium, and large defense companies and small to midsize manufacturing companies. Needless to say, I never knew what I should be spending my time on.

The problem with this is twofold:

1. You only have a limited amount of your most precious resources—time and money—and if you spread them over too many products/services or customers, you will not have enough invested in any one of them to be successful.

Deciding what your business is or will be is the most important single decision you have to make.

2. If you are not clear on what your business is, you will confuse—and lose—prospective customers.

You need to select a central focus of your business, the primary reason for your business' existence. You define this focus by continually asking yourself the five questions on the previous page.

Here are some examples of businesses that are focused:

- North Coast Kids designs and manufactures distinctive (stylish yet practical) children's clothing, distributing nationwide to upper-end department store chains and boutiques.

- ZPC develops, implements and maintains personalized, conservative financial plans for high income (greater than $100,000) individuals/families who reside within ten miles of Weston, Kentucky.

- Zuckerman and Associates guides moderately sized businesses in NE Ohio to become (more) successful through: 1) helping owners and managers chart their business' future course, 2) building effective management teams, and 3) training owners and managers in the guiding principles of running a business.

You know you've succeeded in establishing focus when two things happen: 1) You can describe your business to someone in one or two sentences and they understand it, and 2) You can talk with a prospective customer, and, as soon as you understand her needs, know immediately whether there's a match between what she needs and what you offer. In fact, the absolute test of whether you're clear on the focus of your business is when you send a prospective customer to a competitor because you know you don't offer what she wants.

Most people understand this concept intellectually, but somehow when sales are down or when the business is just getting started or even when the business experiences explosive growth, they forget it. Everyone they meet represents a possible sale and they run from pillar to post trying to follow up on a dozen leads at the same time.

This is very expensive, very stressful and very dangerous for your business and your health. If you don't believe me, talk to someone in a business without a focus. They'll tell you things like: "The business is not working," or "There's no consistency here," or "I don't know what to do to make things right" or "*Everything* is top priority." And if you look at their sales, they're either flat or very erratic.

You can probably think of examples where this is *not* the case. For example, if you're just getting started, your newness may carry you to a certain level. Or if there's an overwhelming demand for what you're offering (and not a lot of competition), dumb luck can carry you for a while. But these are the exceptions rather than the rule.

Some of these exceptions combined with inaccurate media reporting have led to what I call "the lottery theory of business success," which says that if you just find the *right* product or the *right* customer or the *right* investor, your business will succeed. I've seen companies continually change the products they sell or the markets they sell to, hoping they'll strike it rich with the next one or the one after that. This is not how business works, yet every day many people lose a lot of time and money following this path. If you want to grow, you must have a focus and a plan.

You need to select a central focus of your business, the primary reason for your business' existence.

How You Will Run Your Business

This section is a straightforward description of how you will run your business. The questions that need to be answered are listed below. As you answer these questions, you may again want to consult with your business advisors.

- What is the status of your business? A start up? A going concern? An expansion? A takeover of an existing business?

- What is your business form: sole proprietorship, partnership, corporation, cooperative? Appendix VI has brief descriptions of each of these business forms. You should ask your attorney and your accountant for advice before making your decision.

- When will (did) your business open?

- What hours of the day and days of the week will you be (are you) in operation? Think about what makes sense for the business and also for you personally.

- Is your business seasonal? If it is, or if the hours will be adjusted seasonally, make sure the seasonality is shown in your replies to the previous question.

Historical Information

This information helps the reader understand where you've been and provides the basis for your future direction. If you've been successful, highlight it here so the reader is predisposed to believe in your future success. If you've learned some important lessons, this is a good place to briefly discuss them in a positive manner.

The questions that need to be answered are:

- How long have you been in business? If you have spent the last three years developing your product—even if you're not open for business—it is important to note it here.

- Have you been marketing the same products to the same customers? If not, what was different? What did you learn that caused you to change?

- What have your sales and profits been? Have they been increasing? Decreasing? Staying the same?

- What have you learned about your market? Your product? Your industry?

Even if you haven't officially opened for business, you may have taken actions which will lead toward your future success, such as:

- Developing your product. You may have spent the last ten years designing and sewing clothes for your children, which led to your idea of starting a children's clothing business. Sound implausible? Paul Newman claims to have developed his spaghetti sauce by making huge batches of it as Christmas presents for years.

- Doing market research. You may have been helping relatives, friends, and colleagues make better use of their computers and have gotten a clear picture of what kind of computer support people need, want and would be willing to pay for.

- Selling your product. You may have sold your handmade dolls at craft shows and gotten excellent ideas of what does and doesn't sell and what kind of dialogue you need to have with a prospective customer to get them to buy.

There are many actions you may have taken which have given you insights into your business and helped you to set your business direction. You may be tempted to discount some of these actions, thinking, "Well, I wasn't really in business then." But think of how much more you know now compared to when you started.

Why Your Business Will Succeed

The fact is that your business will succeed or fail because of factors within your control (e.g., whom you select as your target market; how much time and energy you put into your business; your ability to get the supplies, information and personal connections you need; your ability to communicate with your target market, etc.); and factors outside your control (e.g., what is happening in your industry and the economy in general, the strength of your competition, government regulations which impact your business, etc.). You must understand all these factors to be able to control the success of your business.

1. You will be successful for a variety of reasons. Here are some generic examples:

   Your experience or knowledge of your business or industry
   Your experience or knowledge of business in general
   Your plans for meeting the needs of your target market
   The level of service you provide
   Your location, promotion or pricing
   The strength of the competition
   Your ability to control costs, or to manage people, or to sell
   Your ability to develop your product or service
   Your overall management skills
   Your relationship with suppliers
   Long-term contracts with customers, especially if they're already in place
   The amount of money available to you to start or expand your business
   Your demonstrated perseverance and professionalism

   As you look through this list, find the factors that pertain to your situation. Describe specifically how they apply to you and how you will use them in running your business.

   You may need to come back to this after you've completed Chapter Four.

2. Have you spoken with other people in this kind of business? What did you learn from them? You can learn more from talking to people in your business or industry (including competitors) than almost anything else

you do. Ask such questions as: What is the day-to-day reality of being in business? How much time do you spend on the business? How long did it take you to become successful? What kind of profit can I expect? What are the most difficult parts of this business and why? How can I find qualified suppliers or sales reps or personnel, etc.?

Needless to say, you're best off learning these things *before* you start your business, but it's never too late.

3. What will be unique about your business? Business is competitive—and standing out from the competition is increasingly important. Keep asking yourself this question as you build your business. For now, you probably have a handle on the answer, but you will understand it much better after you complete the section on competition in Chapter Three.

4. Have you spoken with prospective suppliers to find out what help they will provide? Some of you will need to purchase materials or inventory in order to produce, acquire or create your product or service. Your suppliers can be a surprising source of information, support and even money. Suppliers usually know what your competitors are doing and what's going on in the industry, and they're generally pretty open about this information. Sometimes they will also provide you with managerial or technical help. For instance, store fixture suppliers provide free layout advice, lighting companies give hints on effective use of store lighting, and so on.

In addition, many suppliers provide what is known as "trade credit." Trade credit bears some similarity to a store charge account. Your supplier may give you the merchandise today in exchange for your promise to pay in the future. For example, if you need fabric to produce your monogrammed tote bags, the fabric supplier might sell you the fabric today with the expectation that you will pay in 30 days. This is like giving you a 30-day loan on the cost of the fabric, which can be very helpful if you can't get a loan from a bank. Common terms for trade credit look pretty unusual if you've never seen them before. An example is "2/10, net 30." This means that you get a 2% discount off the price of the items if you pay within ten days after you receive them; otherwise you must pay the total amount in 30 days.

It can't hurt to ask your suppliers for trade credit; however, it's not often available until a business has been in operation long enough to establish a reputation for paying on time.

5. Do you already have firm contracts in place? If you have a contract-type business, firm contracts—or even letters of intent—add credibility to the likelihood of success. For example, suppose you're starting a stress management business providing relaxation training, biofeedback, therapeutic massage and exercise. You could greatly increase your chances of success by getting letters of intent from physicians saying they intend to refer their high-stress patients to you, or by getting contracts with businesses that will provide your service as a benefit to their employees, or by signing a contract with a local wellness center saying you will refer customers back and forth to each other.

You're best off learning these things before you start your business, but it's never too late.

If you do have these documents, make sure you include copies of them in the Supporting Documents section of your business plan.

Putting Together Your Description of Business

If possible, confine your business description to one page. This requires that you combine the information you have just prepared into three or four very clear, very brief paragraphs.

Sometimes you've spent so much time thinking about your business that you forget that other people don't know what you're talking about. Make sure your first sentence is a straightforward statement of what business you're in. It starts with your company name and is written in the present tense. Use the statements of focus on p. 38 as examples.

Remember that some people who read your business plan will not be familiar with your industry's jargon. What may seem like common terminology to you will confuse your banker or other funding source. Ask someone outside your industry to read your business description. Then ask them the six basic questions:

1. What is the primary function of my business?
2. What am I selling?
3. What makes it unique?
4. Who am I selling to?
5. Why do they buy it?
6. Why will my business be successful?

If they can answer those six questions about your business, you have succeeded with this section of your business plan.

DESCRIPTION OF WHAT YOU'RE OFFERING FOR SALE

As you consider what you're offering for sale, the most obvious thing is your product or service. For example, if you own a children's clothing store, you're offering children's clothes; or if you own a dry cleaning shop, you're offering dry cleaning services. What may not be so obvious is that customers are making their buying decisions on more than just your product/service and your price.

For example, suppose you own a convenience store. There's nothing special about your products, and they're priced higher than the grocery store, yet people buy them anyway. Why? Because you're right around the corner, you're open at odd hours of the day and night, your customers can drive right up to your front door and there's rarely a line at the cash register. In other words, you're *convenient*. The way you do business distinguishes you from conventional grocery stores, and since there are customers who want the convenience you provide and are willing to pay your prices, you have a profitable business. This convenience is called a benefit and *benefits are what customers buy*.

It is critical to determine the benefits you provide to your customers, for they are central to your ability to successfully create sales.

It is also critical to understand how to provide these benefits. You do this with what is known as features, i.e., characteristics or attributes of your product or service and of the way you run your business. Taken together, the features and benefits of your business define what you're offering for sale.

Remember that some people who read your business plan will not be familiar with your industry's jargon.

Product/Service Features

Start by listing your products and/or services in Figure 5. If you have a large number of products with similar characteristics, group them together as product lines (i.e., groups of products with similar features) and list the product lines. The same should be done with services.

For example, if you owned a women's shoe store, you would carry hundreds of different pairs of shoes, but you might describe them in your business plan as four product lines: women's dress shoes, casual shoes, sandals and boots.

Similarly, if your company provided training services, you might have several "service lines," such as sales training, supervisory skills training and training in writing business letters.

Or you might need to identify your product lines in terms of customer groups. For example, if you owned a florist shop, your product lines might be floral arrangements for hospital gift shops, funeral parlors and the general public.

After you have listed your product/service lines, use Figure 5 to list the features that characterize each of your products or services.

For products, these features include such things as size, shape, quality, texture, color, complexity (or simplicity) and so on. For example, if you produce and sell porcelain jewelry, your product features could be: handmade, each piece is unique, colorful, color combinations to go with "seasonal" colors, high quality, and each piece is signed. Or if you own a shoe store, your product features could be: trendy, comfortable, latest colors, professional looking and large selection.

For services, your features include such things as the result of doing the service, the amount of time it takes to perform the service and any written documents (e.g., handouts, workbooks, reports, etc.) you provide when you perform the service. For example, if you provide financial planning services, your service features could be: result is a financial plan geared to the acceptable risk level of the client, takes an average of 20 hours of a planner's time and four hours of the customer's time to prepare a plan, we provide quarterly newsletters and annual plan updates. If you provide dry cleaning services, your service features could be: result is clean clothes, we complete the process in no more than three days, we spot check all garments prior to cleaning, we hang all garments and cover with plastic bags (or, on request, we box sweaters), and we inspect all garments when the customer brings them in to make sure our dry cleaning process won't damage the fabric.

Now fill in the remainder of Figure 5, Product/Service Features.

Other Features of Your Business

In addition to product/service features, all businesses have other features necessary to provide the benefits desired by their customers. Some of the more common are listed below with a brief description of what they mean, with two examples, one based on a shoe store and one based on a dry cleaners.

Use Figure 6 on page 49 to define the other features for *your* business. As you develop these features, keep the following things in mind:

1. *Consistency.* There must be consistency among all the features or you will confuse your customers and lose sales. For example, if you sell high quality, expensive clothing for professional women, it would be inconsistent to have

untrained salespeople and a store in a run-down neighborhood. People expect knowledgeable service and a professional atmosphere when they are paying high prices for professional clothing. Conversely, if you are offering inexpensive, moderate quality clothing to middle income families, it would be inconsistent (and needlessly expensive) to be located within a row of elegant, exclusive shops.

2. *Market Needs*. It logically follows that your list of features must be developed to meet the needs of your customers, not your own needs. And the only way to do this is to know what your customers' needs are. To some extent, the only way you will really find out what the customers' needs are is to begin your business. But it's awfully risky and potentially devastating to your business to leave this to chance. Your best bet is to put yourself in your customers' shoes, take your best guess as to which features are important to them and do as much research as you can—in the library, with a survey, by asking people—to validate your intuition. This research is described more in Chapter Three, Your Market.

3. *Competition*. Taken together, your product/service features and the other features of your business will distinguish you from your competition. For example, if you sell shoes, chances are your shoes are very similar to the five other shoe stores in the same mall. By providing a high level of service—such as making sure the shoes fit right or assisting the customer in finding the right shoes for her outfit or simply having polite and helpful sales clerks—you will distinguish your business from the competition.

My experience has been that just being very clear about your business features and benefits will set you apart from the competition.

For those of you who are selling your expertise (e.g., professionals, consultants), there are some peculiar problems which make this assessment inherently more important and more difficult.

First of all, what you're selling is intangible; your customers can't see the result until after they've invested their money in you. Worse yet, the result usually involves some kind of change for the customer, and, regardless of how beneficial it is, change is always painful.

In addition, the customer expects—and rightly so—that you will not only provide the solution to her problem, but will also help her to diagnose the problem.

What makes this even worse is that most people distrust experts. Particularly, they believe that experts (doctors, lawyers, all kinds of consultants) charge more in fees than they are worth. The result is that most people will acknowledge their need for expertise, but few are willing to pay for it.

Perhaps the greatest difficulty is the way most experts think about themselves. They're so enamored with their expertise that they believe they are somehow immune from having to develop products or product/market matches or lists of business features. They believe it's sufficient to tell a customer that they are selling expertise or advice, and they think the customer is foolish if she doesn't buy their advice, which, of course, would make a dramatic difference in the customer's business (or life or health). This description may not fit you, but it

Table 1.

FEATURE	DESCRIPTION	SHOE STORE EXAMPLE	DRY CLEANERS EXAMPLE
Level of Service Features	Detailed description of the care, concern and responsiveness you demonstrate to your customers.	Exceptionally polite and knowledgeable sales staff trained to correctly fit shoes and help customers determine if shoes fit properly. Help select shoes to match clothes. Merchandise may be returned at any time.	Polite and friendly staff. Know customers by name. Twenty-four hour service. Special attention to customers, e.g., move buttons over on request.
Place of Business Features	Location and set up of your place of business (e.g., office, factory, facility, etc.).	Located in suburban mall. Attractive display, well lit. Play quiet classical music. Tastefully decorated.	Located in row of stores around the corner from a trendy neighborhood. Convenient parking. Clean. Motorized clothes rack with numbering system to make clean clothes easy to find.
Personal Appearance Features	Personal image portrayed by you and your staff.	Formally dressed. Clean, neat. Well-groomed.	Neatly dressed. Clean.
Price Features	The way in which you price what you're selling.	Mid- to high-priced shoes.	Priced competitively.
Process Features	The process by which you produce your product or provide your service (step by step description).	Not relevant.	1. Intake at front door. 2. Clean garment. 3. Press garment. 4. Assemble on hangers or in bags. 5. Move to conveyor. 6. Return to customer. NOTE: Each step can be described in much more detail if necessary for clarity.
Distribution Features	The way in which you get what you're selling into the hands of the ultimate consumer (relevant primarily in manufacturing where you often sell through a wholesaler or retailer rather than directly to the consumer yourself).	Not relevant.	Not relevant.

certainly used to fit me. And I can tell you from personal, expensive experience—it doesn't work.

People want to buy *something*. They don't want advice, they want results. They don't want a report, they want a solution to their problems. They want confidence that if they hire you, they will get that result. They don't want to keep pouring money down what looks like a bottomless pit. It's your job to give them that confidence, and then deliver on the result.

Here's what you need to do:

1. First decide what your business focus is going to be. Select what you're going to offer and whom you're going to offer it to. Remember that you'll have a difficult time surviving if you overextend yourself by providing too many services to too many markets.

    This is probably the hardest thing you'll have to do. Keep working at it and refining it. You'll know you've got it when you can describe to someone in one sentence precisely what it is you do.

2. Divide your process (i.e., the way you provide your expertise) into small, manageable chunks of work. You may think of it as tasks or phases or projects or products. For example, if you're a computer consultant, Phase 1 might be helping the client define what she wants to use her computer for; Phase 2 might be selecting the hardware and software to meet her needs; Phase 3 might be purchasing the system; and Phase 4 might be training the client to use it. If you're an accountant, you might provide tax return preparation, bookkeeping services and financial statement preparation.

3. Develop a written, step-by-step description of the process you use to provide each of these tasks or phases. Include the timing the handouts, the nature of customer interaction—whatever is involved in what you do. The clearer you are about how the process works, the more easily you'll be able to describe it to the customer and the more prepared you'll be to provide it effectively.

4. Use Figure 6 as a guide to your business features. As an expert, you will most likely focus on process features, level of service features and appearance features.

Benefits

Even if you understand your product/service business features to the tiniest detail, you will miss the boat entirely if you don't know what benefits the customer is buying.

Benefits are the real value that the customer gets from buying your product/service from you. Features make the benefits possible, but benefits are what the customer buys.

Some examples of benefits are:

1. *Shoe store.* You may think you're selling trendy shoes. Customers think they're buying sophistication, peer approval and sex appeal (the benefits)—and they choose your store because it's convenient and the clerks are helpful (features).

People want to buy something. They don't want advice, they want results.

Figure 5.

Product/Service Features

Product/Service #1 _____

Features _____
_____
_____
_____
_____
_____
_____

Product/Service #2 _____

Features _____
_____
_____
_____
_____
_____

Product/Service #3 _____

Features _____
_____
_____
_____
_____
_____

Product/Service #4 _____

Features _____
_____
_____
_____
_____
_____

Use additional paper as necessary.

Features make the benefits possible, but benefits are what the customer buys.

2. *Bookkeeping Service.* You may think you're selling bookkeeping services. Customers think they're buying the reassurance of accurate business records, relief from drudgery and extra time for other activities (the benefits)—and they choose your bookkeeping company because you pick up and deliver information and records, your staff is cheerful and friendly and you aren't constantly calling customers to bother them with details you can handle yourself (features).

3. *Consulting Business.* I used to think I was selling strategic and business planning services. Customers indicated to me they were buying direction, growth and control for their company and a sounding board for themselves as owner (the benefits)—and they bought from me because I listen to them, I care about them and I understand how profitable businesses operate (the features).

What benefits do you offer? Perhaps you help your customers to increase sales or decrease expenses. You may be the "safe" alternative because you have a history of delivering your service on time and within budget. If you sell to consumers, they may be buying time savings or keeping up with "hot" trends. If you aren't sure what benefits you offer, talk it over with your business advisors or, better yet, with your current customers and get their opinion. Over time, as you think about and operate your business, this whole concept of benefits will become much clearer.

Putting It All Together

Now it's time to consolidate all this information for your business plan. Start by listing your products/services and describing their features and the other business features you are offering. Then discuss the benefits with your customers and write them down. Finish with specifying why your customers will buy from you (and not your competition). The entire section should be no more than one page and will probably be less. But all the thought you've put into it will enable you to answer any questions posed by your funding sources, customers, suppliers and others.

When you are finished, give copies to your business advisors. Ask them to make sure it is in language that any businessperson (including your banker) can understand. Then ask them the three big questions:

1. What am I offering?
2. What are the benefits to my customers?
3. Why will my customers buy from me?

If they can answer those questions after reading the description of what you're offering for sale (without additional explanation from you), then this section of your plan is complete.

Figure 6.

Distinguishing Features

Level of
Service Features
_____
_____
_____
_____
_____
_____

Place of
Business Features
_____
_____
_____
_____
_____
_____

Personal
Appearance
Features
_____
_____
_____
_____
_____
_____

Price Features
_____
_____
_____
_____
_____
_____

Process Features
_____
_____
_____
_____
_____
_____

Distribution
Features
_____
_____
_____
_____
_____

## CHAPTER THREE

Your Market

The essence of business is this: You need customers who will buy your goods and services, at a price that yields a profit, in sufficient numbers and over a sufficient period to keep your business healthy and growing.

These customers—the ones who buy your goods and services—are called your market.

There may be many people (or businesses) interested in what you have to offer. And if you had unlimited resources (time and money), you might be able to reach all of them to try to convince them to buy what you are selling. It's easy to see this would be a very expensive and unprofitable task.

Businesses, therefore, divide their market into groups of people with similar characteristics, behaviors and attitudes and aim their sales efforts at one or more of these customer groups. This process of dividing your market into groups is called "market segmentation"; the customer groups that are the target of your sales efforts are called your "target markets."

The better you understand the characteristics of your target market(s), the better able you are to meet their needs, communicate effectively and price appropriately. Even the simplest analysis is more effective than none.

Your first challenge is to define your target market. In defining your target market you must answer three questions:

- How can you best characterize your target market?

- Why do these people buy from you?

- How many target markets should you have?

The idea here is to describe the characteristics, behavior and attitudes shared by the majority of your customers.

For example, if you are selling children's clothing, one group of customers might be young mothers in the middle income group who value sturdy, washable clothes at reasonable prices. Another group of customers might be older mothers in the upper middle income group who are willing to pay high prices for sophisticated-looking children's clothes. And if you're the clothing manufacturer, your actual customers are distribution companies or retail stores, not the mothers at all.

If you sell public relations services, one group of customers might be professionals (i.e., doctors, dentists, lawyers) located within 20 miles of your office (or home), with no more than five employees and $300,000 sales, who want a simple brochure they can send to prospective new clients. Another group might consist of large manufacturing companies with $200 million in sales and 1,000 or more employees, who want a glossy, full-color brochure for each of their products.

Your first challenge is to define your target market.

Additional market segmentation categories are listed on the worksheets on the following pages (Figures 7 and 8). Use this as a starting point for defining your target market. If you are already in business, start characterizing your current customers by going through your invoices or customer lists or whatever data you have. Most business owners are surprised when they begin to count the number of people in different categories who actually buy from them—their actual customers often don't match their perception of who their customers are. For example, Mary Lou Allen thought most of her gift shop customers were women, but discovered that more than half were men!

If you are not in business yet, start with those people whom you feel will probably be your best customers when your business gets started.

If you are still not sure how to get started, begin by imagining your customers. Who are they? What do they look like? What are their interests? If possible, observe and/or survey your current customers or the people who you believe will be your customers. Refer to Chapter Two, page 31, Doing The Research, for ideas. In particular, determining a market's characteristics is a favorite task for business school classes. Approach a marketing professor at a local university and see if you can get her or him to take on your market characterizations as a class project.

Lastly, keep in mind that finding your target market often requires some experimentation and trial and error. This is true whether you're starting a small business or running a large corporation. Think of this as a starting point, a vehicle for making cost-effective decisions on things like advertising and sales strategies. It doesn't have to be perfect, it just has to be done.

Some notes on market segmentation:

- For some of the characteristics, it's easier and more appropriate to list a range of answers rather than a discrete answer. For example, you might list the age of your average customer as 25 to 40 rather than 32 years old. Remember to keep the range small enough to be useful.

- Some of you may have dual customers, i.e., the person who buys from you is different from the ultimate user of the product/service. For example, if you manufacture children's clothing, you probably sell to clothing stores who then sell to parents, grandparents or kids. You must, therefore, understand the characteristics—and the needs—of both the store buyers and the ultimate consumers.

- Those of you who sell to large companies or organizations may find you need to understand three or four different groups of people/organizations for each target market: the organization, the users of the product or service within the organization, the people who make the purchase decision (generally the department heads of the users) and the people who handle the administrative details of the purchase (sometimes called procurement or purchasing department). For example, if you sell catering services to large companies, you may need to prepare separate market segmentation worksheets for the companies themselves, the food service managers, the executives who typically use catering services and the purchasing agents who actually write out the contracts. This may seem overwhelming—but once you get used to thinking about it this way, it will be easy to keep straight.

Target markets / organizations/employers / parents of employers

A customer survey is one of those projects that costs you little and gains you a lot.

Figure 7.

Market Segmentation—Consumer

Use this worksheet when your customers are individual consumers.

Characteristics	Primary Customer Group	Secondary Customer Group
DEMOGRAPHIC	*Employers Organizations*	*Parents who need child care services*
Age		
Gender		
Occupation		
Income Level		
Religion		
Race/Ethnic Group		
Education		
Social Class		
Other:		
Other:		
GEOGRAPHIC		
City/Town		
Country		
Size of Population		
Climate		
SPECIAL INTERESTS OR NEEDS:		
IDEAL CUSTOMER BECAUSE:		

Earlier you described the features and benefits you would like to provide to your customers. Now you must look at your target markets—the people you expect will buy your goods and services—and make sure they will be willing to purchase these features and benefits. This is crucial—people will only buy goods and services they need or want, regardless of what it is you want to sell them.

How can you find out why people buy from you (now or in the future)?

If you are already in business, ask your customers. You can ask them personally or request that they fill out a survey. For help with preparing a survey, call your local Small Business Administration office and ask for the nearest Small Business Institute program. Or ask for a SCORE counselor. Or call the marketing department at a local college. They will all advise you for free. A customer survey is one of those projects that costs you little and gains you a lot.

If you are not in business or if you want to target a new market:

- Ask people who fit your target market category. Ask them why they purchase from your competitors. Ask them what their interests are, what is important to them.

- Read—magazines are full of articles about why people buy and what triggers their purchasing decisions. Ask your librarian which magazines would be most likely to deal with your products and/or the market you are trying to serve.

- Attend trade seminars. By contacting trade associations for your industry, you can find out when and where these seminars are given. (Again, refer to the section on Doing the Research for more information on trade associations, seminars and magazines.)

- Talk with other business owners and managers.

- Network with other women in business.

Now for the important part: Make sure there's a match between the features and benefits you are offering and the features and benefits your target market wants to buy.

If you are like most other businesspeople, there will not be an exact match the first time around. You can do one of two things: you can modify what you're offering or you can target a different market.

It is much better to make this discovery before you get started than after you have sunk a lot of time and money into your business. And if you have thoroughly defined your product and your target market, it may be relatively easy to make the modifications needed to match them up. It may be as simple as providing additional training for your salespeople to meet your market's need for knowledgeable service. Or having office hours in the evening to meet your market's need for convenience. Or changing the color of your children's clothes to meet your market's need for appearing trendy. Or increasing the price of your product to meet your market's need for appearing extravagant. In fact, modifying your basic products and services to fit customer demands can be one of the most powerful marketing tools you have.

Compare the market you identified in the market segmentation worksheets with the features and benefits you defined earlier. Then make the appropriate

Modifying your basic products and services to fit customer demands can be one of the most powerful marketing tools.

Figure 8.

Market Segmentation—Business

Use this worksheet when your customers are businesses.

Criteria	Primary Customer Group	Secondary Customer Group
Type of Business (Manufacturer, retail, wholesale, service)		
Standard Industrial Classification		
No. of Employees		
Annual Sales		
Location		
Organization Structure		
Purchase Decisionmaker		
Others Who Influence Purchase Decision		
Special Interest or Needs		
Ideal Customer Because		

If you are selling to a large organization, you may also need to understand up to three different groups of people: 1) the users of your product/service, 2) the people who make the purchase decision and 3) the people who handle the administrative details of the purchase. In this case, fill out the "Market Segmentation—Consumer" form for each group.

changes to match what you're offering for sale with the market needs. It will probably take some extra homework to get this done. But it's a lot less expensive and time-consuming than making the changes after you've already started your business.

How Many Target Markets Should You Have?

You may have more than one market you wish to target. There are only two limits on choosing target markets. The first is "natural selection," i.e., there are only so many groups of people that will want to purchase your goods or services at a price that yields you profit.

The second is your time and money. Since each target market has distinct needs and wants, each will require a different marketing strategy, different advertising campaign and, perhaps, even a different twist on the product or level of service or other features of your business. Preparing, executing and monitoring these diverse areas takes time and money, and if you are like most people, you have only a limited amount of these resources. So start with your best one or two target markets. When you have done as well as you can with these, focus on your next best (and so on) and grow your business effectively and profitably. Business owners are notorious for being very optimistic about their market share.

Your first challenge was to figure out who your customers are (i.e., define your target market). The next step is to make sure there are enough of them to keep your business healthy and growing.

There are three questions you have to answer:

- What is the size of your market(s)?

- Is your market size increasing, decreasing or staying the same?

- What percent of the market do (will) you have?

What is the size of your market(s)?
There is a substantial amount of data available about numbers of people in different locales, age groups, income brackets, occupations and so on. Two excellent places to start are the library (for national or regional data) and your Chamber of Commerce or regional development board (for local data). You can also obtain information from trade publications, marketing consultants, other business people, schools and colleges. (See page 31, Doing the Research, for guidelines on getting the information you need.)

If you are marketing to businesses, these same resources have information on number of companies, size of companies, and so on.

Is your market increasing, decreasing or staying the same?
The sources that helped you find the size of your market can also help you determine its growth pattern. In addition, newspapers and magazines routinely report this kind of information. The key question you want to address is: What social, political, regulatory, economic and technological changes are taking place that could impact your industry, your market or your market's perception of and desire for your products/services? For example, many companies are beginning to offer products and services for older Americans as our society ages. Or the

Business owners are notorious for being very optimistic about their market share.

Figure 9.

Buying Habits of Your Target Market

Answer the questions which are appropriate for your business.

Criteria	Primary Customer Group	Secondary Customer Group
Who makes the buying decision?		
How much will they pay for your service?		
How many units will they buy each time a purchase is made?		
How many times must you contact them before they make a purchase decision?		
When will they buy?		
Is your business seasonal?		
How will they finance their purchase?		
Market Description:		

market for video stores, which was non-existent in the early 1980s, has mush-roomed since the arrival of inexpensive VCRs (and may disappear with the advent of new interactive computer technology). And many high-end restaurants have gone out of business in these recessionary times, especially since Yuppies have started having children.

If you can't find any other data on future growth, you can always extrapolate based on historical information adjusted with your best assessment of the changes that are taking place in your geographic market area.

This information is of extreme importance to your funding sources, who have their own sources of information on what's happening in your industry. You may even want to contact a banker to get this data.

What percent of the market do (will) you have?

Your percentage of the total market is called your market share. It is calculated either in sales dollars or in units sold, and it is generally calculated on an annual basis. For example, if the total market for bookkeeping services in your local area is $1 million per year and you sell $75,000 worth of bookkeeping services, then your share of the market is (75,000/1,000,000) x 100, or 7.5%. If 10,000,000 bibs are sold annually across the U.S. and you sell 125,000 bibs per year, your market share is (125,000/10,000,000) x 100, or 1.25%.

Calculating market share can be largely a matter of judgment. It is dependent on the number of competitors, whether your business is national or local, how you've defined your market, and so on. Business owners are notorious for being very optimistic about their market share.

The best way to determine what is realistic is to talk to other businesspeople, especially those in the same industry. This is where you can get a lot of help from your local SCORE chapter, Small Business Development Center, Small Business Institute, SBA office and library. It is also a good idea to talk with your banker and see what her or his thoughts are. You may be very nervous about picking up the phone and calling these people. Remember that they are just people—even if they have imposing titles—and most will be glad to help you.

Once you have defined your customers and are confident there will be enough of them—now and in the future—for your business to profitably grow, the next step is to understand their buying habits.

For example, do they buy seasonally? Ice cream stands do a booming business in the summer and almost no business in the winter.

Who makes the buying decisions? The purchasing agent in a large company may handle the paperwork for purchasing your carpet cleaning service, but the decision on whom to buy from is usually made by the facilities manager.

Figure 9 has a list of questions about the buying habits of your customers. Answer the questions for each product, product line, service or service line.

Putting It All Together

Now consolidate all the information into a written description of your market that will be incorporated into your business plan. Start by describing your market—who they are, the characteristics they share, their needs, wants or desires. Then describe your market size and whether it is growing, shrinking or staying the same. Finish with a brief description of your market's buying habits. For most small businesses, this entire section will be no more than one page and will probably be less. But all the thought you've put into it will enable you to answer any questions posed by your funding sources, customers, suppliers and other significant people.

When you're finished, give copies to your business advisors. Ask them to make sure it's in language that any businessperson (including your banker) can understand. Then ask them the four big questions:

1. To whom am I selling?

2. Why are they buying?

3. Is my market shrinking, growing, or staying the same?

4. What are their buying habits?

If they can answer those questions after reading your market description (without additional explanation from you), then this section of your plan is complete.

Now that you have thoroughly defined your target markets, have confidence that you will have enough customers to be profitable and understand their buying habits, it's appropriate to ask yourself:

• How can I find these people?

• How will I attract them and keep them as customers?

• How can I expand my markets?

These questions will be covered in Chapter Four.

COMPETITION

Business is inherently competitive. There will always be other companies, stores or individuals who are in competition with you for your customers' dollars. Even in the unlikely event that you have a new or unique product or service, competitors will soon be attracted to your line of business when they see that you are profitable.

If you want to have a growing, profitable business, you must know what your competitors are doing. You want information such as:

• What products/services do they sell?

• What do they believe are their customers' motivations for buying?

• Who are their target markets?

• What do they believe are the shared characteristics of their target markets?

• At what price do they sell?

And so on. In other words, you want to know about your competition all the things you just figured out about your own company.

Competition may seem to you to be a little like warfare—you spy on your competitors and encroach on their turf before they do it to you. In some cases

You want to know about your competition all the things you just figured out about your own company.

this is a reality of business, and women must learn to do it well if their businesses are to grow.

But the best competitive strategy is rarely to take a cutthroat position with your competitors. Better to understand your target markets' motivations for buying, to provide product and service features which appeal to those needs and wants, to communicate this to your target markets—and do these three things more effectively than your competitors. In order to do this you must know what your competitors are doing.

There are other important reasons for observing your competitors:

- You may find there are market segments whose needs are not being met by anyone. You can set up your business to meet the needs of this market segment (sometimes called "market niche").

- You may learn new ways of doing business that will work for you.

- You may learn more about your target markets' buying habits.

- You can avoid opening a business in a market that is already adequately served.

- You may avoid errors that your competitors have already made.

The key to effective competitive assessment is to set up a structured approach for gathering and cataloging information about your competitors. There are four elements to this approach:

- Identify your competition

- Describe your competitors in a way that will be useful to you

- Compare your competitors' businesses to your business

- Obtain current information on competitors

Identifying Your Competition

Who is your competition?

1. *Anyone who sells similar products/services to your target market.*
   For example, if you sell recordkeeping services to small professional businesses, you are in direct competition with other companies which sell recordkeeping services to small professional businesses. Your competitors might include other small recordkeeping businesses such as yourself and accounting firms which also supply recordkeeping services to their customers.

2. *Anyone who sells similar products/services to other market segments.*
   Companies which currently sell recordkeeping services to small manufacturing companies could easily start marketing to small professional businesses if it looked sufficiently profitable. Therefore, you must be aware of the strategies and trends of businesses selling to other market segments.

3. *Anyone who sells alternative products/services to your target market.*
   Most businesses can now purchase easy-to-use computer programs for doing their own recordkeeping. You are therefore in competition with the companies selling these programs since they are providing your target market with an alternative to your services.

4. *Anyone who could sell similar products/services to your target markets.*
   Markets are continually changing. When you are successful, you will undoubtedly attract competitors into your line of business.

It may seem like an enormous task to identify and monitor your competitors. Getting the preliminary information will probably be time-consuming, but following up and expanding on the information will become second nature.

Describing Your Competition

Your goal is to describe your competition's products/services, target markets, operations, management and financing. It may take a while to get all this information, and you will probably never have perfect information. But the more you can find out, the better your business will be.

Make a list of competitors for each of your products/services. Then start files on each of your top five competitors. (A plain manila folder for each competitor will suffice.) For each competitor you'll want to know:

- Years in business
- Number of employees
- Dollar sales
- Unit sales
- Market share
- Financial strength
- Profitability
- President/owner
- Outside advisors
- Key employees
- Target markets
- Pricing
- Advertising themes
- Promotion/public relations efforts
- Significant changes (new people, products, etc.)
- How this competitor competes with you

If you are like most people, you will not get all this information in detail before you complete your initial business plan. Don't let this be a stumbling block to completing the plan. Do as much as you can now and routinely update the information as you run your business.

Competition Comparison

The next step is to compare your business with competing businesses in areas which are important to your customers. Figure 10 provides a format for doing so. Not all the areas shown in the figure will be important to your customers—and there may be other areas not shown in the figure which are critical. Have your business advisors help you select the categories which make sense for your business—then fill out the figure.

By comparing the results with your knowledge of your market's needs and wants, you can determine how you stack up against the competition. You may find that you need to alter your basic strategy or change existing operations to compete more effectively. For example, when Sally Steiner did this exercise for her tailoring business, she discovered that she provided better service, higher quality and faster turnaround time than her competitors, but she charged more than 30% less. She is now in the process of increasing her prices so she can finally become profitable.

Remember, you won't be able to compete in every area. Choose the areas where you can gain a competitive advantage, one based on your business' strengths (level of service is often most important). Try to match your strengths against your competitors' weaknesses.

Obtaining Competitor Information

Now that you know the information you need, how can you go about getting it? There are many ways to get information about your competitors. Some of them are unethical and you should never get so wrapped up in the success of your business that you resort to these methods.

If you are in a retail business, the easiest way to get competitive information is to shop their store. This will allow you to see their products, their level of service and their place of business. You can probably deduce their target markets and their marketing strategy by observing them. If they seem disorganized and confused, they probably are.

If you are in a manufacturing business, you can probably see or even purchase your competitor's products at the places where they're sold. You can also talk to material suppliers, sales reps and store owners or buyers (who buy competing products) to get information about your competition.

If you are in a service business, it is more difficult to get such direct information. The Yellow Pages and newspaper advertisements are readily available. You can also get information by asking your competitor's customers if they're satisfied with the service—just be open and aboveboard about why you are asking.

Many of your competitors will attend the same trade seminars. In fact, you are likely to meet and become friendly with them. It may become evident that they have selected different target markets and you may be able to share infor-

Figure 10.

Comparing Myself to My Competitors

PREPARED BY:	DATE:
COMPETITOR:	

Describe your competitors:		How do you stack up?
Price		
Quality		
Level of service		
Location		
Advertising		
Other yardsticks		

mation. (Be careful, though, not to give away information which may impact your future plans.)

Once you've gathered the information about your competition, write it up in paragraph form. Include one paragraph about each of your top competitors (direct and indirect), describing their strengths and weaknesses and how you compare with them.

## CHAPTER FOUR

Management

Studies have shown that 98% of businesses fail due to poor management. But they don't tell you what "good management" means. The purpose of this section is to describe the process of sound business management, define the areas of business which must be managed and tell you what belongs in your business plan under the heading "Management."

Management textbooks define management as performing the following five functions:

1. *Planning:* Setting objectives, allocating resources and establishing strategies for attaining objectives.

2. *Organizing:* Determining what tasks must be done, when, by whom and with what resources to attain the objectives.

3. *Staffing:* Hiring personnel and assigning the right person to the right job.

4. *Directing:* Supervising the staff to make sure the work gets done efficiently and effectively.

5. *Controlling:* Monitoring the results of these activities, analyzing them for deviations from the anticipated results and modifying future activities accordingly.

This definition is very comprehensive, and as a business owner you will do all of these things. However, I find it easier to think of management as a five-step process.

1. You set goals.

2. You decide what you (or your employees) are going to do to reach those goals.

3. You do it.

4. You look at your results and compare them to your goals.

5. You incorporate what you learned in #4 into your thinking and go back to #2.

In real life, most people do #3 and a little bit of #2. In other words, most people take action without thinking through what they're trying to achieve and without evaluating their options (if they even believe they have options) for achieving it. They waste their hard-earned experience and limited time laying blame for poor decisions rather than taking the time to learn valuable lessons. They let the daily crises of their business control their direction rather than planning the direction that will take them toward their goals. And they end up in the 98% whose businesses fail due to poor management.

You can be different. You can take the management of your business into your own hands or you can let your daily crises manage your business.

It's not hard to plan, it just takes time—concentrated, thinking time—on a routine basis and a willingness to take the risk of owning up to your goals.

The first step is to set goals. The second step is to understand the various facets of business for which you must go through this process. Each step is outlined in this chapter.

SETTING YOUR GOALS

In Chapter One you wrote down your dreams for your business and its future. You need to turn your dreams into concrete goals.

A goal is a definitive statement of what you'd like to achieve in the future. Effective goals are measurable, easy to understand, and expressed in writing. Your business plans and activities will be developed and implemented to accomplish these goals so you (and your employees) must be very sure of what the goals are and what they mean. As a minimum you should provide a timetable and, if you have partners or employees, assign responsibilities.

I'd like to digress here and tell a personal story. I used to be one of those women who went through life without goals. My self-image was low because I never gave myself credit for accomplishing anything—even though by other people's standards I had accomplished a lot. I would feed myself all of the old lines that many women feed themselves: "It was no big deal." "Anyone could do what I did." "It didn't take any special talent."

About ten years ago, I decided to take karate lessons to get myself in shape and to reduce my fear of being physically defenseless. In karate classes, everyone wore a colored belt. Each color symbolized a different level of achievement with white as the lowest level, black as the highest and five colors in between. Every three months each student took a test to see if he/she was ready to move up to the next color belt.

I remember my first test. I was terrified. I had to do my karate exercises in front of my teacher and the entire class, and I had to break a wooden board with my hand. Before the test I had knots in my stomach. I fed myself more lines: "I'm not good enough." "I don't know enough." "Maybe I should go home and forget the whole thing."

Well, I passed the test. I wasn't the best in the class, but I tried hard and I was good enough to pass. I even broke the board with my hand (after ten tries and a very sore hand). I was promoted from white belt to yellow belt.

But here's the best part of the story. When I went to my next lesson, I could see that I was better than the new white belts. I couldn't deny it because I had visual proof. I couldn't use my old stories that I wasn't that good or that talented or that anyone could do it. Not everyone could. But there was just no denying that I had done it—I worked hard at it, I developed the ability, and I achieved my goal.

Effective goals are measurable, easy to communicate, easy to understand and expressed in writing.

Figure 11.

Personal and Business Goal Summary

Some suggested areas for goals are shown. Limit your goals to the most important.

1. List your personal goals.	For next year:	In three years:
A. Financial		
B. Family		
C. Personal Attitude		
D. Health		
E.		
F.		

2. List your business goals. Fill in those that are pertinent to your business.
For next year: In three years:

1. QUANTITATIVE GOALS:	For next year:	In three years:
A. Sales ($)		
B. Number of Clients		
C. Profit ($)		
D. Profit (% of Sales)		
E. Market Share		
F. Number of Employees		

2. QUALITATIVE GOALS:		
A. Market Position		
B. Kind of Business		
C. Target Markets		
D. Business Culture or Style		
E. Other (specify)		

3. Potential conflicts between personal and business goals:

By taking the test and continuing in karate, I learned two valuable lessons: 1) I am capable of taking pride in my accomplishments and undoing my habit of negative self-talk, and 2) I have control over my life; my success doesn't come from someone else—it comes from my own actions. In my mind, I learned both of those lessons by accomplishing a *measurable* goal, i.e., a goal for which the results—success or failure—can be measured.

As women, we often find that it takes a strong conscious effort to break the habit of negative self-talk and to take responsibility for our own success. (For those of you who don't know what self-talk is, it's the little voice in your head that at this very moment is asking "What's self-talk?") Self-talk has a tremendous influence on our behavior, and studies have shown that more than 80% of it is negative. So while our conscious mind is telling us to "go for it," our unconscious mind may very well be saying, "Forget it! You can't (or shouldn't or won't) succeed." Without our even being aware of it, we unconsciously sabotage our own businesses. My personal experience is that setting goals is one excellent mechanism for breaking negative self-talk and its accompanying self-sabotage. It provides a measure that even our unconscious mind can't deny, and it validates our ability to be in the world in any way we want to be.

When writing measurable goals, specify the result you're trying to achieve and the time frame for achieving it. That way you can evaluate after the specified time whether or not you've succeeded. For example:

Non-measurable goal	Measurable goal
Increase sales	Increase sales of Product A 15 percent by December
Get more clients	Have 20 new paying clients by this time next year
Appear more professional	Produce promotional brochure and refurbish office within four months

The first step toward achieving goals is to be absolutely clear about what you want.

On page 67, you'll see a worksheet for summarizing your business and personal goals for next year and for three years from now. It may seem unusual to include your personal goals in your business goal summary. But your business is a reflection of you, so it makes sense to develop your business plans and activities with your personal priorities in mind. If you want to work at home, fine. Plan for it. If you want to bring your children to work with you, fine. Plan for it. You may find that you cannot achieve all of these goals immediately or even within the next year. But the first step toward achieving them is to be absolutely clear about what you want.

Now fill out the worksheet.

Are you having difficulty defining all of your goals? It's often frightening for both women and men to write down their goals for the first time. To some it seems like guesswork—like committing to something they don't know anything about. To others, goal-setting feels like a major commitment that could be setting them up for failure. And to others, success itself seems frightening—somehow unfeminine—and they avoid goal-setting because they fear the success it might bring. If you are immobilized by trying to prepare goals, go back to Chapter One, Dealing with Fear (page 18), and analyze your fears. Remember that you have already done a lot of work just to get to this chapter and you probably know more than you realize. Don't let negative self-talk get in the way. Goals aren't meant to be straitjackets. They simply provide you with a way to measure what you've achieved, to pat yourself on the back when things go right and to evaluate why some things didn't go as planned. Think about other times you have set goals and achieved them. You can do it.

THE SEVEN FACETS OF BUSINESS

On page 30, we covered the seven areas that must be managed: product development, marketing, sales, operations, personnel, finance and management itself.

In each of these areas you must decide what you're going to do to reach the goals you just developed. Your strength may lie in one or two of these areas, and you may know little of the remaining five or six. The purpose of this chapter is to describe them in a way that enables you to write a clear plan for how you will manage each area.

As you read through this section and develop your plans, keep in mind that all these areas must be managed and they all take time. Large companies assign the responsibility for each facet of business to separate people (e.g., manager of product development, manager of marketing, and so on). As a small business owner, that's a luxury you can't afford. Even if you are the only employee of the business, all facets of the business must be managed. Many people don't realize this when they start their business.

For example, Rae Ann Smith was considering opening an engineering consulting business. She had strong communication skills, had always thought about starting her own business and believed she could get a consulting contract from her current employer. Rae Ann felt this was particularly good timing for her because she had just had her third child and was anxious to work part time so she would have more time for her children.

What Rae Ann hadn't considered was:

- While the consulting contract from her current employer looked promising, she couldn't count on it for long term—in hard times consultants are often the first people to be taken off the payroll.

- On average it takes a consultant two hours of marketing and sales to get one hour of billable business. Therefore, if she wanted to work 24 hours per week, she could only count on eight hours of billable time. At $50 per hour, that adds up to $400 per week, considerably less than she could earn at her current job and not enough to meet her personal financial needs.

- As a business owner, Rae Ann would have to define her business and products and develop a market niche—things she had never done before. She would also have to continually upgrade her "product" and her skills in order to stay current with the technology. In the past, her employer had handled and paid for all product development and training.

- Since she would be working for herself, Rae Ann would have to take care of (or hire someone to take care of) all of the "operations" aspects of her business. For a consultant, this is not very detailed, but it does include such things as recordkeeping, billing, typing, filing and so on.

- Rae Ann would incur expenses that she does not have on her current job, including business cards, stationery, office supplies, legal advice, accounting support, advertising and promotional materials, and so on.

Rae Ann was somewhat discouraged when she began to understand that starting a business required more than getting one contract. She realized that she had to reconsider her personal goals and her financial needs before she could make a sound decision. Rae Ann is now considering whether she would be willing to start her business and have it grow very slowly while her children are young. She now knows she needs to manage all facets of her business, but believes she can do it within her time constraints by stretching out the work (and the fees). This will require her to live off savings for a while.

You may also be getting discouraged as you look at the long list of things that must be managed in order to run a viable business. While I can't shorten the list, it helps to remember that there are many things you do in life that take just as much planning and attention as running a business, and you do them successfully without an enormous amount of training. Raising children certainly fits this description. You learn as you go along, you juggle many different aspects of raising children at the same time, you try new activities if the old activities don't produce the desired results and you don't give up because you've never done it before or because you've made some mistakes. You take a big risk when you decide to raise children, but most of us do it anyway. It's no different from starting a business.

Product Development

In Chapter Two you developed a clear understanding of your product or service and all of the features that you're offering for sale. This is a critical part of the business planning process. Take the time now to review the list of distinguishing features you developed in Figure 6. Make sure you're still satisfied that: a) you have a thorough understanding of what you're offering for sale and b) your product/service (including the entire list of features) will provide benefits that are desired by your customers.

Ideas for developing new products and services are not always something you plan for. Most often they come from listening to current and prospective customers talk about what they do and don't like about your products and services.

For example, Deirdre Arons thought she was selling three "products": computer hardware selection, computer software selection and computer training. However, after operating for a year she discovered most of her clients hired her to figure out how to make the computer equipment that they already owned do what they originally purchased it for and then teach them how to use it for that application. Deirdre developed the capability to do that more rapidly and effectively, and now she has a single product: computer applications development and training. She recognized that her clients were telling her what service they wanted to buy from her, and she modified her business accordingly.

Sometimes the best new product ideas come from the most unexpected sources. If you listen and are open to suggestions, current customers will suggest

Some of your best information may actually come from the people who don't buy from you.

modifications or major changes to your existing products as well as new, complementary products to round out your product/service lines. Some of your best information may actually come from the people who *don't* buy from you. By finding out why they didn't buy, you can get a wealth of information on their needs related to whatever it is you're selling.

Whether you're already in business or just getting started, you may also have your own new ideas for products. Perhaps you're currently limiting yourself to only one product/service because you don't yet have the time or money to focus on more than one product line. However, as soon as the product line becomes profitable you plan to add another.

For example, Diane Pushin manufactures bibs for children. She knows there is also a demand for bibs for the elderly. The manufacturing process for both bibs is almost the same, but things like color and style will have to be developed for the adult market. Initially it seemed to Diane that it would be simple to pursue both markets at the same time since the products are so similar. As she thought about new product development, however, she realized each market requires a different marketing plan, sales plan and financial plan as well as a substantial amount of Diane's personal time. Although Diane wants to push forward in both areas, she is waiting until her line of children's bibs is profitable before starting to develop and market the adult bibs.

The keys to new product development are:

- Recognize that the market's needs are *always* changing in response to the social, political, regulatory, economic and technological changes that are taking place in our society. In order to be successful, your products/ services must be responsive to these changing needs. Therefore, you must routinely evaluate, develop and/or make available new products.

  At the same time, *please* do not use this as an excuse to continually change your product lines in hope of finding the "magic" product that will guarantee you your fortune (aka "the lottery theory of business"). New product selections should always be based on a thorough understanding of your market.

- For each new product or service, develop a complete understanding of what you are selling. In other words, read through Chapter Two again for every product or service you're considering.

  If you are in a service business, you must be absolutely clear about what you are providing and how you will provide it. Product development includes developing an understanding of the benefits your new service will provide as well as developing the procedures, handouts, seminars, worksheets, supply list and so on that are needed to provide the new service.

  If you are in a retail or wholesale business, you must thoroughly understand the features and benefits of your new product lines and train yourself or your employees to be able to describe them effectively to your prospective customers. You must consider the level of service, guarantees, and so on that you will provide with the new product lines.

  If you are in the manufacturing business (including home-based crafts businesses), product development includes developing the product to meet the customers' needs and developing a manufacturing process which will consistently produce that product to your specifications.

In order to be successful, your products/services must be responsive to change.

- Regularly evaluate whether you are truly making a profit on each of your products/services. If you've been in business for a while, you may be spending much of your energy on products/services which are no longer profitable. These products may hold great sentimental value for you because they're the ones that got you started in business, but if they're not profitable, it's time to drop them in favor of newer, more profitable products.

It is now time to write your product development plan. You will want to mention:

- your focus on current (or initial) product lines

- your plan to listen routinely (at least once per week) to your customers or prospects for new product/service ideas

- any new product/service ideas that you are currently considering along with your expected time frame for development, market testing and introduction

First write it. Then do it.
Begin by answering these questions:

1. What new products or services are you currently developing (i.e., *other* than those that you've already defined)? Note: You may not be developing any, which could be very appropriate for your business. Remember, it's better to achieve profitability on one product/service than to spread yourself too thin over several.

2. To whom will you market each of these new products or services?

3. How do these new products or services fit with your business focus? with your business strengths?

4. How will these new products or services make your business more profitable?

5. What are your projected time frame and costs for developing these products or services? Market testing? Introduction to prospective customers?

6. What new products or services are your competitors developing?

Write one or two paragraphs containing your responses to the above questions.

Marketing

You attract markets through promotion, pricing and location.

Back in Chapter Three, you defined your target markets. Now you must address the following important marketing questions:

- How can I attract and keep these markets?

- How can I expand my markets?

You attract markets through promotion, pricing and location.

You keep markets by continuing to satisfy their needs at a price they're willing to pay.

You expand your markets by finding other people just like your current customers who are willing to buy what you have to offer.

Marketing is not an exact science. You may want someone to tell you the "right" answers about how to promote your business, how to price, where to locate and how to determine your markets' needs, but there are no right or wrong answers in marketing; there is only what works and what doesn't work for your business. And your marketing success comes through a combination of research, timing, hard work, learning from others, luck and, most importantly, learning from your own past mistakes. To quote a successful businessperson:

Interiewer: To what do you attribute your success?

Businessperson: To making the right decisions.

Interviewer: How did you learn to make the right decisions?

Businessperson: I got experience.

Interviewer: How did you get experience?

Businessperson: I made the wrong decisions.

Marketing is more than a series of plans and decisions—it's an attitude, a way of thinking that says:

> *I am in business to serve the customer. Every decision I make takes the needs of my customer into consideration. I will see to it that everyone in my company is attuned to customer needs.*

Maintaining a marketing attitude can be very difficult.

It is hard to pinpoint your customers' needs. Your target market is not homogeneous, so each person's needs may vary. As your customers are constantly bombarded with new ideas, new technologies and new choices, their needs and desires keep changing. And no matter how much research you do on people's needs, our nature as human beings is that our actual behavior is unpredictable.

It is also hard to keep someone else at the center of your business when you're up to your eyeballs in internal business problems. During times of stress, many of us ignore customer needs, refuse customer requests and feel imposed upon by "demanding" customers.

Maintaining a marketing attitude takes time, creativity, foresight, research, planning, constant attention and discipline. Why should you do it? Because it's the only way to effectively grow a business.

Let me give an example. I recently tried to buy a television from a local electronics store. At first, the salesperson was too busy taking care of paperwork to pay attention to me. Finally I got him to show me the three televisions in my size and price range, and I asked what the differences were between the three. His answer: "They're all basically the same except for the cabinet. Just decide which cabinet you want and I'll get your television from the stockroom." I'm not convinced this person really wanted me to buy a television.

Needless to say, I went to another store, was shown the same three televisions, and asked the same question. This salesperson answered: "Before I can answer that, tell me when, where and how often you plan to use the television, because that will help us decide which one is right for you." I was sold before I even answered the question because I trusted this person to have my needs in mind when he made his recommendation. And since I originally told this story in the first edition of *On Your Own*, the first store has gone out of business.

Here's another, subtler example. I once worked with a woman in an artwork services business. Her routine complaint was that prospective customers never returned her calls when they said they would. She had gone to all the trouble of describing her business to them and telling them how she could help them with their artwork needs, and they did not seem to care how their lack of follow-through affected her business. What she never understood is that it's not their job nor their responsibility to care about her—she's just one more person trying to sell something to them. But if she wants their business, it's her responsibility to care about them.

Why should you have a marketing attitude? Think of the last time *you* did business with a company that didn't have one.

Now on to the three areas of marketing that you have to plan: promotion, pricing and location.

Promotion

Start by setting promotion objectives. Here is a long, but not complete, list of possibilities. Next to each option is an example of how to carry out the objective based on an upscale houseware retail store selling name-brand cookware, bakeware, small appliances and gadgets directly to consumers.

1. *Penetrate specialized markets.* Gear marketing efforts to women and men who enjoy foreign cookery (e.g., Chinese, French, Italian, etc.).

2. *Sell more to present customers.* Target promotional campaigns to people who have purchased from you before. Or plan to sell more than one item to people who are ready to make a purchase.

3. *Specialize in terms of products or services.* Provide cooking classes and specialized products to your niche market. You might have classes in Chinese cookery and sell seven kinds of woks, porcelain bowls and spoons and the largest selection of Chinese cookbooks in the area. Or you might have classes in microwave cookery and sell the latest microwave cookware and cookbooks.

4. *Change your business' image.* During a recession, when people are not spending much money on upscale cookware, you might offer more conventional cookware at discount prices. (Note of caution: This is an expensive decision that is difficult to pull off and should not be taken lightly.)

5. *Penetrate geographical markets more deeply.* Open two new stores in your city.

6. *Create "top-of-mind" awareness.* Develop advertising, publicity and public service campaigns so that everyone in your geographical area knows your store by name.

Create "top-of-mind" awareness.

Figure 12.

Promotion Options*

Paid Advertising
Radio
Television/Cable
Print
  Newspapers
  Magazines
  "Shoppers"
  "Yellow Pages"
  Special directories
  Trade or industry directories
  Outdoor billboards
  Show programs

Direct Mail
Letters
Newsletters
Sales or product/service
  announcements
Flyers
Postcards
Brochures
Coupons

Public Relations
News releases
Articles in magazines, journals, etc.
Open houses
Speaking engagements
Interview shows
Sponsorship of community events and
  activities
Seminars
Workshops
Club memberships
Public Service Announcements

Telemarketing
Inquiry handling
Direct marketing by phone
Service: customer complaints,
  follow-up, special offers

One-on-One Selling
Presentation materials
Personal letters
Customized proposals
Some telemarketing
Sales personnel training

Sales Promotions
Discounts
Loss leaders
Coupons
Contests

Specialty Advertising
Matchbooks, keychains, and other
  novelties
Calendars
Datebooks

Facilities
Site location and shared
  advertising
Signage
Window displays
Point-of-purchase displays
Fixtures and layout of store
Lighting

Other Types of Promotion
Flyers
Posters
Handouts
Blimps and balloons
Sandwich boards
Free samples, etc.

*From *The Market Planning Guide*, by David H. Bangs,
(Dover, NH: Upstart Publishing, 1990)

7. *Expand demographically.* Once you have successfully penetrated the market for women ages 25–55, target women over 55 with cookware and gadgets designed to make cooking for one or two much easier.

8. *Increase sales of specific products or services.* Promote your small appliances.

9. *Announce a new product, new location, new personnel and so on.* Promote the fact that you now have a master chef assisting you in selecting your cookware inventory.

10. *Create image of community support.* Support your local public radio station and volunteer your time to visible local charities.

Each of these objectives (and associated examples) has implications in how you promote your business, price your products, train your salespeople, spend your valuable resources (time and money), not to mention where you locate andhow many salespeople you hire.

For instance, if you plan to sell more than one item to each person ready to make a purchase (#2), you may have to add salespeople, provide meaningful sales training, add soft lighting and music so your store is a comfortable place to shop, provide discounts for multiple purchases, promote your personalized service, and so on. If you plan to promote your small appliances (#8), you may have to stock more inventory provide technical training to your salespeople on how to demonstrate, use and/or fix appliances heavily advertise the appliances; provide in-store warranties, and so on.

Review the list of promotion options in Figure 12 to get an idea of what's available to meet your promotion objectives. As you look at the list, pretend you're a customer. Which promotion options would catch your attention? Which options would attract you? Which would annoy you? Write down two or three options that feel right to you from the customer's perspective and that meet your objectives.

See what others in your industry and/or type of business are doing. Read trade journals—how do companies like yours advertise? If you haven't done it yet, scout out your competitors and see how they're promoting themselves. Select the ideas that seem to be working. Would they work for you?

Consider the seasonality and cycles of your business. You may need to do more promoting at certain times of the year than at others. Many small business owners have a two-pronged promotional strategy: they have ongoing, routine promotional campaigns throughout the year and then have special promotion projects to meet special needs.

After you've developed some ideas for promoting your business, talk to your business advisors. See if your ideas make sense to them. Also, get up your nerve and talk to some of your customers. Find out what kinds of promotions they dislike.

Find out the costs of the kinds of promotion you're considering. If you're thinking of print ads, call the newspaper and see what they cost. For direct mailing of brochures, call an ad agency or a marketing consultant to get prices on brochures; then add in the cost of mailing them. If you don't know where to start to get prices, call SCORE. Or make use of the network you've been developing, your business advisors or the Chamber of Commerce. Look in the Yellow

Pages. Also try to find industry averages for advertising and promotion expenses to see if your ideas are in line—your trade association or Small Business Development Center may be able to help with this.

Most of your options cost money, and some are painfully expensive. You will save yourself a lot of work in your financial analysis by making your promotion decisions with a sound knowledge of costs.

Now select the promotional activities you plan to use. As you consider this selection, keep in mind two of the primary rules of sound promotion:

1. Be consistent. Your advertising and promotion campaign should be consistent with the image you're trying to portray. And it should also be consistent with itself. If you develop a logo, use it on all of your company literature and advertising. Even without a logo, make sure your business cards match your business stationery and your promotional pieces and your advertisements, and so on. Use the same type style, the same business name, and the same colors. Otherwise you will confuse your customers.

2. Repeat your message. I frequently hear from business owners who advertised one time in a particular newspaper or magazine and were disappointed at the lack of results. According to Jay Levinson in his book *Guerrilla Marketing Attack*, a person needs to see your message nine times before they act on it, *and* people only actually see or notice one out of three messages. So you need to get your message out 27 times (and in a variety of media) before it will have the effect you desire.

Write your promotional plan answering these questions:

*   What promotional activities will you use?

*   Why do you believe they will work?

Stick with this plan unless there is an overriding reason not to. If you're like other business owners, you're likely to get tired of your "look" just about the time it starts to mean something to your customers. Remember who's at the center of your business—your customers.

By the way, once your business name becomes available to your community, you will begin getting requests to buy advertising in a variety of local newspapers, magazines and newsletters. If you haven't planned for this advertising and you can't think of a compelling reason to change your plan, don't do it.

For example, Debbie Herman thought she was getting a terrific deal when a local business magazine asked if she would advertise her personnel consulting business in their classified section. After all, they said they would be able to help her design her ad for free, and Debbie had heard rumors about how expensive ad agencies are.

Debbie had done neither her research nor a promotional plan when this offer came along. She had no idea what kind of response to expect from such an ad—in fact, it had never crossed her mind to think about the response. She was just starting her business and had a vague notion that people advertised when they wanted to get new customers.

Remember who's at the center of your business—your customers.

What Debbie found out is that business-to-business consultants rarely purchase newspaper or magazine advertising because it doesn't draw new clients. At best, it keeps their name in the public eye. Debbie would have made better use of her money if she had advertised in the Yellow Pages or joined the Chamber of Commerce. After two months and $300, her response rate was zero.

Don't make the same mistake. Research the promotional activities that make sense for your business. Plan for them. *Then* implement your plan.

Pricing

There are no mechanical formulas for cranking out prices. However, there are a few guidelines you can follow that will help provide a price range for you to safely work within.

1. Price = Product + Level of Service + Image + Expenses + Profit. Unless there is an overriding reason not to, your price should at least cover your costs and provide you with some profit. In addition, your pricing will reflect an intangible image factor. In an ideal world, you would be able to assign a dollar value to the perception of your goods and services in the eyes of your current and prospective customers. In the real world, you do this based on research and experience.

    For example, one small business sold a nutritive doughnut made of wheat germ, whole wheat and honey which, when deep fried, did not absorb grease. It was cheap and simple to make, with high profit margins. The business owners received excellent advice from their local business school on how to conduct a market survey. Every customer got a free box of doughnuts for filling out a simple form. Their questions were basic: Why did you buy this product? For its nutritive value? For the packaging? What size package do you prefer? When do you do your shopping?

    The results? The owners discovered that people would pay a high premium for a natural product. They were more apt to buy a medium-sized package (the small packages disappeared too fast, the large ones went stale). Because it was a natural product with no preservatives, it was necessary to know when people did their shopping in order to deal with the constraints of shelf life.

    As women we are notorious for undervaluing ourselves and pricing too low. I know a woman with a manufacturing company who charges 30% below the average price for her product. Even though her business is not profitable, she can't bring herself to raise prices. Many woman consultants charge between $45 and $75 per hour, while men doing the equivalent job charge a minimum of $75 per hour and some upwards of $1,500 per day. Talk to any woman about pricing, and she will tell you how difficult it is to charge higher prices or how she's not worth it or that no one would pay more. We are doing better than we were in the late 1980s, but we still struggle to get over our conditioning that we're not worth as much as men. It's simply not true, so don't buy it.

2. Determine your pricing objectives. Are you trying to buy market share with low prices? Maximize profits? Remain competitive? Build up a new product line?

As women we are notorious for undervaluing ourselves and pricing too low.

As your business grows and increases in complexity, you will want to consider some of these more complex pricing objectives.

3. Establish price ranges. Pages 124-128 describe how to do a break-even analysis. This will give you an idea how many "units" you must sell and at what price to cover your costs, thus helping you establish the low end of your price range.

   You can also include your desired profit levels in the break-even calculation to arrive at the number of "units" you must sell and at what price to cover cost-plus-profit, thus helping you evaluate a reasonable upper end of your price range. Compare the prices you arrive at in this calculation with your sense of what the market will bear. In the end, it is your customers' perception of the value of your goods and services that sets the upper limit on price.

   This calculation will become much clearer when you have the opportunity to go through the section on break-even analysis.

4. Select a pricing strategy. Four common strategies are discussed below. As you read through them, you will encounter several financial terms which you may not have heard before. They are described in more detail in Chapter 5. You may find that you cannot set prices until after you read this section, so don't be too concerned if you don't get it the first time through.

Now, here are the strategies:

A. *Suggested going rate.* In some retail businesses, it is common practice for the manufacturer to suggest a retail price for the products. In fact, they even go so far as to print this price on the package (e.g., books, potato chips). As the retailer, you may choose to sell these products at the price shown, which makes pricing very simple. The biggest drawback to this method is that it takes you and your understanding of the market out of the pricing decision. And we probably all know of stores which sell potato chips for less than the price shown on the package.

B. *Full-cost pricing.* This method is most often used in manufacturing or retail businesses. You calculate the total cost of your product and add a percentage or flat dollar amount for profit. For example, suppose you are in the business of knitting sweaters which you sell to department stores. You determine that the total cost to knit one sweater is $55. You read the trade magazines in your industry and find that the average profit percentage is 10%. You believe your sweaters are slightly above average in style and appeal, so you decide on a 12% profit. You calculate your sweater price to be $62 (55 x 1.12 = 61.60, rounded up to $62).

   One difficulty with this method is figuring out what the real cost of the product is. In the example, the cost of the sweater includes the cost of the yarn, the thread, the buttons and two hours of one person's time to do the knitting. It also includes your costs of being in business, like your rent, the depreciation on your knitting machine, your personal time to supervise the knitters, insurance, telephone, maintenance of the equipment, and so on. The costs of being in business are the same whether you sell five sweaters or five hundred sweaters, so allocating them to each sweater is not straightforward.

Compare the prices you arrive at with your sense of what the market will bear.

Another difficulty is that you are setting a price based on the costs you *think* you'll have in the future, which may or may not turn out to be what the costs really are.

Despite the difficulties, this method provides you with an excellent pricing guideline. You will understand more about how to use this method after you complete Chapter Five.

C. *Gross profit* (also called gross margin or contribution margin). This is another method common in retail or wholesale businesses, and there are two ways of using it. It's not difficult, but you may want to have a calculator handy.

In order to understand this method, you must first know what gross profit is. The term is described in detail in Chapter Five, page 110, but I'll touch on it here. Go back to the sweater example described above. The gross profit is the price you charge minus the direct costs that can be directly associated with the sweater, i.e., the yarn, the thread, the buttons and two hours of one person's time to do the knitting. In other words, it is the profit you can tie directly to each sweater you sell.

Or suppose you sell large appliances and electronics. Your gross profit for, let's say, a refrigerator is the price at which you sell that refrigerator minus the cost to you of buying the refrigerator from the manufacturer.

In each of these businesses, there are other costs besides those mentioned, including rent, utilities, insurance, advertising, and so on—these are the costs of being in business. The problem with using these costs as part of the pricing equation is that the only way you can determine how much of each of these costs to allocate to each sweater or each refrigerator is to know in advance exactly how many units you will sell. You can (and will) estimate this information, but there is no way to know it for sure ahead of time. For this reason, some people use gross profit as the base for determining price because it is not dependent on sales volume. Note that this doesn't relieve you from the responsibility of ensuring that your price covers *all* of the costs of being in business. The section on Income Statements shows you how to do that (page 110).

Now here are two ways to use this method of calculating prices.

The first way is called a *mark-up*—you increase those costs you can directly tie to the product by a markup percentage. For example, suppose you sell large appliances and electronics (refrigerators, stoves, stereos, televisions, and so on), and let's say that you buy refrigerators from the factory at a cost to you of between $750 and $1,200. Based on your knowledge of the market, your other costs of being in business, and some past experience, you set your markup at 60%. This means you price refrigerators at between $1,200 and $1,920 (750 x 1.6 = 1,200; 1,200 x 1.6 = 1,920).

The second way of using the gross profit margin method is called *mark-on*. This assumes you have some information on the percentage of gross profit that is standard for your industry. For example, suppose you've done some research and have determined that for large appliances gross profit is, on average, 40% of sales. The cost to you of the refrigerators is between $750 to $1,200. How can you use this information to calculate a sales price? Use the following formula:

$$\text{Sales Price} = \frac{\text{Cost of Product to You}}{1 - \text{Mark-on}}$$

$$\text{Sales Price} = \frac{750}{1 - .4} = \frac{750}{.6} = \$1{,}250$$

$$\text{Sales Price} = \frac{1{,}200}{1 - .4} = \frac{1{,}200}{.6} = \$2{,}000$$

You would set your price at $1,250 for the bottom-of-the-line refrigerator and $2,000 for the top-of-the-line refrigerator.

By the way, the gross profit for the bottom-of-the-line refrigerator with a 60% markup is $1,200 minus $750, or $450. With a 40% mark-on, the gross profit is $1,250 minus $750, or $500.

The first obvious question is: How do I select the right percentage? If you have experience in the business, you probably have an idea of what the percentage is. If not, contact your trade association and people in other cities in the same business. They should at least be able to provide you with some guidelines for your industry. Talk to your support people and your accountant—they may be able to help you determine what's appropriate for you. Check with your librarian and SCORE counselor—they can guide you to industry averages. And don't be afraid to do some experimentation.

The second obvious question is: How do I know whether to use markup or mark-on? This depends on the information you have available to you for your business and industry. If you know what the average markup is, use that method as a guideline. If you have data on the average gross margin percentage for your industry, use mark-on as your guideline.

Whichever method you choose, don't forget that you must confirm in your income statement that your prices cover *all* the costs of being in business.

D. *Competitive Pricing.* For this method, you look at what your competition is charging and charge either more, less or the same depending on how you believe you compare. This method is often used by consultants. For example, if you're a marketing consultant, it would not be uncommon for you to charge the same hourly rate as other marketing consultants in your area. You get this information by asking other consultants what they charge—many will tell you—and by asking people who've used consultants what the going rate is.

One problem with this method is that it doesn't take into account your value in the customer's eyes. Depending on your client's needs, your service could be more valuable than your competitor's—or it could be less.

Another problem with this method is that it doesn't account for your cost of being in business. Even if you are a consultant working out of your home, you must still pay for books, workshops, brochures, other marketing costs, materials, professional fees, and so on. Plus, it's rare to find a consultant who can bill 100% of her working hours, since it typically takes a consultant two hours of marketing to get one hour of billable time. All of these costs, including your marketing time, should be covered by your fee.

If you're in a retail business or a service business (other than consulting), the problem with this method is that it might engender the feeling that you're only competing on the basis of price, and this causes everyone to lose. We've all seen examples of the gas station price wars in which gasoline prices keep spiraling downward until the gas stations can't afford to provide good service or even be in business anymore. There are many alternatives to price competition, including service location, customization, expertise, image and follow-through. Take advantage of them.

The key to success with any of these methods is to write down your selected strategy and all your assumptions and then *stay flexible*. If you listen to your market, keep your eye on the competition, are willing to experiment and in all cases keep your own cost structure in mind, you should be able to establish optimum price ranges for your products.

Ultimately your price will be determined by your best judgment of what the market will bear, tempered by your experience and your costs. Will you ever find the "right" price? There is really no way to know for sure which price combined with which sales volume will maximize profit. I recently read a true story of a woman who opened an exclusive gift shop. She stocked a large inventory of old-fashioned porcelain dolls with beautiful handmade lace clothes. At $60 per doll, she couldn't sell any of them. One day, on a hunch, she raised the price to $850. Today, she can't stock enough of them to meet the demand.

I love that story, but sometimes I wonder: Did she really find the "right" price? Who knows? Perhaps she would have done even better if she priced them at $1,000, or $500.

Write a brief paragraph describing your pricing policy. You may need to come back to this section after you've completed the section on the Income Statement.

Location

Proper site location is both a marketing decision and an operations decision. Your ideal location will attract customers, fit your business' image, be of ample size and layout to meet your needs, be zoned for your type of business and be priced within your budget.

Many women successfully operate their businesses out of their homes. It is an inexpensive way to get started, and you may find that it helps you meet some of your personal goals. To determine whether it makes sense for you, ask yourself the following question: Will working out of my home negatively impact the image of my business in the eyes of my customers? If the answer is yes, consider other alternatives.

By the way, I used to work out of my home and I did very well in my consulting business. But I was turned down for board positions with local business groups by men who said: "Zuckerman and Associates isn't a *real* business because she works out of her home." (Grrr! I hated that!) Now I have an office

There are many alternatives to price competition, including service, location, customization, expertise, image and follow-through.

outside my home, and I find that people's perception of my business has changed for the better—and my expenses have increased substantially.

If you do plan to locate outside your home, you can find out about available business locations in your area from Chambers of Commerce, industrial development commissions, trade associations, planning commissions, bankers, lawyers and your business advisors. Often they will have information on such things as traffic (i.e., the number of people who walk or drive by the location), average dollar sales per square foot for retail space, total space in the building, vacant space in the building, rental price ranges and contact people.

Also, use your banker as a reference source. Some locations seem to be jinxed, and bankers are apt to know why and will tell you.

Once you have a feel for how much space you need, what kind of image you'd like to portray and what your cost requirements are, talk to a commercial real estate broker who will guide you to several locations which meet your requirements.

The price ranges for different locations may or may not include such things as leasehold improvements (i.e., changing walls, doors, floors, lighting and decoration to meet your needs), utilities, parking, signs, and so on. The length of your lease may also vary from building to building. Make sure you know what each location includes so you are making a realistic comparison among alternatives. The calculations for monthly payments are not always straightforward. Don't go by price per square foot. Find out exactly what your monthly payments will be for the term of the lease.

In some cases, especially for retail stores and restaurants, the following equation holds true:

Rent = The Cost of Space + Advertising

Often you can get more mileage out of locating in a heavily traveled location than you can by expensive advertising. Conversely, all the advertising in the world may not make up for a poor location. Do not go into a spot just because the rent is low.

Once you've made your decision, you can save yourself a lot of money and headaches by having someone knowledgeable in lease agreements negotiate with the landlord on your behalf. Your attorney may be a good choice—lawyers are trained negotiators. This may cost a little money up front, but will probably save a lot in the long run. Regardless of who does your negotiating, make sure all terms of the agreement are in writing and signed by both parties.

For your business plan, answer these questions:

1. What is your business address?

2. What are the physical features of your building?

3. Do you lease or own your space? How much space do you have?

4. What renovations are needed and how much will they cost? Get written quotes from more than one contractor. Include these as supporting documents.

5. Does zoning permit your kind of business in the neighborhood? This has been the cause of great expense and headaches for many businesses. Get

Rent = The Cost of

Space + Advertising

the answer to this question before you make any commitments. And don't believe anyone who says you can get a zoning variance in short order. City and town councils are notoriously slow in making these kinds of decisions.

6. What other businesses (or kinds of businesses) are in the area? It is often wise to locate near similar businesses to take advantage of traffic and nearby services.

7. Why did you pick this site over others?

8. Why is this the right location for your business?

9. How will the choice of location affect your operating costs?

Once you've answered these questions, put the information in paragraph form for inclusion in your business plan.

You have now completed the two parts of your marketing plan: promotion and location. You will develop the third part, pricing, after you develop your business financials.

Sales

As small business owners, most of us come face to face with our prospective customers and ask for a sale. How and how often we do this depends on our type of business, our business goals and our creativity.

There are two major issues which must be addressed in preparing your sales plan: 1) setting detailed sales goals and 2) planning customer contacts.

In Figure 11 you wrote down your sales goals for next year. You can greatly increase the probability of meeting that goal if you break it down into smaller, more manageable goals.

Translate your goal into the average number of units you need to sell.

The first step is to translate your goal into the average number of units you need to sell to meet your goal. Depending on your business, "average number of units" may be defined as average number of sales transactions per day, average number of new clients per month or average number of "widgets" per month. The "unit" is directly related to the nature of what you're selling; the time frame depends on how closely you must manage your cash flow and on your sales cycle (how long it takes from the time you first contact your customer until the time you make a sale).

The second step is to determine how many contacts you need with prospective customers in order to get to that number of units. The third step is to assess whether it is reasonable for you to make that many contacts and sales.

• **Retail Example:** Charlene Brock owns an upscale women's accessory shop. She wants to increase her sales to $250,000 next year. She decides she needs to monitor her average number of sales transactions. However, since no two customers buy exactly the same thing, she is concerned about doing this analysis. By taking a closer look at last year's records, she realizes that she can divide her customers into two groups: Group A buys an average of $50 per transaction and represents 60% of her transactions. Group B buys an average of $200 per transaction and represents 40% of her transactions. Therefore, Charlene knows that in order to meet her sales goal she must have:

3,000 Group A transactions per year $250,000 x 60% = $150,000
$150,000/$50 per transaction = 3,000

500 Group B transactions per year $250,000 x 40% = $100,000
$100,000/$200 per transaction = 500

This sounds like a lot to Charlene, so she decides to look at her weekly sales requirements.

3,000 transactions/52 weeks = 58 Group A transactions per week
500 transactions/52 weeks = 10 Group B transactions per week

Total transactions = 68 per week

From past experience Charlene knows that only one in three people who walk into her store actually make a purchase. Therefore, she must attract an average of 204 people (68 x 3) into her store each week in order to meet her goals. She feels that these numbers are realistic as long as she maintains a knowledgeable, helpful, friendly sales staff and increases her newspaper advertising and promotions.

Charlene plans to set up a weekly monitoring system to determine whether her assumptions about the number of people who enter her store, the number of people who make purchases and the group they fall into remain the same throughout the year. This way she can take rapid corrective action in case her historical data does not hold true.

● **Service Example:** Betsy Mullen sells general cleaning services to local businesses. She sets up contracts in which her client companies pay for nightly light cleaning (dusting, vacuuming and bathroom cleaning) and quarterly heavy cleaning (carpet cleaning, windows and walls). Clients pay on a square-foot basis, with the average client paying $8,000 per year. Betsy currently has ten ongoing clients, or $80,000 worth of business.

Betsy's revenue goal for next year is $150,000. This means she needs $70,000 worth of new business. Betsy feels she needs to target 15 new clients to meet her goal, since not all of the new clients will begin using her services at the beginning of the year.

Competition for cleaning services is fierce in Betsy's community. She believes one-on-one selling is her best marketing approach, and, based on past experience, she assumes she'll have to call on six prospective clients in order to get one new client. This means she needs to call on 90 (6 x 15) companies next year, or eight companies per month. Betsy knows this level of selling will take up a lot of her time, since there is a substantial amount of follow-up associated with each sales call. The more she thinks about it, the more she realizes this is not reasonable, since she must also spend her time developing her advertising pieces, investigating new cleaning techniques, working on company books, training and managing her employees and, of course, cleaning. She believes she can call on four companies per month, so she revises her sales plan and starts thinking about hiring a sales representative.

Betsy plans to monitor her sales successes monthly to see if her assumed averages are correct.

• **Consulting Example:** Pat Green is a communications specialist who develops company literature (business cards, business stationery, brochures and newsletters) and does media planning for small businesses. This is Pat's first year in business, and her goal is to do $50,000 worth of business. She knows this is ambitious, but believes it is possible because she has an excellent referral network through advertising agencies. Pat charges $75 per hour for developing company literature and 15% of the advertising costs for media planning.

From her prior experience in the industry, Pat assumes that 50% of her work will come from brochures ($25,000), 20% from newsletters ($10,000), and 30% from media planning ($15,000). She translates this into the number of clients she needs as follows:

Brochures: On average brochures take 20 hours to prepare. Therefore,

Average brochure price = 20 hrs x $75 per hour = $1,500

To get $25,000 worth of business, Pat needs:

$25,000 / $1,500 per brochure = 16.67, rounded up to 17 brochures

Newsletters: On average, newsletters take about 15 hours to prepare, and Pat expects clients to purchase them quarterly (i.e., four times per year).

Average newsletter price = 15 hrs x $75 per hour x 4 times per year = $4,500

To get $10,000 worth of business, Pat needs:

$10,000 / $4,500 per newsletter = 2.22, rounded up to 3 newsletters

Media Planning: Pat expects her average client will spend $5,000 per year on advertising.

At 15% commission, Pat will receive an average of $5000 x .15 = $750 for each client

To get $15,000 worth of business, Pat needs:

$15,000 / $750 per client = 20 clients

Pat believes she can get half these clients from referrals. The other half she will have to generate herself. Pat knows that this will take a lot of work and a lot of money (for promotional expenses). She's prepared to work 70 hours per week if that's what it takes.

Pat will monitor her sales record each month to make sure her assumptions are within the ballpark.

• **Manufacturing Example:** Julia Ruple and Carrie Schade design and manufacture distinctive children's clothing which they sell to department stores and specialty shops. Although they are just getting started, there appears to be a lot of interest in their line of clothes, and they are shooting for $400,000 in sales in their first year of business. Since their average selling price per item is $15.50, in order to meet their goal they must sell:

$400,000 / $15.50 per unit = 25,800 articles of clothing per year, or

25,800 per year / 12 = 2,150 units per month

Julia and Carrie have hired knowledgeable sales reps around the country to sell their clothing, since they will have their hands full producing the garments. With the sales reps' help they estimate that large department store chains are likely to buy $15,000 worth of merchandise and specialty shops might buy $2,500 worth of merchandise. If the revenue split is 75% department store chains and 25% specialty shops, they would have to sell to:

($400,000 x .75) / $15,000 per dept. store chain = 20 dept store chains, and

($400,000 x .25) / $2,500 per specialty shop = 40 specialty shops

Julia and Carrie think this will be easy; their reps think it will be hard in their first year of operation.

Julia and Carrie have their sales reps provide weekly written forms listing the stores they've contacted, their success rate and any other information that might be useful for marketing purposes.

Note that in this industry it is more relevant to identify the sales dollars per customer rather than the sales volume (i.e., number of units sold) per customer. Julia and Carrie will have to deal with the production of 25,800 articles of clothing in their operations plan.

Also note that Julia and Carrie do not sell directly to the ultimate consumer of their clothing,—they sell to department stores and specialty shops, and they use sales reps to do the actual selling. In business jargon, the sales reps and the stores are part of a "distribution channel." They provide the mechanism for them to distribute their clothing to the ultimate consumer. Finding the right distribution channel can be critical, especially if you are in a manufacturing business. Your trade association can be very helpful in describing what's typical for your industry and in leading you to effective sales reps. Just attending a trade show in your industry can put you in touch with sales reps, as well as other people who can assist you.

Now think about your business.

1. Look at your annual sales goals again.

2. Translate your sales goals into the average number of units you need to sell to achieve this.

3. How many contacts must you make in order to achieve this level of sales?

4. Is this reasonable?

5. Is this consistent with your marketing plan? Your operations plan?

The best salespeople follow this rule: They serve the customer in making the best buying decision.

Now put this information in paragraph form for inclusion in your business plan.

Before we move off the subject of sales, I'd like to talk a little bit about personal selling because it's so important in almost all our businesses.

Many of us think of salespeople as middle-aged used car salesmen with white shoes, a wide tie and a phony smile, and that doesn't fit our own image of ourselves. Therefore we find it hard to go out there and sell ourselves and our businesses. Happily, statistics show that the best salespeople are not those pushy, brassy, slimy characters. The best salespeople follow this rule: They serve the customer in making the best buying decision.

They do this by listening (*really* listening) to their clients' needs and then helping their clients understand how best to meet those needs. The best salespeople thoroughly understand the benefits of what they have to offer and what their markets' needs are, and they use this information to help their customers rather than to sell their customers.

Once you really get this concept, you can think of sales as helping people. You'll relax. You'll come across in a very human way. Your customers and prospects will like you. They will want to do business with you. You'll be pleasantly surprised with the results.

If, after you try this for a while, you are still uncomfortable with your role as a salesperson, it may be wise for you to take a sales training course.

Operations

Operations is the term used in business for doing the work that the company is set up to do. For example:

- For Charlene Brock, the owner of the women's accessories store, operations includes selecting the merchandise, storing it when it arrives at the store, stocking the shelves, ringing up the transactions and returning damaged merchandise.

- For Betsy Mullen, the owner of the cleaning business, operations includes the actual cleaning (vacuuming, dusting, carpet cleaning, washing windows, and so on), as well as routinely checking to make sure the cleaning is up to standards, maintaining the cleaning equipment and buying the cleaning supplies.

- For Pat Green, the communications consultant, operations includes meeting with clients, writing, editing and contacting the media.

- For Julia Ruple and Carrie Schade, the clothing manufacturers, operations includes designing, ordering fabric, cutting, sewing and boxing for shipment.

The key issues for managing operations are:

1. What tasks must be performed and who will do them?

2. When and where will these tasks be performed?

3. How long will it take to perform them? Is there enough time available if you meet your sales projections? What if you exceed your sales expectations?

4. How will you monitor the quality? How will you make sure you produce on time and within budget?

5. How will you keep the costs down? What if you don't meet your sales expectations?

For those of us who are the sole employees of our businesses, the answers to most of these questions are simple. For example, when I was the only employee in my consulting business:

- I did all the consulting, product development, typing, filing and going to the post office.

- I did the consulting work at my clients' offices. All other work was done in my office.

- It took 15 hours per week of operations (12 hours of billable time and three hours of administrative time) to meet my annual sales goals. Using a rule of thumb of two hours of marketing per one hour of billable time, I needed to spend 39 hours on operations and sales. Then, I still had to do product development, marketing and financial management. Those were long work weeks!

- Quality control is not an issue for me since I do all the work myself, and I have seen the success of what I have to offer. I produce on time by working additional hours in the evening, though this sometimes cuts into my family or sleep time.

- I keep costs down by budgeting my expenses and living within my budget.

If you have employees or partners, it is important to be clear about who is responsible for each aspect of the business. The greater everyone's understanding of the five basic operational issues, the more smoothly your operation will run. You will enjoy greater commitment to the company on everyone's part and less likelihood of something falling through the cracks.

Now answer the five questions above for your business. Then put the information in paragraph form for inclusion in your business plan.

Personnel

Personnel management is one of those areas that everyone thinks they can do by themselves, but few people do it well. It doesn't take a human relations expert to place a classified ad in the local paper, talk to the people who send resumes and tell someone they're hired. The trick is to hire someone who will do the job effectively and efficiently and to have them like the job well enough to stay.

The impact of hiring a bad employee or losing an outstanding one cannot be overstated. It causes stress, financial hardship, and it interrupts your business. If you currently have or plan to have employees, you may already have spent a great deal of time worrying about these and other personnel issues.

Many books talk about the mechanics of effective personnel management and personnel planning. These are important, and they are discussed here, too. But perhaps even more important is setting the climate and tone of your business.

The impact of hiring a bad employee or losing an outstanding one cannot be overstated.

Every year, more and more research is done on human relations, including understanding which working environment will encourage people to be their most productive and how things like motivation, job satisfaction, interpersonal styles and communication affect productivity and quality. The difficulty of doing this research is compounded by the fact that the ways to motivate people depend on economic and social situations and expectations, which are always changing.

Given this state of affairs, the best thing you can do to develop a productive, quality work environment is to continually educate yourself in the areas of personnel and human relations management. Go to workshops and seminars. Stay current on how to develop and maintain a productive staff. Then plan and implement changes in your personnel plans and policies which incorporate what you're learning. It will cost some money in the short run, but it will save a great deal more in the long run.

Now for the mechanics.

PERSONNEL GUIDELINES

Hiring and training an employee is expensive, and worth planning for before the action is taken.

1. Add employees only as they're needed. In making your decision to hire, consider your business goals, plans and expected one-year and three-year financial situation. It's surprising how many small business owners hire new employees during a crisis without thinking through how the new employee will fit with the direction of the business. Hiring and training an employee is expensive and worth planning for before the action is taken.

2. Hire the person with the right qualifications and characteristics for the job. Often business owners are inclined to hire the first candidate they feel comfortable with (especially if she's a relative or friend) to get the hiring process over with and get on with business. Or they'll interview several people and select the person they feel is the best of a bad lot.

    Don't make either of these mistakes. Hiring the wrong employee can be extremely costly and potentially devastating to your business (and can put you in a very uncomfortable situation if this person is a relative or a friend). Interview at least three people before making any hiring decision. And keep interviewing until you find the right person. If you have an immediate need because of an impending sales increase or because an employee quit, it may seem expensive *not* to fill it quickly. But when you consider such things as salary, taxes, insurance, training, plus lost customer goodwill and personal stress if the employee doesn't work out, it can be substantially more expensive to hire the wrong person.

    Before you begin interviewing, write a job description (see #3) so you know exactly what qualifications and characteristics are needed to get the job done. Better yet, write it before you place the ad. I cannot stress this enough. I've seen too many people hire the wrong person without really thinking through their situation and put themselves and another human being through needless pain. It is also valuable to have a 90-day trial period for new employees. It can help you correct a mistake early on—a real boon for novice personnel managers.

3. Make sure that all of your employees know exactly what is expected of them. The best way to do this is with a written job description for each

employee (including yourself) outlining duties, responsibilities and criteria for success. The added benefit of a job description is that it forces you to think through all the tasks that need to be done daily, weekly, monthly and occasionally and make sure someone is assigned to each task.

4. Allow for adequate training. Even employees who have experience in such things as sales or sewing or nursing or bookkeeping don't know how to do things in *your* business. By making the time to teach them about your products, markets and values, you will help them to be more effective employees and to feel that the company wants them to grow. When you can afford it, consider sending employees to outside training courses in such things as sales, computer applications, operations or whatever is appropriate for your business. In order to succeed, you must have well-qualified personnel. That calls for serious training efforts.

5. Communicate with your employees openly and honestly. In today's society, people get job satisfaction from feeling they've made an important contribution to the business, that they've really made a difference. One of the most effective ways of getting people to believe this is to communicate with them about how the business is doing and about how their job affects the business. Share the business goals—in fact, let your employees have a say in those goals. Give them feedback—both positive and negative, but always constructive. Verbally tell them how their job, their productivity and their quality leads toward meeting (or not meeting) the goals of the business.

6. Make sure you meet all of the legal and accounting requirements of having employees. Your attorney and accountant will be able to help you in these areas. In addition, keep written records for personnel matters to protect yourself. If you need to prove something in court, written documentation is critical.

7. It's not always necessary to hire full-time people for every job. Some jobs, like bookkeeping, sales and piecework sewing, lend themselves well to temporary employees or even outside contractors. This is an area where you may be able to save some money. But remember that even part-time employees work better if they are kept informed and treated well.

For your business plan, you need to define how many people you need, what they will be doing and how you will compensate them. To do this, answer the questions below, then put the information in paragraph form for inclusion in your business plan.

PERSONNEL QUESTIONS

1. What are your personnel needs now? In the near future? In three years?

2. What skills will your business need?

3. Are the people with those skills available? Where?

4. Will you have full- or part-time employees? How many? Describe.

5. Will your employees be salaried or hourly? How much will you pay them?

Share the business goals—in fact, let your employees have a say in those goals.

6. What fringe benefits will you offer?

7. Will you pay overtime? Describe.

8. Will you have to train people? If so, at what cost to your business (time, interrupted work flow, money)?

If you have no personnel, just add a sentence in your business plan that you have no plans to hire anyone at this time and that you will carefully review your personnel needs every quarter (or whatever time period is appropriate for your business).

Finances

Managing your business finances is such an important facet of running your business that an entire section of this book has been devoted to it. For now, as you prepare your personnel and management plans, keep in mind that you will need to allocate time and resources to such things as:

• *Recordkeeping* (also called "bookkeeping")—Keep track of your revenues and expenses.

• *Balancing your checking account*—If you haven't yet done so, open a separate business checking account.

• *Billing*—In some businesses, you will not get paid unless you submit bills (invoices) for the work you've done.

• *Paying bills*—As in your personal life, bills must be paid or your creditors will come after you.

• *Review*—Use your financial results to identify critical business issues.

Your accountant or your local SCORE or SBDC office can help you set up these and other important accounting systems. Once the systems are in place you'll find it fairly straightforward, but time-consuming, to keep the books, i.e., to enter the information necessary on the right forms or into your computer. If necessary, you can hire a bookkeeping service to help you do this; however, as the business owner, it is *your* responsibility to monitor the books, look for clues about the financial health of your business, note when action should be taken and take appropriate action.

This will all become clearer when you read Chapter Five. Right now it is important to recognize that there is additional work which must be done and be assigned to someone.

Management

So far in this chapter you have done what good managers do: You've set goals and outlined plans to achieve them. Now you have one more plan to prepare—the management plan—in which you describe who will manage each area, what experience these people have that gives you and your funding sources the confidence that they can carry out the plans, how much you will pay yourself and your other managers and what other resources you will make available to support you in managing your business.

The five areas to cover in your management plan are:

1. Personal History of Owner(s) and Key Personnel

2. Related Work Experience

3. Duties and Responsibilities

4. Salaries

5. Resources Available to the Business

PERSONAL HISTORY OF THE OWNER(S) AND KEY PERSONNEL

This segment should include responses to the following questions for yourself and any other managers in your business:

1. *What is your business background?* Include any work experience, even if you weren't paid.

2. *What management experience have you had?* Many women don't have paid management experience, which puts us at a disadvantage when applying for a loan. But most of us have management experience—through volunteer work (such as serving on boards or committees for charitable, civic or religious organizations), outside activities (such as involvement in hobby-related clubs, sports teams, scouting, PTA) or even running a home—that has taught us the skills we need to run our businesses. These skills include such things as:

   • Ability to work under stress and with frequent distractions

   • Ability to get things done under ever-changing conditions

   • Ability to be decisive and lead in times of crisis

   • Ability to coordinate the activities of different groups of people

   • Ability to train people (e.g., your kids) in jobs with which they are unfamiliar

   Remember, the definition of management is setting goals, deciding what you'll do (and what resources you'll need) to meet those goals, and reflecting on what you've learned the next time you decide what to do. Have you chaired a membership committee for your church or synagogue? Taken on the responsibility of den mother for the Cub Scouts? Coached a kids' soccer team? In order to be effective, these jobs generally require good managerial skills.

   I am reminded of Juanita Fletcher's comments in the August 8, 1988, edition of *U.S. News and World Report.* She was applying for a job as a high school English teacher after ten years of staying at home to take care of her kids. After being told by a number of prospective employers that she "hadn't done anything in ten years," she finally decided to stop apologizing for being a mother. She "pointed out to one school district that when nine children from six different families are playing video games at your home and get into a fight, you learn things about patience and handling conflict that you simply cannot glean from a course in teaching methods." She got the job.

You're writing a business plan, not applying for a job, but the concept is the same. Chances are you've had experience as a manager even if it didn't match the typical male experience. Open yourself up to that possibility and write it down.

Include *any* experience you've had in management in general or in managing any of the different areas of business. Have you been on a school board committee long enough to see the committee chair or board president make mistakes that you've learned from? You've probably learned more than you realized from working with good (and bad) managers.

3. *What education (including both formal and informal learning experiences) have you had which has a bearing on your managerial abilities?* Have you taken management courses at the local university or through continuing education? It's never too late to sign up.

4. *Include your age, special abilities and interests, reasons for going into business, where you live, have lived, and so on.* The personal data needn't be a confession, but should reflect where your motivation comes from. For example, if you've grown up in the town in which you'll be starting your landscaping business, you may be strongly motivated to beautify the town. If you've spent 15 years volunteering for the local PTA, you may have seen some gaps in the education process that motivated you to buy an SAT training franchise. If you've been president of your local chapter of the National Organization for Women, you may be strongly motivated to become a consultant to industry and to women in the area of sexual harassment. If you've been running the business for your current boss while being grossly underpaid, you may have enough solid experience and very strong motivation to start a competing business. The strength of your motivation is what will keep your business going when times get tough.

5. *Are you physically up to the job?* Running a business takes long hours for many months or years on end. Stamina counts.

6. *Why are you going to be successful in this venture?* List everything you think you've got going for you (include family support, if you've got it). Just seeing it in print will make you feel terrific.

7. *What is your financial status?* This area is particularly difficult and frustrating for many women, especially single heads of household. The facts are: a) A personal balance sheet must be included as a supporting document in your business plan if the plan is to double as a financing proposal (see Appendix IV for a blank form). And if you expect to get a loan, it should show that your assets (what you own) are worth more than your liabilities (what you owe); b) Funding sources want to see as much collateral as possible to secure their investment. In plain English,

You've probably learned more than you realized from working with good (and bad) managers.

this means the bank will want you to promise them such things as your house and car in case you can't repay your loan. c) You will undoubtedly be expected to personally guarantee the loan. This means even more of your personal assets may be taken if the business fails—even if the business is a corporation.

This is very scary to most people, men and women alike, and it is particularly frightening if you are the sole supporter of your children. You may not be prepared to take the risk.

It may seem to you as if the system is set up to discriminate against women. While individual cases of discrimination do exist, the system is really set up not to discriminate but to protect. The money banks use to make loans comes from the bank's depositors, and, by law, banks have a responsibility to their depositors which makes risky loans illegal. If you are not confident enough of your business plans to be willing to take a financial risk, your bank will not (and should not) be.

Unfortunately, many women don't have confidence, not because their plans are bad, but because they've been conditioned to downplay their abilities, especially in the area of business. Remember that you've spent a lot of time researching your market and preparing product development plans, marketing plans, and so on, to make your business a success. If you are unsure of your plans, have them reviewed by your support people, your banker, SCORE counselor, your accountant and others. This should give you some comfort regarding their soundness. Beyond that, no one but you can decide whether you're willing to take risks for your business.

You will undoubtedly be expected to personally guarantee the loan.

RELATED WORK EXPERIENCE

This segment of your business plan includes (but is not limited to) responses to the following:

1. *What is your direct operational experience in this kind of business?* If you don't have any direct experience, you may want to consider getting a job in this field—and working in it for at least a year—before you start your business. This idea probably sounds extremely unattractive right now. If you've gotten this far in your business plan, you're probably very eager to get started with your business. But there is absolutely no substitute for having prior work experience in the business of your choice. Your assumptions, your financial projections, your knowledge of your products, market and competition will be substantially enhanced and you will have a much greater chance of succeeding if you are not approaching this business for the first time.

2. *What is your managerial experience in this kind of business?*

DUTIES AND RESPONSIBILITIES

If you are the sole employee of your business, this section is straightforward: You will manage all facets of the business.

However, now that you have a better understanding of what this involves, you may find that you don't have the knowledge, ability or time to do this. Depending on your situation, you may want to consider the following: a) signing up for some classes or seminars in your areas of weakness, b) looking for a partner, c) hiring other managers, or d) hiring part-time employees to fill in the gaps.

If you are already planning to have more than one person managing the business, use this section to describe who manages which facet of the business and what specific responsibilities each person has. Be sure to highlight any areas of responsibility that are of particular importance to your business.

If you have a large number of employees, you will need to outline:

- Who does what.

- Who reports to whom.

- Who makes the final decisions.

Allocating duties and responsibilities is critical. Even if there are just two of you, you want to make sure that nothing slips through the cracks because each of you thinks the other is taking care of it. In larger organizations, if the chain of command is unclear to your employees, you will have the worst kinds of personnel problems. Don't give in to the hope that "we can work it out later when we see where the problems are." By then it will be too late.

As you think through these issues, make sure you allot adequate time for:

- Planning and reviewing plans.

- Managing and implementing the plans in each facet of the business.

- Establishing policies.

- More planning.

SALARIES

A simple statement of what the management will be paid is sufficient. The difficulty is to decide what that number should be.

It is important that your salary (and that of your managers) be high enough for you (and them) to meet personal expenses and be motivational, but not so high that you drain much-needed cash from your business.

To help you figure out what you need to live on, fill out the Personal Income Statement in Appendix IV. It is critical that you approach this area realistically. On the one hand, this is not the time to underestimate. If your business can't afford to pay you what you need to live on, and if you have no other income or savings, this may not be the right time to start your business. While many of us dream of becoming rich overnight, the fact is that, for most of us, the high payoff of owning our own business comes in the future, after our business becomes successful. On the other hand, this is not the time to splurge on frivolous expenses. You will make a serious mistake if you depend on your business to meet hefty personal expenses.

Don't give in to the hope that "we can work it out later when we see where the problems are."

Some people find that paying managers (and themselves) modest salaries plus a bonus based on results enables them to motivate people without draining the business.

RESOURCES AVAILABLE TO THE BUSINESS

This is the place to list those businesspeople who will support you in your business and to specify the nature of support they will provide. List names, organizations and type of support. You can plug many gaps in your experience and increase your chances of success by relying on other people's experience. Here are some examples. You may not need all of them, and you may also have others not listed.

1. An accountant—for financial support and tax preparation. You need one.

2. An attorney—for legal support. You need one.

3. A banker—for financial and lending expertise. You would be wise to develop a relationship even if you don't plan to request a bank loan. You never know what your future needs will be or what other services a bank may be able to offer.

4. An insurance agent or broker—for insurance advice. While you may not need one immediately, it's far better to check out possible insurance arrangements now than to find you're not covered when it's too late.

5. A business consultant—for general advice and support.

6. A specialist in your industry—for specific advice and support.

7. Technical and moral support people—for general and specific advice and support.

Once you've completed all the questions on management, rewrite your responses in paragraph form. Keep this section short (no more than two pages), direct and honest.

Now you're ready to pull together all the components of the management section of your business plan. A sample order is as follows:

Management

1. Personal and Business Goals. (Your funding source may not be interested in your personal goals. Use your judgment. If in doubt, ask.)

2. Product Development Plan.

3. Marketing Plan.

4. Sales Plan.

5. Operations Plan.

6. Personnel Plan.

7. Management Plan (Also called Description of Management).

Increase your chances of success by relying on other people's experience.

Your financial plan will be shown in another section of the business plan.

Allow me to interject a brief dose of reality here. All of the plans which you have now developed will take up your two most precious resources—time and money. Presumably you have considered the amount of time it will take you and your employees to carry out the plans you've made.

The financial section of your business plan will help you consider the money it will take to turn your plans into a viable business. As you go through your financials, keep two very important things in mind:

1. Your financials should be based on your business plans.

2. If your financials indicate that your business will not be viable, you may need to review and modify all the plans you just spent so much time developing.

In other words, there's some experimentation involved in preparing a business plan, so don't be surprised if you have to make some rather major changes to your business tactics. It's still better to do this than to uncover your problems after you're knee-deep in alligators and have mortgaged the house, the car and the kids to get your business started or expanded. This is a large part of what management is all about.

APPLICATION AND EXPECTED EFFECT OF LOAN OR INVESTMENT

This may be the first section your prospective funding source turns to.

This section outlines what your funding will be used for and may be the first section your prospective funding source turns to. It describes how the money will be used, why it's a valuable use of money and how you will provide a return on the investment. This information is very similar to the Statement of Purpose at the front of your business plan, but it's presented in much more detail. Even if you plan to finance your business yourself, it is (obviously) sound business practice to know how well your money will work for you.

The objectives of this section are: 1) to give you and your funding source a qualitative insight into the expected effect of the loan on the business and 2) to specify the details of the "deal" as a starting point for discussion between you and your funding source.

The exact figures that belong in this section won't be available until you have worked through the financial data in Section Two of your business plan. However, you should understand the concepts behind this section so you can come back to it later.

You will have to answer the following questions:

1. How is the loan or investment to be spent? This gives the reader a general idea of how you will spend the money and will come straight out of your Sources and Uses of Cash Statement. Most people think they need funding only for major equipment purchases. As you will discover, starting a business requires money for numerous other items, including such things as business stationery, office supplies, insurance, deposits, pre-opening advertising and pre-opening inventory.

2. What major items (including capital equipment and real estate) will be purchased? Your Capital Equipment List (see page 109) will contain all of the major items you plan to own. For this section, just weed out those you will buy with the loan or investment. Then add any real estate purchases.

   For all major purchases, you will also need to list the following:

   a. Who is the supplier? Get this from the Capital Equipment List.

   b. What is the price? Again, this comes from the Capital Equipment List. Plus be sure to include documentation (such as written price quotes or invoices) in your supporting documents. If nothing else, include an advertisement showing the price.

   c. What is the specific model name and/or number of your purchase?

   d. How much did you (will you) pay in sales tax, installation charges, freight or delivery fees? You need to consider the total cost of acquiring the equipment or real estate.

   As you consider the major equipment and, perhaps, the real estate that you need for your business, recognize that there is another way to obtain the use of these items: leasing or renting. Leasing or renting gives you added flexibility—it's usually easy to change to a different equipment model or to move to a new office. (If you own the equipment or the building, you may be stuck). Also, leasing may have some tax advantages (check with your accountant—the tax laws change from year to year) and may alleviate the burden of a large down payment if you're short of cash. Owning, on the other hand, is usually less expensive in the long run. The way to determine which is better for you is to identify the alternatives, find out the costs (including any hidden tax costs) and then run your cash flow statement separately for each alternative.

3. How will the loan make your business more profitable? It costs money to borrow money. Whether you borrow from a bank or from a relative, you will have to pay interest on the loan and, possibly, an up-front loan fee. Make sure the loan earns more than it costs. You should at least have a qualitative sense of what you expect to get out of purchasing whatever it is you're going to buy with the money. Examples include:

   Make sure the loan earns more than it costs.

   • The working capital will enable my business to meet current expenses, offset negative seasonal cash flow as shown in the Cash Flow Projection in the Financial Data section and ensure the continued growth of the business.

   • The knitting machine will save more than two hours of knitting time per sweater. With this machine, less skilled knitters can produce quality sweaters. This will free up my time for soliciting more business and for developing new sweaters.

   • The computer and special software will enable me to save ten hours a month in recordkeeping time, including keeping track of inventory, logging in sales clerk time and doing the books. With better inventory control, I can keep less inventory on hand, thus reducing my cash needs.

- The special software and laser printer will dramatically increase the quality of resumes I produce for my customers. This will allow me to target the executive market and increase my fees by 20%.

4. How will you repay your funding source? Anyone who puts money into your business (including you) will eventually want the money back. Most people will be pretty specific about the time frame in which they want you to return the money and will also want to be compensated for having taken the risk of lending you the money or investing in your business (not to mention the opportunity they lost by NOT putting their money in some other investment, like CDs or stocks).

   For example, if you borrow money from a bank, your banker will expect you to pay back the initial amount of the loan (the principal) plus interest on the borrowed money. If you are lucky enough to find independent investors for your business, they will probably expect compensation in two ways: receiving regular dividends and the option of selling their share of the business after it has become successful. Even if you borrow money from a relative or a friend, you should clearly specify when and how you plan to repay the money and provide them a return on their investment.

Chapter 8, Using Your Business Plan to Get Financing, provides a more detailed discussion of financing. If you are writing your business plan to get up-front cash, you should read it and then have your support people and your accountant help you specify the details of the deal and its impact on your cash flow.

If you are like most people asking for a bank loan, you may not yet know the interest rate or repayment terms of the loan. Nonetheless, you must make some assumptions about what you expect them to be to complete your financial statements and make sure your plan is financially sound. State your assumptions here and use them as a starting point in talking with your banker.

If you are looking for someone to invest in your business, your financing proposal must state the terms of the deal, the expected return for the investor and how the investor will "cash out," i.e., get her or his money. A deal like this is very complex and beyond the scope of this book. If you are looking for such an arrangement, find advisors and an accountant who have put together deals like this in the past, and have them help you put your financial package together.

SAMPLE APPLICATION AND EXPECTED EFFECT OF LOAN

Green Consulting Company plans to borrow $10,500 to be used as follows:

Gateway 2000 486 25 MHz computer with color monitor (incl. shipping)... $2,090
Hewlett Packard Laser Jet IIIP Printer 900
Lotus 123 for Windows spreadsheet software 350

WordPerfect for Windows word processing software.....................................500
Quicken for Windows accounting software..50
Miscellaneous computer accessories (disks, disk boxes, etc.)............................50
Brother Fax 800 550
Pre-opening marketing and promotions (business stationery, advertising). 1,300
Lease deposit plus one month's rent 800
Other pre-opening expenses (office supplies, insurance) 400
Working capital 3,500
TOTAL $10,490

The computer hardware, software and accessories will be used to prepare worksheets, finished documents and reports to our clients, to prepare scripts and handouts for seminars, and to do billing and recordkeeping. The computer equipment will save over $10,000 per year in secretarial and bookkeeping charges. We have selected this level of hardware (which is faster and higher quality than the less expensive hardware) because our clients are company executives who will expect quality products, the faster computing time will save two hours per week which can be used for marketing and the speed and quality of the laser printer will allow us to print multiple copies of handouts rather than having to purchase a copy machine.

The pre-opening marketing and promotion budget will cover business cards, business stationery and initial advertising to let people know we're open for business and to promote our professional business image.

The lease deposit is for the space in a professional office building on the side of town where our clients are located.

The other pre-opening expenses are for initial office supplies to get us started and for liability insurance.

In addition to the money we will borrow, we plan to spend $4,000 of our own money on office furniture and a library, including desks, a conference table and chairs, a telephone system, filing cabinets, bookshelves, lamps and pictures, books, magazine subscriptions, cassette tape series and organization dues.

While we don't know the exact nature of the bank loan agreement, we have run our cash flow projections (in the financial data section of this plan) assuming a fixed interest rate of 8% (the going rate) amortized over three years. As you can see from our analysis, the resulting payments of $329.03 per month can be repaid within the three-year time frame. (Note: The calculation of the monthly payment is complex; call any banker or SCORE or SBDC counselor to have them do this calculation for you.)

SUMMARY

The purpose of this section is to summarize the ideas you've developed in the preceding sections to give anyone who reads your plan (including you) a succinct description of your business and, if appropriate, your funding needs. The idea here is that there will undoubtedly be some readers who will not need (or want) to slog through your entire plan to find out what you're proposing to do, but will want to get the information they need quickly.

Some readers will not need (or want) to slog through your entire plan to find out what you're proposing to do.

The summary should be no more than one page and should clearly state:

- What business you are in, what you're selling and why it's unique

- Where you're located

- Who the owner(s) is (are)

- How much money you need and a general statement of what you will use it for

- Who your target market is and why they will buy from you

- How you will beat your competition

- How your background will help you be successful

- Why your business will be successful

Sample Summary

Green Consulting Company sells market research and consulting services to the polymer industry. Green is located in Akron, Ohio, the hub of the polymer activity in the United States. Cathy Green, the owner, is seeking $10,500 to purchase office equipment, pay for pre-opening expenses and cover working capital for the first year of operation. This amount will be sufficient to enable the client base to grow and stabilize.

Careful analysis of the potential market shows a growing number of small polymer-related companies springing up in Akron. These companies are generally run by an owner-scientist who has developed a unique product application for polymers, but who does not know how to market the product. Ms. Green intends to use her experience in performing and managing polymer market research at the Goodpoor Company and in product management at Airstone Company to market her skills and to service her clients.

Ms. Green has just completed a term as local president of the American Polymer Society and, in that capacity, has developed sound relationships with many of the business owners in her target market, thus increasing her ability to successfully market to them. Ms. Green has also served on the budget and finance committee of the local YWCA and is very familiar with financial controls.

Green Consulting Company will price its services to be competitive with other marketing consultants in the Akron area. Green will compete on the basis of its recognized knowledge of and insights into the polymer industry plus the demonstrated capability of the owner to research the market for polymer products, to prepare successful marketing plans and, most importantly, to effectively implement those plans.

## CHAPTER FIVE

Finances

Many of us are intimidated by the financial side of business. It is an area in which we may have little or no background, and this may be compounded by a fear of math and numbers. In fact, many of us may be tempted to skip this section altogether, but we can't. It is simply not possible to be successful in business without understanding the numbers.

As you read through this section keep four important things in mind:

1. Allow yourself to be a beginner. If you expect yourself to do this the first time as though you've been doing it for years, you will have a problem. Don't criticize yourself unfairly if you don't understand the material the first or even the second or third time through. Don't give in to that voice that says "I can't do this." Many women do it and you can too. Just open yourself up to the possibility of success.

2. Seek help and support if you need it. While this book strives to be as clear as possible, it's not uncommon for people to hear new concepts several different ways from several different people before they understand them. Talk to your accountant, your support people and other women entrepreneurs about any financial concepts you have trouble with.

3. More than half the battle will be learning the terminology. Financial data comes with its own lingo. You may get frustrated when you read whole sentences with two or more words that you don't understand (or, worse yet, with words that obviously mean something different from the definition you've always known). If you get stuck, refer to the glossary or ask for help. Just don't let the jargon get you down.

4. Meet the problem head-on. Work on it. Fill in the numbers. You'll be surprised at how quickly it all begins to make sense once you start to do it. There's nothing like successful activity to breed more successful activity. Or, to quote Eleanor Roosevelt: "You gain strength, courage and confidence by every experience in which you really stop to look fear in the face... You must do the thing you think you cannot do."

Over the years accountants and businesspeople have developed a series of five business forms to make all of the financial data easier to understand and manage.

These five forms (sometimes called "statements") have become so well accepted that now banks require them if you're applying for a loan, small business

It is simply not possible to be successful in business without understanding the numbers.

consultants preach them, large companies include them in their annual reports and small businesses use them to manage their businesses. They are:

1. *Sources and Uses of Cash*—This form describes in broad terms where you will get the money to start or expand your business (hence the term "sources") and what you will use that money for (hence the term "uses").

2. *Capital Equipment List*—This form lists the major pieces of equipment you either own or need to buy for your business, the cost of that equipment and its current value. Capital equipment includes such things as desks, chairs, computers and manufacturing equipment.

3. *Income Statement* (also called Profit and Loss Statement)—On this form you match your sales with your expenses to determine whether or not you will make (or have made) a profit.

4. *Cash Flow Statement*—It may sound strange, but even a profitable business can be in a situation where it doesn't have enough cash on hand to pay its bills. This form allows you to make sure that your cash needs are met on time.

5. *Balance Sheet*—This form shows what you own (assets), what you owe (liabilities) and what you and others have invested in the business (owner's equity) at a particular point in time. It is used to describe the financial health of your business.

Each of the five forms is used in your business in two ways:

1. To predict the future performance of your business. As part of your business plan, you must "guesstimate" your future sales, expenses and overall financial situation. In other words, you must fill out all five forms as you expect them to look in the future. When used this way, the forms are referred to as "projections," "pro formas," "forecasts" or "budgets." (The four terms are used interchangeably.) For example, your "pro forma income statement" is your best estimate of your income statement at some future time. So is your income forecast, your projected income and your budgeted income statement.

2. To evaluate the past performance of your business. As you run your business, you will regularly fill out the form with the "real" results (your actual sales, your actual expenses, and so on). You can then compare the actual results with the predicted results. This comparison is the most useful and powerful management tool available to you. When used in this way, the forms are simply called by their real names. For example, if someone asks to see your income statements they generally mean your most current income statement—probably last month's statement.

Your projected statements (or forms) are a critical part of your business plan. You've already defined your product, your market, your competition and your plans for managing your business. Now you need to translate that information into hard numbers to see if the business you've envisioned will really make money.

You may find that it will only make money if you spend less than you want to on your rent or your computer or your advertising. Or you may find that while people love your idea they're just not willing to pay enough for it to cover the cost of being in business. Whatever the result, it is much easier to look at the numbers now and take the requisite steps to make your business a success than to wait until you've poured money and hard work into the wrong business strategy or even the wrong business.

Nonetheless, projecting financial statements into the future is one of the most difficult things a business owner has to do. As a minimum, income statements and cash flow statements must be projected on a monthly basis for the first year and on a quarterly basis (i.e., every three months) for two additional years. This seems like a lot of work, and it is. But it's a lot easier than living with the results if you don't do it.

By the way, men aren't born doing financial analyses either. It doesn't take special brains, but it does take experience to understand the financial statement "clues," ask the right questions, determine what the issues really are and plan activities to correct problems. The best thing you can do is go through these analyses several times with your advisors, ask lots of questions and develop an understanding of them for yourself. It won't take long before you know what's important for your business, can do your own analysis and can determine the activities appropriate for you. The keys are: 1) Don't be afraid to ask questions, even if you think they're stupid. It's the only way to learn. 2) Be open-minded to making changes in your management and operating practices to improve the financial health of your business.

The following pages describe each of the financial forms in detail. If you don't have a calculator, now is a good time to get one.

If you have access to a computer, it is an invaluable tool for forecasting. Any spreadsheet program can be used to create your own pro forma financial statements. Let the computer add up the numbers. It will save you hours of calculating and you can easily look at the effects of changes in your assumptions about the business.

Two more quick notes:

1. By definition, projecting numbers into the future is not an exact science. When you do it, round your numbers to the nearest five or ten dollars. It will be much easier to keep track of, much easier for your funding source to read, and a much better use of your time than tracking down all the numbers to the nearest penny.

2. According to standard accounting practice, negative numbers are shown in parentheses. In other words, "-$100" is shown as "($100)."

Projecting financial statements into the future is one of the most difficult things a business owner has to do.

SOURCES AND USES OF CASH

For those of you who need to borrow money, this form succinctly describes where you will get the money (your sources of cash) and what you will do with it (your uses of cash). Even if you're planning to fund your business yourself, it's wise to complete this form so you have a clear picture of where your money is going.

Figure 13 provides a format for your sources and uses of cash statement. Each item in Figure 13 is described below. As you read through the description of each item, fill in the numbers that are appropriate for your business.

Don't be overly concerned if you're not 100% sure of the numbers right now—you can firm them up later as you get more information. However, for your final business plan—the one you present to a funding source—don't rely on guesses if you can get exact prices or firm estimates. If you must make an estimate, specify how you arrived at your figures.

"Uses of Cash" are divided into three categories:

1. *Pre-Opening (Or Expanding) Uses of Cash*—the cash you need to start or expand your business.

2. *Operating Uses of Cash*—the cash you need to operate your business.

3. *Capital Equipment*— the cash you need to purchase equipment after you've opened for business (or for expanding).

Pre-opening uses of cash include:

- Opening Inventory—If you're in the retail or wholesale business, this is the inventory you need on your shelves before you open your doors.

- Capital Equipment—This includes your office equipment, business machines, store fixtures, production equipment and vehicles. This is covered in greater detail later in this chapter.

- Property—You may plan to purchase property for your business. The cost of that property is shown here.

- Renovations—Whether you purchase property or rent space, you will probably need to modify your place of business to make it suitable for your particular needs.

- Pre-Opening Marketing and Promotions—As a minimum you will need business cards and business stationery. You may also need special signs, advertising, balloons, and so on to announce the fact that you've opened for business.

- Deposits—Most building owners require lease deposits. You may also need to pay deposits for your telephones and rented office equipment.

- Other Pre-Opening Expenses—Includes such things as pre-opening office supplies, signs with your name or your business' name on them, business licenses, business insurance, accounting fees to set up your recordkeeping system, costs to hire personnel and any other expenses you anticipate prior to opening (or expanding).

Use your knowledge of your business and the plans you described in Chapter 2 to fill in these numbers now.

Operating uses of cash include:

- Working Capital—This is the money you need to keep your business operating until you generate enough cash from sales to be able to pay your bills. The explanation of working capital is lengthy, but stick with it because the notion of working capital is critical to your business.

Figure 13.

Sources and Uses of Cash

USES OF CASH

Pre-opening (or expanding)

Opening inventory .... _____

Capital equipment .... _____

Property .... _____

Renovations .... _____

Pre-opening marketing and promotions .... _____

Deposits .... _____

Other pre-opening expenses .... _____

Total .... _____

Operating

Working capital .... _____

Contingency funds .... _____

Total .... _____

Capital Equipment

(post-opening or expanding) .... _____

Total Uses of Cash .... _____

SOURCES OF CASH

Savings .... _____

Loans from relatives/friends

1. .... _____

2. .... _____

3. .... _____

Loan from bank .... _____

Other .... _____

Total Sources of Cash .... _____

The idea is this: Even after you've bought everything you need to start your business and you're ready to open your doors, you will continue to incur bills which must be paid before you generate enough sales to cover them.

For example, let's say you're starting a children's clothing store. You have $15,000 saved up to start your business. Your pre-opening expenditures look like this:

Opening inventory	$ 8,000
Fixtures and equipment	3,000
Renovations	500
Pre-opening marketing and promotions	1,500
Deposits	500
Other pre-opening expenses	1,000
TOTAL	$14,500

You're ready to go and you have $500 in your checking account.

The first month you're open most people don't know about you yet, so you sell only $400 worth of children's clothes. This means you now have $900 in your checking account. But you have bills to pay:

Rent	$ 350
Utilities	150
Salesclerks	400
Advertising	100
Bookkeeper	100
TOTAL	$1,100

You have to pay $1,100, you only have $900 in your checking account, and you haven't even drawn a salary. *This situation is not uncommon.* It will probably continue for at least a few months, maybe longer, while you get your business off the ground. The money you need to cover these cash requirements is called working capital, and you must plan for it before you open because you must have it available to you in order for your business to survive. You get working capital in the same way you get your start-up cash: you take it out of personal savings or you borrow it or you convince someone else to invest it.

How do you determine how much working capital you need? This is what your cash flow statement is used for. It is described in detail later in this chapter. When you get to that section, you will determine the number that belongs in Figure 13 for your business.

● Contingency Funds—The second operating use of cash is for unexpected, unpredictable cash needs. For example, you may find that you need to attend a seminar or trade show that you hadn't planned for or hire additional salespeople to maintain quality service, or you may be audited by the IRS or sued by a supplier, or your sales might be less than you projected. No matter how well you plan, events almost always arise that are not part of your plan. It would be a mistake not to have additional cash on hand to cover them.

Capital Equipment (post-opening) includes the capital equipment that you need to purchase during the planning period in order to fulfill your management plans (i.e., your product development plan, marketing plan, sales plan, etc.).

By now you should understand that in order to start or expand your business you need more than just the money to buy that computer or other major piece of equipment you have your eye on. You need to finance all of your pre-opening expenses and all of your operating expenses, including money for contingencies.

The next question is: Where will the money come from?

Chapter Eight, Using Your Business Plan to Get Financing, describes in detail the ways to get the money you need. For now you probably have some idea of where you anticipate getting the money. Fill in the Sources of Cash section of Figure 13. Remember that your total sources of cash must be at least as large as your total uses of cash in order for your business to survive.

CAPITAL EQUIPMENT LIST

Your capital equipment list describes all of the equipment, furniture and fixtures you need to start your business. Technically capital equipment is equipment you use to provide a service or to sell, store and deliver merchandise; or to manufacture a product. Generally it refers to those major items that you buy for your business which last more than a year.

For example, your desk is considered capital equipment because it is a major piece of furniture that you will use for more than a year. Your pens, pencils and paper are not capital equipment because they are not major pieces of equipment, even though they might last more than a year.

Examples of capital equipment are:

- Office furniture and business machines, e.g., desks, typewriters, computers, adding machines, filing cabinets, bookshelves

- Store fixtures, e.g., display cases, lighting fixtures, refrigeration units

- Machinery used to make products or provide services, e.g., sewing machines, stoves and ovens, medical equipment

- Vehicles used for business

If you are unsure of whether something is capital equipment, check with your accountant.

The reasons for listing your capital equipment are:

- To get clear on the equipment you need and how much it will cost

- To understand your insurance needs since you will probably want to insure some or all of your capital equipment

- To make it easy to calculate your depreciation expense (a definition of depreciation and its impact on capital equipment is discussed on page 122)

Use Figure 14 to help you list the capital equipment you need for your business. Include the equipment you plan to buy and the items you already own.

As you compile your list, consider the advantages of leasing some of the equipment rather than buying it. You may not be aware that much of your equipment—including furniture—can be leased or rented. The advantages of leasing are that it gives you added flexibility if you want to change equipment in a few years and it generally doesn't require much down payment, which is great if you're short of cash. The disadvantage is that leasing can be very expensive. Your accountant will be able to help you understand the ramifications of this decision.

INCOME STATEMENT

By now you should realize that even after you purchase your capital equipment there are many costs that your business will incur as you develop your goods and services; market and sell them; produce, create or buy them; and manage your business. The sample income statement on page 112-113 matches these expenses with your business revenues to show you whether or not you will make a profit.

Explanation of Sample

(Line 2) *Total Sales:* The revenues which you take in from the sale of all your products/services.

(Line 3) *Cost of Goods Sold:* The costs which are directly related to your level of sales. If you are in a retail or wholesale business, cost of goods sold is the cost of inventory plus the cost of the bag, box or package in which the customer takes home the merchandise. If you are in a manufacturing business, cost of goods sold is the cost of materials and labor that are used in producing your products. If you pay a sales representative a commission (i.e., a percentage of sales), that figure is included in cost of goods sold because you can attribute the commission directly to the level of sales. The test you apply to determine if a cost belongs in the cost of goods sold category is: "Would I still pay this if I didn't sell any of my goods or services?" If the answer is no, then the expense fits the category.

If you are in a service business, you probably have very few, if any, costs that are directly attributable to your providing that service, so your cost of goods sold may be small or even zero. Some examples of costs of goods sold for a service business are: (a) If a training company hands out a notebook to each person in the training class, the cost of that notebook (paper, printing, binding, the notebook itself) is considered cost of goods sold because that cost is incurred every time a training class is given. (b) A housecleaning company uses a certain amount of cleaning supplies every time it cleans a house. The cost of these supplies are considered cost of goods sold.

(Line 8) *Gross Profit (also called Gross Margin):* This is simply sales minus the cost of goods sold. Why is this number important?

- It tells you how much money you have left over—after you've paid for producing or acquiring the product—for spending on the other expenses of doing business.

Figure 14.

Capital Equipment List

Office Equipment/Business Machines	Model	Purchase Date	Cost
_____	_____		
_____	_____		
_____	_____		

Total .... _____

Store Fixtures	Model	Purchase Date	Cost
_____	_____		
_____	_____		
_____	_____		

Total .... _____

Machinery Used to Make Product	Model	Purchase Date	Cost
_____	_____		
_____	_____		
_____	_____		

Total .... _____

Vehicles	Model	Purchase Date	Cost
_____	_____		
_____	_____		
_____	_____		

Total .... _____

Figure 15.

Sample Income Statement

	JAN	FEB	MAR	APR	MAY
1. SALES					
2. Total Sales					
3. COST OF GOODS SOLD					
4. Materials					
5. Labor					
6. Other					
7. Total Cost of Goods Sold					
8. GROSS PROFIT					
(Sales – Cost of Goods Sold)					
9. OPERATING EXPENSES					
10. Salaries and Wages					
11. Payroll Taxes and Benefits					
12. Rent					
13. Utilities					
14. Advertising and Promotion					
15. Office Supplies					
16. Postage					
17. Telephone					
18. Professional Fees					
(Legal, Accounting, et al)					
19. Repairs and Maintenance					
20. Car/Travel					
21. Depreciation					
22. Others:					
23. TOTAL OPERATING EXPENSES					
24. OTHER EXPENSES					
25. Interest					
26. TOTAL EXPENSES					
27. PROFIT (LOSS) PRE-TAX					
28. TAXES					
29. NET PROFIT (LOSS)					
Explanation of Income Statement Projections					

Figure 15. Continued

Sample Income Statement

JUN	JUL	AUG	SEP	OCT	NOV	DEC	TOTAL

- It is often used to see how efficient your operations are when compared to similar businesses or to your overall industry. Your librarian can direct you to gross profit figures for your industry.

(Line 9) *Operating Expenses (also called Administrative Costs or Overhead)*: These are the expenses of running the business. This is where you account for your expenditures in product development, marketing, sales (unless you pay on commission—see Cost of Goods Sold), personnel, management and the part of operations not accounted for in Cost of Goods Sold. You incur these costs whether you sell one "unit" or one hundred "units."

As you can see from the sample income statement, operating expenses include such things as your salary and the salary of the other people who work for you, rent, telephone, advertising, and so on.

(Line 24) *Other Expenses*: These are non-operating expenses. The most common of these (and probably the only one you have) is the interest you pay the bank if you have a bank loan.

(Line 26) *Total Expenses*: These are all of your business expenses. The figure is calculated by adding together operating expenses (23) and other expenses (25).

(Line 27) *Profit (Loss) Pre-Tax*: This is the figure on which your taxes will be determined. It is calculated by subtracting total expenses (26) from gross profit (8).

(Line 28) *Taxes*: Your accountant can provide you with a percent of your pretax profit to include in this category.

(Line 29) *Net Profit (Loss)*: Pre-tax profit (27) minus taxes (28). This is the "bottom line," the profit which your business will make.

Explanation of Income Statement Projections: It is important to have a written explanation of how you arrived at the numbers (including calculations and assumptions) on your pro forma income statement so you can remember what you did at a later time and can explain it to your funding source. The best way to do this is on a line-by-line basis. If you use standard accounting paper to do your statements, the line numbers will already be on the paper.

You can buy standard accounting paper at any business supply store. (Note: If you're doing your analysis on a computer, just include a column of line numbers down the left-hand side.)

You *must* have these notes of explanation in order to take your business plan to a funding source. (And they will take more room than what is allocated in Figure 15, so plan to use more paper.)

PROJECTIONS

One workable sequence for preparing your projected income statements is:

1. Prepare a three-year summary.

2. Break down the first year on a month-by-month basis. If your business doesn't break even the first year, you may want to continue monthly

For all projections

state your

assumptions clearly.

projections until it does. (Note: "break-even" means that your profit is zero or greater, i.e., you are not incurring a loss.)

3. Break down years two and three by quarters.

In Chapter Four you described in detail how you will run your business. Your income statement quantifies your business ideas.

For all projections state your assumptions clearly. Do not put down numbers that you cannot rationally substantiate. Get estimates—preferably in writing—for as many expenses as you can. Use conservative sales figures based on your marketing and sales strategies.

Forms for preparing your pro forma income statements are supplied in Appendix V. These forms are designed to be generic; there may be some areas unique to your business that require different expense categories or an expansion of the sales or cost of goods sold areas. For example, you may want to divide sales into retail sales and wholesale sales. Or you may want to divide cost of goods sold into raw material, labor and purchased goods. Update the forms so they fit your business. If you're not sure how to do this, talk to your accountant and your support people.

In case you get stuck putting together your projections, the key areas of the income statement are described in more detail on the following pages.

Projecting Sales

Whether you've been in business for a while or are just starting a business, your sales forecasts are the basis for most of your financial planning. They are also the most difficult to estimate. For many people, sales forecasting is a stumbling point: either they feel they can't do it and they never get farther than this in their business plan or they pull numbers out of thin air without any justification or they work backward from their costs and calculate the sales they need to make a profit. Don't let this be you!

There are many ways to calculate total sales. Several methods are listed below. Choose the way that makes the most sense for your business or be creative and develop your own way. You may even try a variety of ways. The important things are that: a) you understand how the sales figures are derived, b) they are based on your market research and market assumptions and c) you correct them over time if your estimates prove to be incorrect.

Sales forecasts are the basis for most of your financial planning.

Ways to calculate sales:

1. Compare your business to already existing businesses and then modify for the things that will make you different. The library and your local Chamber of Commerce have information on such things as average sales in a particular industry, average retail sales per square foot for your geographical area, and so on. Call them, tell them what you're trying to do and ask them for help. Start with these figures and then modify for such things as differences in your market, seasonality of your business, the time it will take for people to realize you're open for business, and so on.

2. Get information on sales from similar, non-competing businesses in other cities. While most business owners are (understandably) reluctant to part

with such data, they may be willing to share it if you convince them that you will never be a competitor of theirs.

3. Make your best estimate of your market share percentage and multiply that by the total market to get your sales. Your local library and Chamber of Commerce will be able to help you get the demographic data you need to determine the size of your total market. To estimate your market share percentage, use your knowledge of the business, your common sense and as much research as you can dig up.

For example, Kerry Shay writes and produces newsletters tailored to particular industries, which her client companies use as public relations and marketing tools. Kerry's target market includes FIRE (Finance, Insurance, and Real Estate) and service businesses in her geographic area with sales ranging from $250,000 to $5 million. In order to project sales for her business, Kerry called the business librarian at her local library and asked for assistance. The librarian directed Kerry to Dunn and Bradstreet's *Donnelly Market Profile Analysis*, where she found that there were 7,500 companies that fit her target market description.

Kerry then asked a marketing class at the local university to help her with a telephone survey. They called 200 companies and found that 20% were interested in newsletters. It followed, then, that there might be 1,500 companies in Kerry's target market (7,500 x 20%) interested in newsletters.

Kerry knew she had two direct competitors and at least ten indirect competitors. She also knew that it would be very difficult and costly to reach all of the companies in her target market to sell them on the benefits of newsletters. Therefore, she conservatively estimated that she could capture 2% of the market, or 30 companies (1,500 x 2%) the first year, 3% the second year (45 companies), and 4% the third year (60 companies). Kerry planned to closely monitor sales to see if her estimates were reasonable.

4. If you're already in business, look at your sales trends for prior years on a month-by-month basis. This is the best indicator you have for what future sales are likely to be. Then, consider those factors within and outside your control which might impact sales, such as:

| Factors within your control: | Promotion | Staffing |
| | Pricing | Product Development |

| Factors outside your control: | Economic | Social |
| | Technological | Competitive |

Write down your assumptions regarding these factors on a separate sheet of paper and use them to adjust last year's sales to determine next year's projections. This is not a straightforward process because change is difficult to quantify, but take your best shot at it—you'll be far more successful than if you leave it to chance.

For example, if you're in the athletic footwear business, you need to consider trends in physical fitness in your sales projections so you don't get caught selling off a huge inventory of running shoes when walking shoes or aerobic shoes are more "in." Or if you're in the printing business, the proliferation of desktop publishing systems is likely to impact your sales projections. Or, if you're a house painter, a continued recessionary economy could have a detrimental impact on sales.

To determine monthly (or quarterly) sales, divide the annual sales figure by 12 (or 4 for quarterly) and then adjust this figure based on such things as slow periods (including start-up) and peak periods (like Christmas for retailers).

Use Figure 16, Sales Forecasts, to help you solidify your sales assumptions and to divide your annual sales into monthly and quarterly numbers. You can duplicate Figure 16 and prepare it individually for each salesperson and/or product and service line that is appropriate for your business. Depending on your assumptions, you may not need to calculate sales units in order to determine sales dollars—by all means don't do extra work if you don't have to.

When you work on your monthly and quarterly sales projections, there is one more issue regarding sales which may be important for your business: When do you officially "recognize" (i.e., record) a sale on your income statement? If you're in a cash business—a business in which every transaction is immediately paid for in cash (check, major credit card)—this issue doesn't matter to you. But if you extend credit in your business, this issue can have a significant impact on your success. Businesses which routinely extend credit include:

- Service businesses which do the work and then bill their customers

- Retail businesses which offer store credit cards

- Manufacturing businesses which allow their customers to pay them over an extended period of time

Let me digress and say that the extension of credit is not a decision to be taken lightly. It's like a loan to your customers—you're letting them use your money at 0% interest. In some industries, however, this is the accepted standard, and you may have to extend credit in order to be in business.

Now, back to the issue at hand. You "recognize" a sale (i.e., record it on your income statement) when two things occur:

1. The services are rendered, and

2. You receive either cash or a promise to pay

For example, suppose you're in the telemarketing business, i.e., you call people on behalf of your customers and ask them if they're willing to buy a product. A scenario might look like this:

January: You sign an agreement with Silver Widget Co. to provide them with telemarketing services.

You hire three temporary employees to do the work.

February: Your temporary employees make the calls, and you give the results to the president of Silver Widget.

You send an invoice to Silver Widget.

March: Silver Widget sends you a check which you deposit in your checking account.

When do you officially "recognize" a sale on your income statement?

Figure 16.

Sales Forecast—Year 1

Total Annual Sales (Units): _____

Based on the following assumptions:

1. _____
2. _____
3. _____
4. _____
5. _____

Total Annual Sales ($): _____

Based on the following assumptions:

1. _____
2. _____
3. _____
4. _____
5. _____

	JAN	FEB	MAR	1st QTR TOTAL	APR	MAY	JUN	2nd QTR TOTAL
# of Units								
Sales $								

	JUL	AUG	SEP	3rd QTR TOTAL	OCT	NOV	DEC	4th QTR TOTAL
# of Units								
Sales $								

Assumptions for distributing sales by month:

1. _____
2. _____
3. _____
4. _____
5. _____

Figure 16. Continued

Sales Forecasts—Years 2 & 3

Total Annual Sales (Units) Year 2:

Based on the following assumptions:

1. _____

2. _____

3. _____

4. _____

5. _____

	1st Quarter	2nd Quarter	3rd Quarter	4th Quarter	TOTAL
# of Units					
Sales $					

Total Annual Sales (Units) Year 3:

Based on the following assumptions:

1. _____

2. _____

3. _____

4. _____

5. _____

	1st Quarter	2nd Quarter	3rd Quarter	4th Quarter	TOTAL
# of Units					
Sales $					

Question: Do you account for the sale in January, February or March?

Answer: You show the sale in your February records because you did the work in February ("services are rendered") and you sent an invoice which automatically elicited a promise to pay.

By the way, you might have noticed that you had to pay the temporary employees in February, but you didn't get paid until March. The money you need to cover such expenses is called working capital (described earlier in this chapter.)

Now, fill in the Sales Forecasts by month for year one and by quarters for years two and three.

Projecting Cost of Goods Sold

Cost of goods sold is one of the easiest parts of the income statement to fill in. You simply determine how much it costs you to produce, acquire or create the sales you projected in Figure 16. The nature of the calculation depends on the type of business you're in.

• For retail or wholesale businesses, the cost of goods sold is the cost of inventory plus the cost of the box, bag or container in which the customer takes home the merchandise. The simplest and most effective way to prepare projections is to use averages.

For example, suppose you're in the children's clothing business. Let's say you plan to sell girls' dresses for $30 and your research tells you they will cost $15 each. Your cost of each sale (before including your operating costs) is 50% of the selling price. After including the price of the box, your cost of goods sold might be 51% instead of 50%. Therefore, if you projected January sales at $15,000, your January cost of goods sold would be $7,650 (51% of $15,000).

Chances are, you plan to sell more than just girls' dresses in your store. You might sell girls' and boys' dress clothes, girls' and boys' play clothes and children's accessories (such as bibs, socks, baby booties, and so on).

Also, don't forget about the merchandise which you will probably have to sell at sale prices. This occurs when you need to move out last year's styles to make room for this year's styles or when you want to get rid of defective merchandise.

The way you handle these situations is by calculating what's called an average weighted cost of goods sold. Using the children's clothing store as an example:

Item	Projected Sales Revenue	Cost Per sale	Total Cost Of Goods Sold
Dress clothes	$30,000	40%	$ 12,000
Play clothes	75,000	50%	37,500
Accessories	6,000	30%	1,800
Sale items	50,000	80%	40,000
TOTAL	$161,000	57%	$ 91,300

In the example, the total average cost per sale is not an average of the individual cost per sale percentages. Rather it is weighted by the projected sales revenue in each category. It is calculated by dividing the total cost of goods sold by the total projected sales revenue (91,300/161,000 = 57%).

Now make this calculation for your retail or wholesale business. Then multiply the total average cost per sale by your projected sales in each year, month or quarter to arrive at the figure that belongs in the cost of goods sold category for your income statement.

• For manufacturing businesses your cost of goods sold includes the cost of raw materials plus labor plus purchased goods that it takes to produce one "unit" of product. This total cost per unit is then multiplied by the number of units you expect to sell in each time period to determine the total cost of goods sold for that time period.

For example, suppose you are in the business of producing children's bibs. In order to produce each bib, you need the following:

Raw Material	Cost Per Bib
Bib fabric (6 bibs/yd)	$0.83
Collar fabric (3 inches/4 bibs)	0.06
Thread (75 ft/bib)	0.10
Label (in 10,000 label lots)	0.03
Labor (@ $5.00 per hour)	
Sew edge, collar (2 minutes)	$0.17
Decorative stitch (2 minutes)	0.17
Packing, storage (40% of other labor)	0.14 [.40 x (.17 + .17)]
Other Purchases	
Cutting @ $100/hr (50 bibs/minute)	$0.03
Sew applique and label	0.58
Sales Commission	
Sales rep (15% of the $6 wholesale price)	0.90
TOTAL	$3.01

In this example I have assumed that you will sew most of the bib yourself (within your company), but will contract out cutting the fabric and sewing on the applique and label.

If you anticipate selling 1,000 bibs, your cost of goods sold is $3,010 (1,000 x $3.01).

If you are producing more than one product, calculate the cost of goods sold for each individually, then add them together for your income statement.

• For service businesses the cost of goods sold is generally either very small or zero. The test you use to determine whether an expense fits in this category is to ask: If I didn't sell any of my service, would I still incur this cost? If the answer is no, the expense fits in the cost of goods sold category.

For example, let's say you're selling supervisory training services. You operate out of a small office which you rent monthly. When you give your training course, you rent a conference room at a local hotel. If no one signed up for your training service in June, would you still have to pay the June rent at your office?

The answer is yes since your landlord would not be likely to let you out of your lease for one month just because you didn't sell anything. Therefore rent is NOT a cost of goods sold. Now, if no one signed up for your training course in June would you still have to pay to rent the hotel conference room? If no one signed up, you would not rent the room and you would not have to pay for it. Therefore the cost of the motel room IS a cost of goods sold because you only incur the cost when you sell your service.

If you are in doubt about whether or not you have cost of goods sold in your service business, talk with your accountant and your support people—they can guide you.

Now calculate the cost of goods sold for your business.

Projecting Operating Expenses

Most of your operating expenses are fairly straightforward to estimate.

For example, you can find out what it costs to lease space in your area by calling a commercial realtor or by checking with your local Chamber of Commerce.

You can estimate your telephone costs by assuming how many calls you'll make and calling the telephone company to get their rates.

You can estimate your advertising and promotion expenses by reviewing your marketing plan and getting price quotes from classified ad departments, advertising agencies, marketing consultants, and so on.

Fill in the operating expense portion of the income statement now. If you have any doubts, be conservative and make your estimates higher than you currently expect them to be. As always, document your assumptions on a separate piece of paper. And don't be shy about asking your business advisors for advice.

There is one tricky part of operating expenses which may apply to your situation: depreciation. For most small businesses, especially service and retail businesses, depreciation has only a minimal impact. Your accountant can help you figure out how to calculate it when tax time comes around, but it won't make a whole lot of difference in projecting your income statement and using it to manage your business.

If you're in a manufacturing business and have a lot of equipment, depreciation may have more relevance to you.

A description of depreciation is provided here so you can talk knowledgeably to your accountant and banker when they bring up this subject.

Think of depreciation as a gift from the government. It's an amount of money that the government allows you to deduct from your profit before calculating your taxes. In other words, the gift is in the form of a tax break.

On paper this "gift" represents the wear and tear on your capital equipment. For example, suppose you buy a $10,000 computer for your business. After you use it for a year, it's not worth $10,000 anymore—let's say it's worth $8,000. The government allows you to deduct the difference—$2,000—from your profit before calculating your taxes. If you're in the 15% tax bracket, this means an extra $300 in your pocket when tax time rolls around. This $2,000 is called depreciation.

Realistically it would be impossible to readily calculate a dollar amount that accurately represents wear and tear on your equipment. Recognizing this, the

Think of depreciation

as a gift from the

government.

government has set up guidelines on the amount it allows you to call depreciation and deduct from your profit. These guidelines are based on the nature of the capital equipment as well as the applicable tax laws in any given year. Your accountant will be well versed in how to make this calculation.

The important things to remember about depreciation are:

1. Depreciation shows up on your income statement as an expense, but it is not out-of-pocket cash. Rather, it is an expense that the government allows you to show on your income statement for the purpose of reducing your taxes.

2. In the government's eyes, depreciation represents the annual wear and tear on your capital equipment.

3. For most small businesses, depreciation does not have a large impact on the success or failure of the business. It is more important to manage your expenditures on capital equipment in the first place.

Projecting Profit

Theoretically you don't project your profit; rather you calculate it after projecting your revenues and expenses.

Realistically, however, you can use your profit projections to determine whether your business plans (i.e., your marketing plan, sales plan, operating plan, etc.) will result in a profitable business. If not, you have the opportunity to modify your plans—while they're still on paper—to result in a business that will make money. As you review your profit projections, consider the following:

• Don't be surprised if you incur a loss for at least six months (and, more likely, for one to two years). In fact, if you don't you probably have been overly optimistic about your sales and expenses.

• There are three ways to make your net profit more positive: increase gross profit, decrease expenses or both.

• Recognize that there might be a distinction between net profit and your personal income (i.e., the amount of cash that you can take out of the business for your personal use). The reasons for this are very complex and beyond the scope of this book—your accountant can explain them to you if you are interested. The important thing is to use your cash flow projections rather than your income projections as the judge of how much money will be available for your personal expenses.

• If the business doesn't look good on paper, it's not likely to become "good" as you operate.

If your profit projections don't look large enough for the financial health of the company (as well as for you personally), the first place to look for increasing your profit is decreasing your expenses. The question you want to ask yourself is: How can I operate with less? This is a very difficult issue because most of us want to start with the best for our business. But remember that you won't be in business very long if you can't control your costs.

The question you want to ask yourself is: How can I operate with less?

Perhaps you can start with a smaller computer system—you can always upgrade later. Maybe family members will work in your store for a few months at no charge. You may be able to start your business in your home or share an office with a friend in business. Business support companies are popping up all over which can provide you with copying services, telephone answering services, typing services, and so on without your having to invest in copy machines, secretaries and expensive office equipment. It's nice to start out with a lot of really slick things, but it's even nicer to take steps that increase your chances of business success.

You may be tempted to increase your profit by changing your estimate of sales. Move in this direction with caution. Chances are that your first estimate of sales is the most accurate. If you start making changes in this area just to make the profit look good, you may avoid changing your expenses on paper only to find that you must change them as you begin operating. It's much better to look those changes squarely in the face when you're not up to your knees in the day-to-day problems of the business.

Evaluate your pro forma income statement and make the changes necessary to prove to you and your funding source that your business will succeed.

BREAK-EVEN ANALYSIS

Break-even analysis is a financial tool that you can (and should) use to effectively operate your business. It answers such questions as:

- What level of sales must I reach before I start making a profit?

- What will happen to my profit if I increase or decrease the price for my goods and services?

- What will happen to my profit if my sales fall short of my projections?

You use break-even analysis to determine the level of sales at which you incur neither profit nor loss—this is called the break-even point. When sales fall below the break-even point, you are not making a profit. Used in this way, a break-even analysis provides you with a sales target to shoot for.

A break-even analysis provides you with a sales target to shoot for.

In order to do break-even analysis you must divide all of your costs into two broad categories: variable and fixed costs. Variable costs go up when your sales go up, go down when your sales go down, and are zero when you have no sales at all. For example, if you owned a bookstore but didn't sell any books, your variable cost would be zero. If you sold five books, you would incur the cost of those five books. If you sold 500 books, you would incur the cost of those 500 books, which is 100 times the cost of five books. Fixed cost remains the same regardless of your volume of sales. For example, your bookstore has to pay rent and electricity whether you sell five books or 500 books.

Take a look at your Year One pro forma income statement. You may remember that I defined all the costs in your costs of goods as variable costs—they all vary with the level of sales—so put a V to the left of those entries. I defined operating costs as fixed costs, so put an F to the left of those entries. If you have other costs, such as interest, these are also fixed, so put an F to the left of those entries. Now look again at your operating costs. In your particular situation, it may be that some of those costs are both variable and fixed. For example, your telephone costs may have a fixed component—the basic monthly charge—and a variable component—the long distance toll calls that are directly tied to sales. These costs that have both variable and fixed components are called semi-variable. In most cases it is not worth the extra effort to separate out the amount of semi-variable costs that's fixed from the amount that's variable. If you have semi-variable costs, you should either:

- very quickly and arbitrarily allocate them as either fixed or variable, or

- add up all the semi-variable costs and assign half to fixed and half to variable.

Do this now. As you continue reading, you should know which of your costs are variable and which are fixed.

The break-even equation is this:
Break-even point = fixed costs divided by contribution margin*

> Where fixed costs = sales − variable costs
> Sales = your projected sales for the period
> Variable costs = the sum of all your variable costs during the period

*Contribution margin is another word for gross profit. It is also called gross margin.

If you're not used to dealing with equations, this may be a little intimidating, but you will quickly see how to do the calculation once you try it.

- Example #1: You're an image consultant operating out of your home. You charge $60 per hour for your service. Your variable costs are zero because you have no expenses that are tied directly to your volume of service. Therefore, for every hour that you can bill your time, 100% of the price ($60/hr) contributes to your operating costs plus, once they're covered, your profit.

Another way of saying this is that your contribution margin is $60.00, since sales - 0 = sales (refer back to the definition of the break-even equation).

Suppose your fixed costs are $1,000 per month, including the interest and depreciation on your $2,000 computer system.

Break-even = $1,000 ÷ $60/hr = 16.67 hr

In other words, you need to bill 16.67 hours per month to break even.

- Example #2: You own a camera store and your fixed costs are $7,000 per month. You have a variety of cameras that sell at different prices, but your contribution margin percentage is a constant 45%. (Contribution margin percentage = [sales - variable costs] ÷ sales. Sometimes, especially in retail businesses, this number is readily available. In the section entitled Projecting Cost of Goods Sold, I described a way to calculate your cost of goods sold as a percentage. Your contribution margin is equal to 100% - cost of goods sold percentage.) You need to use a minor variation of the break-even equation:

> Break-even point = fixed costs/contribution margin percentage
> (in sales $)   = $7,000/45%
>   = $15,556

In other words, you need to sell roughly $15,500 worth of cameras per month to break even. Note that if you use your contribution margin percentage in the equation, the break-even point is calculated in sales dollars. When you use the contribution margin dollars (not the percentage) in the equation, the break-even point is calculated in sales volume.

● Example #3: You own a retail store that sells gift baskets. While each basket is unique, the average gift basket sells for $35, and, on average, your variable costs per basket look like this:

Basket and decoration $4.50
Food 13.50
TOTAL $18.00

Therefore, from each $35 sale, $18 is taken out to pay your variable costs, leaving $17 to contribute to your operating costs and, once they are covered, to your profit. This $17 is called your contribution margin.

Now suppose your fixed costs were $5,000 per month. How many baskets would you have to sell to break even?

Break-even = fixed costs/contribution margin
= $5,000 ÷ $17
= 294 gift baskets

In other words, you would have to sell 294 gift baskets each month at an average of $35 apiece to break-even.

Now, how else can you use this information?

It's clear that if you sell fewer than 294 gift baskets per month, you will show a loss. But what happens if you sell more than 294 per month?

For every gift basket over 294, you show a profit of $17 per basket. Therefore, if you sell an additional 50 gift baskets, your monthly profit will be $850 (50 x $17).

Pricing Considerations

Perhaps you feel that the price of gift baskets is too high to draw sufficient customers. What happens if you lower the price?

At $33.25/ basket: Contribution Margin = $33.25 − $18.00 = $15.25
Monthly break-even = $5,000/$15.25 = 328 gift baskets (rounded)

Lowering your price by $1.75 increases the break-even point by 34 gift baskets per month. Or, put another way, lowering your price by 5% increases your break-even sales volume by 12%. The question you want to answer is: Can I sell 12% more gift baskets at the lower price of $33.25 per basket?

Now suppose you'd like to increase your profit by raising the price of gift baskets. What happens at the higher price?

At $36.75/basket: contribution margin = $36.75 − $18.00 = $18.75
Monthly break-even = $5,000/$18.75 = 267 gift baskets

Raising your price by $1.75 decreases the break-even point by 27 gift baskets. Or put another way, raising your price by 5% decreases your break-even sales volume by 9%. The question you want to answer is: Will sales fall by more than 9% if I raise the price of gift baskets to $36.75?

Profit Considerations

Suppose you want to earn a monthly profit of $4,000. If gift baskets cost an average of $35 apiece, how many gift baskets must you sell to meet your profit goal? This is the equivalent of tacking on an additional $4,000 to your current fixed cost of $5,000 per month. Your goal is to cover your fixed cost plus your profit, or $9,000.

Contribution margin = $35 – $18 = $17
Monthly break-even = $9,000 ÷ $17 = 529

In other words, you must sell 529 gift baskets per month in order to cover your fixed costs and meet your profit goal.

Fixed Cost Considerations

Suppose you want to buy a new computer and software system to help you with your inventory control and bookkeeping. The total package, including training to use the system, costs $4,000. The entire cost is fixed, i.e., it does not vary with your level of sales. How many additional gift baskets must you sell to pay for it? There are two ways to look at this:

1) You can look at it from the perspective of paying for the total project. You know that your contribution margin is $17 per basket sold. Therefore to pay for an additional $4,000 worth of fixed cost, you must sell $4,000/$17 or 235 gift baskets. From past experience, you know how long this will take. Keep in mind that you won't earn a profit until you cover this additional fixed cost.

2) You can look at it on a monthly basis. If you depreciate the equipment on a straight line basis over five years, your monthly depreciation cost is $66.67. If you take out a five-year, 10% loan to pay for the system, your monthly interest cost is $84.99. Therefore your additional monthly fixed cost for the computer system is $151.66 ($66.67 + $84.99). In order to break even you would have to sell an additional $151.66/$17 or 9 gift baskets per month for the next five years.

If you are still confused about how to do a break-even analysis, follow these steps using your Year One pro forma Income Statement:

1) Add all of your fixed costs in the column called "total year one."

2) Add all of your variable costs in the column called "total year one."

3) Write down your expected total sales for year one.

4) Now solve the equation: Contribution margin = sales - variable costs

5) Now solve the equation: Break-even point = fixed costs/contribution margin

As you do your own break-even analysis, keep the following in mind:

- While break-even gives you a sales target to shoot for, once you've gotten there, you're still not in the clear. At break-even, you're not losing money, but you're not making a profit either.

- Depending on how you set up your income statement, your fixed costs may or may not include your personal income. If it is included, then you can rest easy that once you've hit break even you'll be able to take home your paycheck. If it is not included, then make sure you add it to your fixed costs before you calculate break-even so you are targeting a sales figure that will allow you to earn money you need in your personal life.

- For those of you who are considering borrowing a large amount of money, the more interest you have, the higher your fixed costs are and the more you will need to sell to break-even.

- For many businesses it takes more than a year to break-even. Don't be surprised if you fit in this category.

CASH FLOW STATEMENT

Profits are important and you must have them to stay in business in the long run, but even more important to your business is cash. Simply put, you must have cash available to pay your bills when they come due.

Strange as it sounds, it is possible to make a profit and still not have enough cash to pay your bills. Here's an example:

- Suppose you're in the construction business building speculative homes. This means that you build homes on the speculation that, once they're complete, someone will buy them. The market in your area is booming for homes in the $90,000 price range, and you believe you'll have no difficulty selling three homes quickly and at a 25% gross profit. You calculate projected sales to be $270,000 ($90,000 x 3) including $67,500 gross profit ($90,000 x 3 x 25%).

Your peak building time is April through September, when the weather is conducive to outdoor construction, and you need $100,000 of building supplies to get started. But since November through March were very slow months, you only have $30,000 in your business checking account. You ask your supplier to provide you with building supplies in April, and tell her that you'll pay for them in September when you expect to close on the houses. Much to your dismay, she says no. You see, it doesn't matter to her that you believe you'll have $270,000 flowing into your business in September. To her, it's a risk she's not willing to take. And without those building supplies, your $67,500 is only a dream.

As you can see, it is critical to plan for your cash needs to make sure that you have sufficient cash available when you need it. The mechanism for doing this is called a cash flow statement. Your projected cash flow statement will show you:

1. How much cash your business will need.

2. When it will be needed.

3. Where it will come from.

It is possible to make a profit and still not have enough cash to pay your bills.

It will allow you to plan your cash and borrowing needs before you're sitting there with your checkbook, panicking about how you'll pay your bills. By planning in advance, you'll have many more options available to you, at lower costs, and you'll be able to make your borrowing decisions before your business is in crisis.

For the purpose of this analysis, the word "cash" means hard currency or anything that can be readily converted to hard currency, including checks and major credit cards.

Explanation of Cash Flow Statement

Figure 17 shows a sample cash flow statement. A description of each line is provided below.

Cash Inflow: This is all of the cash that you expect to take in for your business.

Cash is generated primarily by sales. However, not all sales are cash sales. Perhaps your business is all cash—but if you offer any credit (charge accounts, term payments, trade credit) to your customers, you need to have a means of telling when those credit sales will turn into cash-in-hand. The timing of this is blurred in the income statement, but made very clear by the cash flow statement.

In addition to sales, cash inflow can also come from investment and loans. Even if you plan to finance your business from savings, that is still an investment into the business which is recorded on your cash flow statement. This allows you to see the results of investing your own hard-earned money.

(1) *Cash from Sales:* This is the cash you take in from selling your products/ services. It includes:

(2) *Cash Sales:* Sales to people who pay immediately in cash.

(3) *Cash from Receivables:* The cash you receive when your receivables come due. For example, let's say you're in the advertising business and you bill your clients on a monthly basis. From past history, you know that 75% of your clients pay within two weeks of receiving your bill and 25% wait another month to pay you. Therefore, a scenario for you might look like this:

> January: Anticipate doing $10,000 worth of work. Will send out bills to clients on January 31. Record $10,000 in sales on January projected income statement.

> February: Estimate receipt of 75% of January's billings, or $7,500. Record $7,500 in cash from receivables in February's projected cash flow statement.

> March: Estimate receipt of 25% of January's billings, or $2,500. Record $2,500 in cash from receivables in March's projected cash flow statement.

> Of course, this scenario assumes that January is the only month in which you do work (hopefully not the case). If you also expect to do billable work in February, 75% of your sales will be added to March Cash From Receivables, and so on.

(4) *Total:* Total cash from sales equals (2) plus (3).

Plan your cash and borrowing needs before you're sitting there with your checkbook, panicking about how you'll pay your bills.

(5) *Cash from Funding Sources:* This is the total cash that you expect to receive from all of your funding sources. It includes:

(6) *Cash From Owners:* All of the cash you will invest in the business. If you will have partners, it includes the cash that they will invest. The cash is shown in the month in which you expect to give it to the business. Note that some of it may be invested prior to opening your doors for business, which fits in the column entitled "Pre-Opening."

(7) *Cash From Loans:* The cash you expect to borrow from banks.

(8) *Cash From Other Investors:* The cash from others willing to invest in your business, such as family, friends, business acquaintances, and so on.

(9) *Total:* Total Cash from Funding Sources equals (6) plus (7) plus (8).

(10) *Total Cash Inflow:* The total of all cash which you expect will flow into your business. For most businesses, this cash comes from sales, investments and loans and equals (4) plus (9).

Cash Outflow: These are all the disbursements you plan to make in cash or cash equivalents during the normal course of business plus any major anticipated cash outlays.

(11 through 19) *Pre-Opening (or Expansion) Expenses:* You already calculated this on page 107. Simply copy the numbers onto rows (12) through (19) of the cash flow statement in the column called pre-opening.

(20) *Cost of Goods Sold:* These numbers come from your income projections. If appropriate, modify the month, quarter or year in which you include this number to represent when you will actually write out the check or pay cash for your inventory, raw materials, labor and so on.

(21) *Operating Expenses:* These numbers come primarily from your income projections. If appropriate, modify the month, quarter or year in which you include this number to represent when you will actually write out the check or pay cash for your expenses. For example, you may have budgeted $1,200 per year for business insurance based on a phone call to your insurance agent. On your income statement, you would have divided the $1,200 by 12 to show $100 per month of insurance expense. In reality, your agent requires you to pay quarterly, so your cash flow projections would show four payments of $300 each.

Note that depreciation does not show up on the cash flow statement because it is not a cash expense.

(22) *Owner's Salary:* Show this separately on your cash flow statement so you can see the impact of your salary on the financial health of the business. Also, your investors and/or lenders will want to know how much money you plan to take out of the business and whether or not you've allowed yourself enough money to live on.

(23) through (38): You already have established these numbers for your income statement. Just transfer them directly to your cash flow statement. As described above, it may be necessary to adjust the timing of the numbers (not the numbers themselves)—make sure you record them on the cash flow statement in the month in which you expect to pay them.

(39) *Total:* The sum of (22) through (38)

(40) *Loans:* The effect of loans is reflected in this section of the cash flow statement. If you expect several different kinds of loans (e.g., short-term loan, mortgage, line of credit), you may want to modify the form to show each loan separately.

By definition, you will be required to pay interest for the use of the lender's money. In addition you will have to repay the principal (i.e., the original amount of the loan). The specific terms of each loan are different. For some loans you'll be required to pay back some interest and some principal every month—this is how home mortgages work. For other loans you will be required to pay monthly interest for the term of the loan and repay the principal at the end of the loan. The details of your loan will be worked out with your banker. The results are recorded in rows (41) through (42).

(43) *Other Capital Equipment:* Any other capital equipment you expect to purchase during the plan period.

(44) *Taxes:* Taxes are part of the cost of doing business, and if you show an income, you have to pay taxes. The amount and timing of taxes varies from business to business and from year to year. Ask your accountant for help.

(45) *Total Cash Outflow:* (19) plus (20) plus (39) plus (41) plus (42) plus (43) plus (44). This is the total cash flowing out of your business.

Cash Flow Needs: This section highlights the cash you will need to operate your business.

(46) *Net Cash Flow:* (10) minus (45). As the calculation implies, this number tells you whether you have more money coming into your business or going out of your business, and by how much. This is the number that's critical to your business, because you must have more money coming in than going out in order to survive.

(47) *Cumulative Cash Flow:* (46) plus last month's (47). This sums up the net cash flow on a monthly basis, adding the present month's cash flow to last month's cumulative cash flow. The more negative the number is, the more money you will have to borrow in order to meet your cash obligations. In fact, for the purposes of this plan, you can use the largest negative number as a guideline for calculating your working capital. This is not the accountant's definition of working capital, but it is easy to use and a good rule of thumb.

Checking Account Reconciliation: Here's where you find out whether or not your business plan makes sense from a cash flow perspective. This shows you how your cash flow projections will impact your business checkbook.

(48) *Opening Balance:* Start with whatever you expect to have in your checking account at the start of the plan period. Thereafter, the opening balance for the current month equals the closing balance from the prior month.

(49) *Cash Inflow:* Copy from line (10).

(50) *Cash Outflow:* Copy from line (45).

(51) *Closing Balance:* (48) plus (49) minus (50). Evaluation of this area will give you an idea of what your checkbook will look like over time.

Figure 17.

Cash Flow Statement—12-Month, Year 1

		Pre-Opening	JAN	FEB	MAR
CASH INFLOW	1. CASH FROM SALES				
	2. Cash Sales				
	3. Cash from Receivables				
	4. TOTAL				
	5. CASH FROM FUNDING SOURCES				
	6. Cash from Owners				
	7. Cash from Loans				
	8. Cash from Other Investors				
	9. TOTAL				
	10. TOTAL CASH INFLOW				
CASH OUTFLOW	11. PRE-OPENING (OR EXPANSION) EXPENSES				
	12. Opening Inventory				
	13. Capital Equipment				
	14. Property				
	15. Renovations				
	16. Marketing & Promotions				
	17. Deposits				
	18. Other				
	19. TOTAL				
	20. COST OF GOODS SOLD				
	21. OPERATING EXPENSES				
	22. Owner's Salary				
	23. Other Salaries & Wages				
	24. Payroll Taxes & Benefits				
	25. Rent				
	26. Utilities				
	27. Advertising and Promotion				
	28. Office Supplies				
	29. Postage				
	30. Telephone				
	31. Professional Fees				
	32. Insurance				
	33. Repairs and Maintenance				
	34. Car/Travel				
	35.				
	36.				
	37.				
	38.				
	39. TOTAL				
	40. LOANS				
	41. Interest Payment				
	42. Principal Payment				
	43. OTHER CAPITAL EQUIPMENT				
	44. TAXES				
	45. TOTAL CASH OUTFLOW				
CASH FLOW NEEDS	46. NET CASH FLOW				
	47. CUMULATIVE CASH FLOW				
CHECKING ACCOUNT RECONCIL-IATION	48. OPENING BALANCE				
	49. + Cash Inflow				
	50. - Cash Outflow				
	51. CLOSING BALANCE				

Figure 17. Continued

Cash Flow Statement—12-Month, Year 1

APR	MAY	JUN	JUL	AUG	SEP	OCT	NOV	DEC	TOTAL

Figure 18.

Cash Flow Statement—Quarterly, Year 2

		1st Qtr	2nd Qtr	3rd Qtr	4th Qtr	TOTAL
CASH INFLOW	1. CASH FROM SALES					
	2. Cash Sales					
	3. Cash from Receivables					
	4. TOTAL					
	5. CASH FROM FUNDING SOURCES					
	6. Cash from Owners					
	7. Cash from Loans					
	8. Cash from Other Investors					
	9. TOTAL					
	10. TOTAL CASH INFLOW					
CASH OUTFLOW	11. PRE-OPENING (or expansion) EXPENSES					
	12. Opening Inventory					
	13. Capital Equipment					
	14. Property					
	15. Renovations					
	16. Marketing & Promotions					
	17. Deposits					
	18. Other					
	19. TOTAL					
	20. COST OF GOODS SOLD					
	21. OPERATING EXPENSES					
	22. Owner's Salary					
	23. Other Salaries & Wages					
	24. Payroll Taxes & Benefits					
	25. Rent					
	26. Utilities					
	27. Advertising and Promotion					
	28. Office Supplies					
	29. Postage					
	30. Telephone					
	31. Professional Fees					
	32. Insurance					
	33. Repairs and Maintenance					
	34. Car/Travel					
	35.					
	36.					
	37.					
	38.					
	39. TOTAL					
	40. LOANS					
	41. Interest Payment					
	42. Principal Payment					
	43. OTHER CAPITAL EQUIPMENT					
	44. TAXES					
	45. TOTAL CASH OUTFLOW					
CASH FLOW NEEDS	46. NET CASH FLOW					
	47. CUMULATIVE CASH FLOW					
CHECKING ACCOUNT RECONCIL-IATION	48. OPENING BALANCE					
	49. + Cash Inflow					
	50. - Cash Outflow					
	51. CLOSING BALANCE					

Figure 18. Continued

Cash Flow Statement—Quarterly, Year 3

		1st Qtr	2nd Qtr	3rd Qtr	4th Qtr	TOTAL
CASH INFLOW	1. CASH FROM SALES					
	2. Cash Sales					
	3. Cash from Receivables					
	4. TOTAL					
	5. CASH FROM FUNDING SOURCES					
	6. Cash from Owners					
	7. Cash from Loans					
	8. Cash from Other Investors					
	9. TOTAL					
	10. TOTAL CASH INFLOW					
CASH OUTFLOW	11. PRE-OPENING (or expansion) EXPENSES					
	12. Opening Inventory					
	13. Capital Equipment					
	14. Property					
	15. Renovations					
	16. Marketing & Promotions					
	17. Deposits					
	18. Other					
	19. TOTAL					
	20. COST OF GOODS SOLD					
	21. OPERATING EXPENSES					
	22. Owner's Salary					
	23. Other Salaries & Wages					
	24. Payroll Taxes & Benefits					
	25. Rent					
	26. Utilities					
	27. Advertising and Promotion					
	28. Office Supplies					
	29. Postage					
	30. Telephone					
	31. Professional Fees					
	32. Insurance					
	33. Repairs and Maintenance					
	34. Car/Travel					
	35.					
	36.					
	37.					
	38.					
	39. TOTAL					
	40. LOANS					
	41. Interest Payment					
	42. Principal Payment					
	43. OTHER CAPITAL EQUIPMENT					
	44. TAXES					
	45. TOTAL CASH OUTFLOW					
CASH FLOW NEEDS	46. NET CASH FLOW					
	47. CUMULATIVE CASH FLOW					
CHECKING ACCOUNT RECONCIL-IATION	48. OPENING BALANCE					
	49. + Cash Inflow					
	50. - Cash Outflow					
	51. CLOSING BALANCE					

As with your income statement, you also need a written explanation of how you arrived at the numbers (calculations and assumptions) in your pro forma cash flow statement.

The concepts behind the cash flow statement will become much clearer to you as you prepare your own statement.

You prepare a cash flow statement by modifying the financial statements you've already prepared—i.e., your income statement, your sources and uses of cash statement, etc.—to account for the timing of when cash actually changes hands as you receive revenues, pay bills or otherwise spend or receive money. There is some number juggling involved in this and the concepts behind it are described in the guidelines below. If you've never prepared a cash flow statement before, you would be wise to find someone to help you through it the first time, such as your accountant, your banker, a SCORE or SBDC counselor, a business consultant, one of your support people or an associate who is familiar with preparing financial statements.

By understanding the details of your cash flow statement, you'll be in a strong position to make informed management and financial decisions for your business. However, don't get so immersed in the details that you ignore the larger question: Do you have enough cash to pay your bills and take advantage of opportunities as they arise?

Here are some guidelines for preparing your cash flow projections:

1. Start with the easy part. Look at the operating expenses on your income statement and make a note next to those for which you actually write out a check on a monthly basis. Transfer those numbers directly to the cash flow statement (lines 21 through 39) in the month in which you expect to pay them.

2. Look again at the operating expenses on your income statement. For each expense category that you have not yet transferred to your cash flow statement, determine when cash payments will actually be made (i.e., in which month or months you will actually write the checks). Chances are there will be some areas for which you're not sure of the answer, especially if you're just starting your business. This is where getting assistance from an expert will really pay off. Let someone help you work out the details, then write down your assumptions. If you can't find anyone who can help you, make your best guess and write down your assumptions. You probably won't be exactly on target, but if you have a record of what you assumed, you will be able to make the necessary adjustments to your statements as you operate your business.

3. Now turn to the sales section of cash inflow (lines 2 through 4). If all of your sales are cash sales, this is very easy. Just transfer the monthly sales figures from your income statement directly to your cash flow statement (line 2).

   If your business operates on credit (i.e., if you allow people to pay you later for goods or services provided today), you have to estimate when you will actually receive the cash for the sales you recorded on your income statement. (Remember, there are times when you will record sales on your income statement even though you haven't received payment for the work performed or goods provided.)

This calculation can be very simple or very complex depending on the nature of your business. An example is shown on page 129 under the section on Cash from Receivables. The idea is to evaluate each number in the sales row of your income statement and determine when, on average, you expect to actually get the cash into your checking account. Then record the results in the appropriate months of the cash flow statement. If you're confused, seek help. Keep asking questions until you understand how to do the evaluation for your business, and don't forget to record all the assumptions.

4. Consider the cost of goods sold entry (line 20). Remember, cost of goods sold is the variable cost associated with providing your product or service to the customer. It generally consists of labor and materials (for manufacturing businesses) or inventory (for retail and wholesale businesses). For service businesses, it is not uncommon for cost of goods sold to be zero.

    If you don't have any cost of goods sold in your income statement, you will likewise not have any in your cash flow statement, so just leave that row blank. If cost of goods sold is pertinent to your business, read on.

    As with sales, cost of goods sold is often recorded on the income statement in a different month from when you actually pay for the labor, materials or inventory. The idea is to evaluate each number in the cost of goods sold row of the income statement and determine when you will write the checks to pay for these expenses. Then record the results in the appropriate months of the cash flow statement. At the risk of sounding like a broken record, seek help and document all assumptions.

5. Now turn to line 44, taxes. Many businesses pay taxes quarterly, but every situation is different. Check with your accountant for reasonable assumptions for your business. Be sure to consider federal, state and local taxes if you will incur all three.

6. Now you're ready to take your first cut at your cash flow. Before you do the next few calculations, make several copies of the cash flow statement as it stands right now. Save the original and make your calculations on the copies.

    There are still some rows you haven't filled in, including Cash from Funding Sources, Pre-opening Expenses, Loans and Other Capital Equipment.

    First, calculate the net cash flow for each month. Net cash flow equals total cash inflow minus total cash outflow.

    Next, determine cumulative cash flow for the entire year. For most businesses, this number will start out negative and become more negative for at least the first four to six months. If it continues steadily downhill, keep projecting on a monthly basis until the cumulative cash flow begins to turn toward a positive figure. (If it never turns upwards don't start the business unless your business advisors have shown you where your numbers have gone wrong.) For the first month, cumulative cash flow equals net cash flow. For the second month and beyond, add the new month's net cash flow to the previous month's cumulative cash flow to arrive at the new month's cumulative cash flow.

For most businesses, cash flow will start out negative and become more negative for at least the first four to six months.

7. You can now calculate how much capital your business needs. Or, said another way, you can now calculate how much money you need to put into the business to meet your cash obligations. In order to do this, you will be using both your Cash Flow Statement and your Sources and Uses of Cash Statement (from page 107). First, some explanation.

You need capital for four things:

- Pre-opening expenses, including opening inventory, capital equipment, property, renovations, pre-opening marketing and promotions, deposits and "other." You calculated these in Figure 13, Sources and Uses of Cash.

- Working capital. As discussed earlier, working capital is the money you need to pay your bills when the money you take in from sales lags behind the money you pay out for expenses. To calculate working capital, take the largest negative number in the cumulative cash flow on your cash flow statement and increase it by 20% (i.e., multiply it by 1.2) to be safe.

- Other capital equipment. If your management plans (i.e., your product development plan, marketing plan, etc.) call for you to purchase additional capital equipment during the year, you will need additional capital to pay for it.

- Contingency. Even though you've already tacked on 20% to your working capital, it doesn't hurt to arrange to have additional money available for your business' use. Regardless of how careful and/or experienced you are, it's rare to have the foresight to think of all your business needs in advance, and it's even rarer to be on target with your sales and expense projections the first time through. Your best bet is to find an advisor in your industry to help you determine a reasonable contingency figure. As a guideline, add another 10% of your working capital projections for contingencies.

Now go back to your sources and uses of cash statement (on page 107) and fill in: Working Capital and Contingency; then calculate Total Uses of Cash. Total Uses of Cash represents the amount of money you need to invest, borrow or have someone else invest in your business in order for you to make it the first year.

Are you surprised? I've talked to a number of people who start out thinking all they need is the money to buy a new computer or sewing machine and they could get their business started. Or, if they only had six months' worth of operating expenses they could build a business. This evaluation tells you how much you *really* need to get your business started or expanded. By understanding the cash flow concept, you will put yourself way ahead of the many other people out there trying to build a business.

8. Also in your Sources and Uses of Cash Statement, make some assumptions about your sources of cash. You know how much money you (and, if you have them, your partners) are prepared to invest in the business, so include that in the sources of cash part of the statement. Then, subtract your

investment from the sum of uses of cash to find out how much additional money you need for your business.

You may not know yet where you will get this money—whether you will borrow it or find someone to invest in you—and what the terms of the deal are. The deal that makes sense for you depends on when you need cash, how much you need and what you need it for. This is an important issue, and you will want to discuss it with your support people, your accountant, any other financial advisors and your banker. Chapter Eight, Using Your Business Plan to Get Financing, describes the basics of business financing and gives you advice on approaching your banker.

The simplest deal, and a good starting point for most small businesses, is to assume that you borrow it all up front from a relative, a friend or a bank at the going rate of interest. Unless you have reason to believe that your deal will be more complex, make this assumption and fill in the two loan sections on one of the clean copies of your cash flow statement (lines 7, 41 and 42). If you are not familiar with calculating loan payments, have your SCORE counselor or accountant or another advisor help you.

Now, use your Sources and Uses of Cash statement to fill in the pre-opening expenses (lines 11 through 19), other capital equipment (line 43) and cash from funding sources (lines 5 through 9) of your cash flow statement. Recalculate your net cash flow and your cumulative cash flow. If you've done this right, your cumulative cash flow should be consistently positive.

9. Complete the cash flow statement by doing the checking account reconciliation. Again, if you've borrowed enough money, your checking account should always be in the black (i.e., be positive).

10. Now that you know how much money you need, you are ready to use your cash flow statement to manage your business and to get financing. This is discussed in more detail in Chapters Seven and Eight.

BALANCE SHEET

The balance sheet lists your business assets (what you own) and your business liabilities (what you owe) and portrays the net worth of your business at a given moment in time.

It's easy to understand the concept behind the balance sheet if you think of it from the perspective of your personal finances. For example, suppose your financial situation look like this:

PERSONAL ASSETS	CURRENT VALUE
Checking Account	$800
Savings Account	5,800
House	65,000
Car	6,000
Jewelry	2,500
Furniture	3,000
TOTAL	$83,100

PERSONAL LIABILITIES	BALANCE OF LOAN
Mortgage	$50,000
Car Loan	2,000
VISA Balance	800
Loan from Aunt Harriet	3,000
TOTAL	$55,800

Your personal net worth is the difference between what you own and what you owe:

Net Worth = $83,100 - $55,800 = $27,300

Balance sheets for companies look similar to the analysis above except they list assets and liabilities which are applicable to business. The main headings are the same for all businesses and are shown in the sample balance sheet in figure 19. The details of your balance sheet should be designed based on your individual business needs. Have your accountant, banker or SCORE advisor help you do this.

The balance sheet equation is:

Total Assets = Total Liabilities plus Net Worth

This equation always holds true.

A brief description of each category follows. See the glossary for definitions of the remaining terms.

1. *Current Assets:* These are items owned by the business that could be converted to cash in the normal course of business within one year.

2. *Fixed Assets:* These are items owned by the business with a useful life of more than one year. When you buy an item qualifying as a fixed asset, it is considered an investment in the business and NOT an expense. The amount you paid for the item appears on the balance sheet as an asset and not on the income statement as an expense. In general, your capital equipment is a fixed asset.

3. *Depreciation:* The notion of depreciation was discussed earlier in the section on your income statement. Recall that depreciation is the amount of money the government allows you to call an operating expense based on the fact that you are using up your capital equipment. Depreciation also shows up on the balance sheet. The idea is this: Since you have (supposedly) used up some of your capital equipment, it is no longer worth as much as you paid for it, so its value on the balance sheet is decreased by the amount you've called depreciation. For example, suppose you bought $10,000 worth of office equipment two years ago. Each year the government allows you to claim $2,000 in depreciation expense on your income statement. Your balance sheet entry for your office equipment would look like this:

Equipment	$10,000
Minus Accumulated Depreciation	4,000
(2 years x $2,000)	
TOTAL	$6,000

Figure 19.

Sample Balance Sheet

ASSETS (What your business owns)	LIABILITIES (What your business owes) Plus NET WORTH (the value of your business)
Current Assets	**Current Liabilities**
Cash _____	Accounts Payable _____
Accounts Receivable _____	Accrued Expenses _____
Inventory _____	Taxes Payable _____
Prepaid Expenses _____	Short-Term Notes Payable _____
TOTAL _____	TOTAL _____
Fixed Assets	**Long-Term Liabilities**
Fixtures and Equipment _____	Mortgages _____
Minus Accumulated Depreciation _____	Long-Term Notes Payable _____
	TOTAL _____
TOTAL _____	
	TOTAL LIABILITIES _____
	NET WORTH _____ (what your business owes you)
TOTAL ASSETS _____	TOTAL LIABILITIES PLUS NET WORTH _____

In other words the current value of your office equipment as reflected on the balance sheet is now $6,000 rather than the original $10,000 purchase price. (Its market value may actually be more or less than the $6,000.) As you annually depreciate the office equipment, its value as an asset continually decreases on the balance sheet by the same amount.

4. Current Liabilities: These are the financial obligations that you must meet within one year.

5. Long-Term Liabilities: These are the financial obligations that are due in more than one year and include such things as mortgages, intermediate and long-term bank loans, equipment loans, and so on.

6. Net Worth (also referred to as "owner's equity" or "retained earnings"): This is the value of the business. As with your personal net worth, it is calculated by subtracting liabilities from assets. You can also calculate it as follows: The money you've invested in the business (capital) minus what you've withdrawn from the business (owner's withdrawal plus dividends) plus what the business has earned (profit or loss).

There are several reasons for preparing a balance sheet:

- To make sure your business net worth is increasing over time. If it is decreasing, you are probably making some grave management errors which should be corrected quickly.

- To assess the financial health and stability of your business. You do this by comparing your current balance sheet to those of prior years and those of businesses similar to yours. Balance sheet analysis, described further below, can provide excellent clues on how to improve the management of your business.

- Because your banker wants one. Even if you don't see a need for a balance sheet for your business, you may be required to prepare one if you want a bank loan.

Now that I've discussed the balance sheet theory, here's a small dose of reality.

If you're a home-based business, especially a service business, the lines between your personal assets and liabilities and your business assets and liabilities can get very blurry. It's probably not possible—and likely not worth the time—to separate the two. You're much better off preparing a statement of personal net worth than a business balance sheet. (Forms for this are in Appendix IV.) Your main concern is that you're getting more out of the business than you're putting in. If your personal net worth is decreasing over time and you determine that it's because of your business, then it's time to make some major changes in how (or whether) you do business.

In a non-home-based business, especially in a micro-business, your balance sheet may or may not have importance in assessing the financial health of your business, and using it to do this is not cut and dried. There are very few rules of thumb and, for a small company, a single transaction can greatly skew the results.

Your banker, credit manager, SCORE or SBDC counselor or your accountant can best help you determine whether you even need a balance sheet and how to prepare one for your size and type of business. Whomever you use, make sure she or he is well-versed in analyzing your type of business and willing to answer questions.

Balance Sheet Analysis

I've described some of the balance sheet analysis below to help you discuss it intelligently with your financial advisors. For explanation purposes, refer to the example balance sheet from a children's clothing store, Small World, run by Jennifer Johnson.

ASSETS		LIABILITIES + NET WORTH	
Current Assets		Current Liabilities	
Cash	$1,750	Accounts Payable	$8,450
Accounts Receivable	0	Accrued Expenses	700
Inventory	12,620	Total	$9,150
Prepaid Expenses	300		
Total	$14,670		
Fixed Assets		Long-Term Liabilities	
Capital Equipment	$3,250	Long-term Notes	
Minus Accumulated		Payable	$5,280
Depreciation	650	Total	$5,280
Total Fixed Assets	$2,600		
		Total Liabilities	$14,430
		Net Worth	$2,840
Total Assets	$17,270	Total Liabilities Plus Net Worth	$17,270

1. *Working Capital.* I've discussed the concept of working capital in the section on cash flow. The accountant's definition of working capital is current assets minus current liabilities. Small World's working capital is $14,670 - $9,150 = $5,520, which is a fairly comfortable position to be in.

   A low or negative working capital position is a major danger signal. Possible corrective actions include getting a working capital loan, selling off some fixed assets, financing accounts payable by arranging to spread payments over a longer term or arranging for new equity investment. The solution that's best for you is dependent on your particular situation. Your business advisors will best be able to guide you in making an appropriate decision.

2. *Comparison.* Comparison of your balance sheets from one year to the next highlights trends and spotlights weak areas. If you are just starting your company, this option is not open to you; however, if you are expanding an ongoing business you may be able to reconstruct past balance sheets and work with your advisors on this analysis.

A low or negative working capital position is a major danger signal.

3. *Ratio Analysis.* This technique permits comparison in terms of percentages rather than dollars, thus making comparisons with other companies more accurate and informative. There are many different ratios used by accountants and financial analysts. Your advisors will guide you in which ones will help you in your particular business. Among the more useful ratios for business are:

A. *Current Ratio.* This measures the liquidity of the company, i.e., its ability to meet current obligations (those coming due during the current year). It is calculated by dividing current assets by current liabilities. For Small World, the current ratio is 14,670/9,150 = 1.6. While many industry analysts like to see a current ratio of 2.0, Small World's situation is not that bad. The important thing is to determine what's causing the current ratio to be so low and to take action to raise it.

B. *Quick Ratio.* (also called "Acid Test"). This is another measure of liquidity and is calculated by dividing the most liquid assets (cash, securities, and possibly accounts receivable) by current liabilities. For Small World, the quick ratio is 1,750/9,150 = 0.19. This compares to a rule of thumb of 1.0. Small World's Quick Ratio looks terrible because so much of its current assets are tied up in inventory. If Small World has any difficulty at all selling its inventory, it will have a rough time finding enough cash to meet its short-term obligations.

Remember that the rules of thumb are far from infallible since your numbers are dependent on your industry and your particular situation. The objective behind balance sheet analysis is to detect areas of potential weakness and evaluate them to see if you need to make changes. It is NOT to make wholesale changes in your business based on rules of thumb.

You can get industry averages for these and other ratios from:

• The library, local business school and Chamber of Commerce. They have a significant amount of available data.

• Trade associations. There are many around which can provide you with the information you need.

• Annual statement studies, which your banker will usually have, are available from Robert Morris Associates. Your library may have these.

• Dun & Bradstreet publishes key business ratios for partnerships, proprietorships and corporations. Your library may have these also.

Ask your banker and accountant for help finding current figures.

You have probably figured out that it's difficult and unnecessary to project your balance sheet way out into the future (like you do with your cash flow statement and your income statement). If you're just getting started, prepare a balance sheet as you expect it to look at start-up. If you've been in business for a while, prepare one as your business currently stands. You can use this balance sheet to evaluate the current financial health of your business. Even more important, you can use it three months from now (or six months or a year) to compare to your future balance sheet and improve your judgment about how well your business is being run.

SUPPORTING DOCUMENTS

This is the place to include any information which documents and supports the information contained in your business plan. Such documentation might include:

1. Resumes of company principals

2. Personal balance sheets of company principals

3. Cost of living budget for company principals

4. Credit reports

5. Letters of reference

6. Job descriptions

7. Letters of intent (these are letters from customers stating their intent to purchase from you when you get started or grow)

8. Copies of leases

9. Contracts

10. Legal documents

11. Any other document which you feel might increase the credibility of your plan

Documents 1 through 5 are required by most lenders when you apply for a loan. If you don't provide them with your financial proposal, your prospective funding source will have to go to the trouble of calling you to ask for them. Better to make life easier by including them at the outset. Forms for 2 through 4 are included in the Appendix.

As you're deciding whether or not to include something, remember what you're trying to do here: You're providing the evidence that will give both you and your funding source confidence in your financial projections. So, it's worth your time now to go that extra mile to get written documentation to back up as many of your numbers as you possibly can.

## CHAPTER SIX

Compiling Your Business Plan

Now that you've completed all the pieces of your plan, it's time to put them all together into a single document you can use to manage your business and apply for financing.

If you haven't done so yet, buy a three-ring binder and a three-hole punch. That way you can readily compile your plan yet leave room for flexibility. Your plan is not meant as a straitjacket. You will move forward with your business, learn which of your assumptions are correct and learn what works for you. As you modify your business plan in your mind, you also want to be able to update your plan on paper.

On the next page is a checklist for all the things that should be included in your business plan. Use it to see what you've completed and what's left to be done, then fill in the gaps.

You have probably put together your business plan over a period of time and may have modified your ideas as you've mulled them over in your mind and gathered new information. For your plan to have any value, all of the pieces must individually make sense and collectively support each other. For example, if your marketing plan shows how you will double sales next year, your operations plan must show how you will deal with the increase in work.

Most important is that your financial projections be thoroughly supported by your written description of how you will be in business. This is common sense, yet it is surprising how many people will write about how they want the business to be and then fill in the numbers based on pure guesses or on someone else's recommendations and never go back to check that the two match. The financial parts are the quantitative representation of the written description of your business. The two parts should mesh and support each other.

Follow this very important step: Read through the entire business plan and make sure that the different parts of the analysis fit together and the business plan contains all the information a business plan should have.

The different areas of your business plan must make sense, support each other logically and coherently and leave the reader with a concise, convincing statement that the project and plan are feasible.

For example, if your income projections show a marked increase in sales in year two, marketing and sales plans should discuss how you will cause that to happen, and your operating and personnel plans should discuss how you will accommodate the accompanying increase in work.

Or if your operating plan discusses your move from a home-based office to rented office space, your income and cash flow statements should reflect the increase in operating expenses.

In addition, your business plan should answer all the questions in the checklist plus deal with any other areas of emphasis that are unique to your business.

Your financial projections must be thoroughly supported by your written description of how you will be in business.

Figure 20.

BUSINESS PLANNING CHECKLIST—IS YOUR PLAN COMPLETE?

DESCRIPTION OF BUSINESS
_____1. Business form: proprietorship, partnership, corporation or cooperative?
_____2. Type of business: retail, wholesale, manufacturing, service or consulting?
_____3. What is the product and/or service? What makes it unique?
_____4. Is it a new business? A takeover? An expansion? A franchise?
_____5. When is your business open?
_____6. Is it a seasonal business?
_____7. How long have you been in business?
_____8. What have you learned about your business from past operations or (if you're a start-up) from outside sources?
_____9. Why will your business be profitable?
_____10. What are your personal and business goals?

PRODUCT/SERVICE
_____1. What are you selling?
_____2. What benefits are you selling?
_____3. What is unique about your goods or services?
_____4. If you are a consultant, what process will you use?

MARKET
_____1. Who buys from you?
_____2. Are your markets growing, steady or declining?
_____3. Is your market share growing, steady or declining?
_____4. Have you segmented your markets? How?
_____5. Are your markets large enough for expansion?
_____6. What social, political, regulatory, economic and technological changes are taking place that could impact your industry, your market or your market's perception of and desire for your products/services?

COMPETITION
_____1. Who are your nearest direct competitors?
_____2. Who are your indirect competitors?
_____3. How are the businesses similar to and different from yours?
_____4. What have you learned from their operations? From their advertisements?

PRODUCT DEVELOPMENT PLAN
_____1. What other products/services (if any) are you currently considering?
_____2. What is your time frame for developing and introducing them?

MARKETING PLAN
_____1. Who will actually buy from you (e.g., do you sell to distributors, wholesalers, retailers, businesses, consumers?) and how does this impact your marketing plan?
_____2. How will you attract and hold your target market and increase your market share?
_____3. Are you planning to enter or leave any markets?
_____4. How do you price your products?
_____5. Where are you (will you be) located?

Figure 20. Continued

BUSINESS PLANNING CHECKLIST—IS YOUR PLAN COMPLETE?

_____6. Why is this a desirable area? A desirable building?

_____7. What kind of space do you need?

_____8. Are there any demographic or other market shifts going on in your area that could impact your marketing plan?

SALES PLAN

_____1. Who will do the selling in your business? (You? Company salespeople? Independent sales representatives?)

_____2. What are your weekly, monthly and quarterly sales goals?

_____3. What other checkpoints have you established for reaching those goals?

_____4. What sales approach will you use?

OPERATIONS PLAN

_____1. How will you organize the flow of work through your business? (This is especially important if you have several people doing different parts of the overall tasks, such as in a factory or a print shop or a flower shop.)

_____2. How will you assure that all tasks are performed? Performed on time?

_____3. How will you monitor quality?

_____4 How will you keep costs under control?

PERSONNEL PLAN

_____1. What are your current personnel needs?

_____2. What skills will your employees need in the near future? In three years?

_____3. What are your plans for hiring and training personnel?

MANAGEMENT PLAN

_____1. How does your background/business experience help you in this business? For your own use: What weaknesses do you have and how will you compensate for them? What related work experience do you have?

_____2. Who is on the management team?

_____3. What are their strengths and weaknesses?

_____4. What are their duties?

_____5. Are these duties clearly defined? How?

_____6. What additional resources are available to your business?

APPLICATION AND EXPECTED EFFECT OF LOAN (INVESTMENT)

_____1. How will the loan (investment) make your business more profitable?

_____2. Will you buy or lease your equipment, location or cars?

_____3. Do you really need this money? Or can you make do without?

FINANCIALS

_____1. Have you completed your financial projections? (As a minimum, you should have P&L and cash flow projections for three years.)

_____2. Will you need additional cash? If so, how will you get it?

_____3. Have you shown that your business will be profitable?

## PART 3

Using Your Business Plan

## CHAPTER SEVEN

Using Your Business Plan To Manage Your Business

You now have completed your business plan. You may have prepared it for a variety of reasons, including getting money and getting organized.

Whatever the reason, it would be a shame—and a great waste of your time—NOT to use it for its most logical purpose: to manage your business.

If you think back to the definition of successful management, it is this:

1. You set goals.

2. You decide what you (or your employees) are going to do to reach those goals.

3. You do it.

4. You look at your results and compare them to your goals.

5. You incorporate what you learned in #4 into your thinking and go back to #2.

Think of your financial projections and your detailed business plans (i.e., product development plan, marketing plan, etc.) as a set of goals and an action plan to reach those goals. You will take these and other actions as you start or expand your business. To be an effective manager you must look at the results of running your business, compare them with your business plan and modify your plans accordingly.

The fact is you *will* make decisions. Some will be based on your plan and some will be based on your hunches. Some you will give thought to and some you will make in a hurry. Some will work for you and some will not.

As you move forward with your business you will be enthusiastic, scared, energetic, exhausted or all of these.

In order to stay on top of your business and avoid getting mired in crises, you need to routinely look at what you've accomplished, what worked for you and what needs to be changed.

Some areas need to be evaluated on a weekly basis, some monthly, some quarterly, some semi-annually and some annually. This section lists the questions you should consider during each time frame and provides some issues for you to consider as you go through the questioning process.

As you read through this chapter, get out your calendar and schedule each review that is appropriate for your business.

Think of your financial projections and your detailed business plans as a set of goals and an action plan to reach those goals.

WEEKLY BUSINESS PLAN REVIEW

Sales Plan Review

Every business has "checkpoints" on sales, i.e., data that can be gathered and checked on a regular basis to assure that the business will meet its annual sales goals. The sooner you can check how you're doing according to the plan, the better able you are to take effective corrective action. At the extreme, if you waited until the end of the year to see whether you met your annual sales goals, it would be too late to fix any problems.

The idea is to select a measurable goal which, on a weekly basis, will give you some idea of the progress you're making toward your sales goals.

For a retail business, the most common checkpoints are the number of weekly sales transactions and the average dollar amount per transaction. This is because a retail business expects to make sales on a daily basis, so weekly averages are meaningful. The calculation for this was discussed in Chapter Four, in the Sales Plan section.

For a consulting business, the sales cycle tends to be very long (i.e., a long period of time from contacting a potential client to making the sale to getting paid), so weekly transactions are generally not meaningful. This doesn't let you off the hook for monitoring your sales-related activities. Your weekly checkpoints might be such things as number of phone calls made to prospective clients, number of visits, number of letters sent out, and so on. After you get some experience, you will know what these numbers have to be to meet your annual sales goal. You should also set up monthly checkpoints that include such things as number of new clients and number of billable hours. Determine what is meaningful for your business. Then keep track of it.

Other service businesses (e.g., housecleaning, in-home health care) fall somewhere between retail and consulting. Depending on your business, useful checkpoints might be number of telephone calls (or visits) made to prospective customers, number of letters sent out, number of new contracts, and so on. Talk to your business advisors and let them help you determine which checkpoints make sense for *your* business. Be creative. Think about your past experiences in this (or a similar) business. Then establish your checkpoints and keep track of your actual figures on a weekly basis.

Manufacturing businesses vary, and useful checkpoints may be any of those described for other kinds of businesses.

If you have sales reps or salespeople, you will probably want them to be involved in the weekly checkpoint evaluation.

As with all parts of your business plan, you'll have to live with these checkpoints for a while before you can tell how useful they are. Give them a chance. Develop your "checkpoint budget," i.e., the numbers you think you can achieve each week (and each month, if necessary). Compare with your actual numbers and take the action you need to make your business grow. If they don't work, don't give up the concept—just try new checkpoints. It won't take you long to find something that will work for your business.

Once you've established your checkpoints, ask yourself the following questions on a weekly basis:

Develop your "checkpoint budget," i.e., the numbers you think you can achieve each week (and each month, if necessary).

1. How many contacts (sales transactions, customer calls, prospective client visits, and so on) have I made?

2. What was the result of #1?

3. How does this compare to my goal?

4. Do I need to make changes to my sales approach?

You will need to tailor these questions to your particular situation. For example, if you're in the retail business you might ask yourself these questions:

1. How many customers came into my store this week?

2. How many sales transactions did I make this week?

3. What was the average value of my sales transactions this week?

4. How do my answers to #1 through #3 compare with the assumptions in my sales plan?

5. Do I need to make any changes in my sales approach to increase my sales?

MONTHLY BUSINESS PLAN REVIEW

Financial Plan Review

The first area to evaluate monthly is your financial data. This gives you the clearest picture of what your business has accomplished and what areas need attention. The idea is to compare your actual sales and expenses with those you projected in your business plan. Then carefully evaluate all deviations, both positive and negative, develop an understanding of the reason for their existence and take corrective action in a timely manner. This evaluation is called a Budget Deviation Analysis, or BDA, and it's done every month for your income and cash flow projections.

BDA is a direct control on your business operations. It will help you hold down costs and increase profits at a time cost of about one evening per month. (If it takes longer than this, see your accountant or recordkeeper about changing procedures so you have ready access to the actual data.) BDA is an essential tool and should not be ignored even if everything is going well.

The forms on pages 156-159 are BDA forms which you should modify to suit the particular needs of your business. Do this by using the same heading across the top and changing the left hand column to match your budgeted income and expense categories. You may want to break the categories down further for greater control.

Once you've done the analysis, experience will tell you which deviations—and of what magnitude—are significant for your business. The first few times you do it, discuss it with your business advisors and seek their advice in determining what's important and what you should do about it. Then make the necessary

Compare your actual sales and expenses with those you projected in your business plan.

Figure 21.

BDA—Income Statement, Year-to-Date

From the Income Statement for year-to-date	A. Actual for Year-to-Date	B. Budget for Year-to-Date	C. Deviation (B-A)	D. % Deviation (C/B x 100)
1. SALES				
2. Total Sales				
3. COST OF GOODS SOLD				
4. Materials				
5. Labor				
6. Other				
7. Total Cost of Goods Sold				
8. GROSS PROFIT				
(Sales – Cost of Goods Sold)				
9. OPERATING EXPENSES				
10. Salaries and Wages				
11. Payroll Taxes and Benefits				
12. Rent				
13. Utilities				
14. Advertising and Promotion				
15. Office Supplies				
16. Postage				
17. Telephone				
18. Professional Fees				
(Legal, Accounting, et al)				
19. Repairs and Maintenance				
20. Car/Travel				
21. Depreciation				
22. Others:				
23. TOTAL OPERATING EXPENSES				
24. OTHER EXPENSES				
25. Interest				
26. TOTAL EXPENSES				
27. PROFIT (LOSS) PRE-TAX				
28. TAXES				
29. NET PROFIT (LOSS)				

Figure 22.

BDA—Income Statement, Monthly

From the Income Statement for year-to-date	A. Actual for Month	B. Budget for Month	C. Deviation (B-A)	D. % Deviation (C/B x 100)
1. SALES				
2. Total Sales				
3. COST OF GOODS SOLD				
4. Materials				
5. Labor				
6. Other				
7. Total Cost of Goods Sold				
8. GROSS PROFIT				
(Sales – Cost of Goods Sold)				
9. OPERATING EXPENSES				
10. Salaries and Wages				
11. Payroll Taxes and Benefits				
12. Rent				
13. Utilities				
14. Advertising and Promotion				
15. Office Supplies				
16. Postage				
17. Telephone				
18. Professional Fees				
(Legal, Accounting, et al)				
19. Repairs and Maintenance				
20. Car/Travel				
21. Depreciation				
22. Others:				
23. TOTAL OPERATING EXPENSES				
24. OTHER EXPENSES				
25. Interest				
26. TOTAL EXPENSES				
27. PROFIT (LOSS) PRE-TAX				
28. TAXES				
29. NET PROFIT (LOSS)				

Figure 23.

BDA—Cash Flow, Year-to-Date

From the Income Statement for year-to-date	A. Actual for Year-to-Date	B. Budget for Year-to-Date	C. Deviation (B-A)	D. % Deviation (C/B x 100)
1. CASH FROM SALES				
2. Cash Sales				
3. Cash from Receivables				
4. TOTAL				
5. CASH FROM FUNDING SOURCES				
6. Cash from Owners				
7. Cash from Loans				
8. Cash from Other Investors				
9. TOTAL				
10. TOTAL CASH INFLOW (9 + 4)				
11. PRE-OPENING (or expansion) EXPENSES				
12. Opening Inventory				
13. Capital Equipment				
14. Property				
15. Renovations				
16. Marketing & Promotions				
17. Deposits				
18. Other				
19. ` TOTAL				
20. COST OF GOODS SOLD				
21. OPERATING EXPENSES				
22. Owner's Salary				
23. Other Salaries & Wages				
24. Payroll Taxes & Benefits				
25. Rent				
26. Utilities				
27. Advertising and Promotion				
28. Office Supplies				
29. Postage				
30. Telephone				
31. Professional Fees				
32. Insurance				
33. Repairs and Maintenance				
34. Car/Travel				
35.				
36.				
37.				
38.				
39. TOTAL				
40. LOANS				
41. Interest Payment				
42. Principal Payment				
43. OTHER CAPITAL EQUIPMENT				
44. TAXES				
45. TOTAL CASH OUTFLOW				
46. NET CASH FLOW				
47. CUMULATIVE CASH FLOW				
48. OPENING BALANCE				
49. + Cash Inflow				
50. - Cash Outflow				
51. CLOSING BALANCE				

Figure 24.

BDA—Cash Flow, Monthly

From the Income Statement for year-to-date	A. Actual for Month	B. Budget for Month	C. Deviation (B-A)	D. % Deviation (C/B x 100)
1. CASH FROM SALES				
2. Cash Sales				
3. Cash from Receivables				
4. TOTAL				
5. CASH FROM FUNDING SOURCES				
6. Cash from Owners				
7. Cash from Loans				
8. Cash from Other Investors				
9. TOTAL				
10. TOTAL CASH INFLOW (9 + 4)				
11. PRE-OPENING (or expansion) EXPENSES				
12. Opening Inventory				
13. Capital Equipment				
14. Property				
15. Renovations				
16. Marketing & Promotions				
17. Deposits				
18. Other				
19. TOTAL				
20. COST OF GOODS SOLD				
21. OPERATING EXPENSES				
22. Owner's Salary				
23. Other Salaries & Wages				
24. Payroll Taxes & Benefits				
25. Rent				
26. Utilities				
27. Advertising and Promotion				
28. Office Supplies				
29. Postage				
30. Telephone				
31. Professional Fees				
32. Insurance				
33. Repairs and Maintenance				
34. Car/Travel				
35.				
36.				
37.				
38.				
39. TOTAL				
40. LOANS				
41. Interest Payment				
42. Principal Payment				
43. OTHER CAPITAL EQUIPMENT				
44. TAXES				
45. TOTAL CASH OUTFLOW				
46. NET CASH FLOW				
47. CUMULATIVE CASH FLOW				
48. OPENING BALANCE				
49. + Cash Inflow				
50. - Cash Outflow				
51. CLOSING BALANCE				

changes: If the deviation is working against you, take corrective action. If the deviation is in your favor, exploit whatever it is that's causing the positive performance.

Included in the charts are both monthly BDA and year-to-date BDA. The year-to-date figures help level out monthly swings in your business. If more expenditures fall in one month than were expected, you may find a corresponding lowering of expenditures the preceding or following month. Used with monthly BDAs, the year-to-date form will save you some unnecessary arithmetic and worry, as well as check the accuracy and effectiveness of your projections.

You will find that "Column D: % Deviation" will magnify small numbers. If maintenance and cleaning are budgeted at $25/month and come in at $50, the percentage deviation is a whopping 100%, while the actual deviation is only $25. That's why you calculate both the magnitude of the deviation and the percentage of the deviation—either one could be important for your business.

Doing the BDA is an excellent use of a computer, which can save a significant amount of time. I use a recordkeeping program called *Quicken* which is very inexpensive, easy to use, readily available and has budget deviation analysis built right into it. If you have a computer, purchase a BDA program or find someone who can help you set up this analysis so the computer will do the calculations for you. Then you can spend your precious time evaluating the reasons for the deviations.

Sales Plan

Almost all businesses have monthly checkpoints which are reviewed in the same manner as weekly checkpoints. Refer to the discussion on weekly checkpoints as a guide to setting your monthly checkpoints. Examples include: number of monthly sales transactions and the average dollar amount per transaction (retail business), average number of phone calls to arrange one sales meeting with a prospective customer or average number of meetings with prospective customers to make a sale (service or manufacturing business). As with weekly checkpoints, use whatever is meaningful for your business. Set your monthly checkpoints now. Then review your monthly progress.

QUARTERLY BUSINESS PLAN REVIEW

Business conditions are dynamic. Over time, things change. Breakthroughs in technology bring new products and services to the market. Your customers' needs and wants change as new products and services become available to them. Your competition changes as new businesses get started and existing businesses modify their strategy based on their interpretation of market conditions. The economy is in a continuous state of flux from local, national and international events.

It is critically important to monitor these changes because they will have an impact on your business. This does not mean that you have to hire someone just to keep track of what's going on in your industry and in the world. But it does mean that over time you must develop an increasing awareness of how things within and outside of your control are impacting your business.

To do this evaluation, set aside an entire afternoon and find a location where you will not be interrupted. This may seem impossible, but the rewards you will reap will more than make up for one afternoon of your time.

Start by doing your monthly and year-to-date budget deviation analyses so you know where you stand financially. Then, reread your dreams and goals and all your plans (product development plan, marketing plan, etc.). With that in mind, write out the answers to the questions which follow. Compare the answers to your original business plan. Don't worry if there are changes—just update the plan if necessary. As you get more experience in planning and operating your business, your plans will be increasingly on target with your operations.

Product Development Plan

1. Are your products/services and your list of distinguishing features meeting the needs and wants of your customers? (Answer for each product or service line.) You thought they would serve the market. Do they? Now that you have more experience, you may find that you need to redefine your service or repackage your product or modify some of the features you offer for sale.

   For example, as part of her telemarketing services business, Sandy Lands trains small business owners to use the phone to contact potential new customers. Lately sales for that portion of Sandy's business have been shrinking, so she did some research. She called some of her old clients, invited them to lunch, and asked them what benefit they got (or didn't get) from her service. As a result, Sandy is changing the way she describes the process to her customers, modifying her training curriculum and charging a higher fee for the service.

   One of my favorite examples is a franchised clothing store for professional women. The local store sells well-tailored, attractive, yet practical business suits at reasonable prices. They also sell blouses and accessories so you can purchase entire outfits at one time. I love their clothes, yet I refuse to shop there. The service is terrible. The salespeople are pushy, uninformed and annoying—completely unprofessional. The store owners desperately need to rethink their level of service features. Rethink your products, services and distinguishing features. Make any changes you think are necessary.

2. Are your products/services profitable today or will they be in the future? (Answer for each product/service line.) Some may no longer be wanted or needed. Retire the losers. Add some winners. You want to put your resources to work where they'll have the best long-term payoff.

   There may be reasons to maintain some unprofitable products/services. For example, you may have loss leaders, i.e., products/services on which you are willing to take a loss because they provide exposure to your high-profit items. (Your local supermarket does this all the time.) Evaluate each product/service and determine how it is benefiting you or hurting you.

3. Should you expand your current product/service lines? Think about what your customers have been saying to you. Are they asking for something

that you're not providing right now but could add very easily? Perhaps there's a complementary product or service that would be a natural fit with your business. List five such products or services right now.

You may also be able to repackage a product or service to appeal to a wider market or to deepen your penetration of your current markets. (A classic example of repackaging is Arm and Hammer™ baking soda. It sells more widely as a refrigerator cleaner and air freshener than it ever did as a baking soda.) How could you do this in your business?

Think about what your customers have been saying to you. Are they asking for something that you're not providing right now but could add very easily?

As you think about whether to expand your product/service line, consider the additional amount of work to handle a new "product-market match." For each match, you provide one product or service to one target market. For example, if you sell word processing services and telephone answering services to small businesses, you are providing two product-market matches. Or if you sell word processing services to small businesses and to large corporations, that's also two product-market matches. The difficulty in adding product-market matches is that each match has a *unique definition* of the six areas of business (product development, marketing, sales, and so on). In other words, for each product-market match, you must make the time and money to develop and execute a unique product development plan, marketing plan, sales plan, and so on.

Claudia Byers went through this evaluation for her personnel consulting business. She currently has two product-market matches—she sells pre-employment screening and personnel consulting to small businesses. Claudia finds that it takes a lot of her time to manage both product-market matches, but it increases her profitability because the products are complementary.

Recently Claudia considered selling staffing services to large businesses. She reasoned that she had access to many employment candidates through her pre-employment screening work, and large companies would be willing to pay more money for her services. On further reflection, Claudia realized that adding a different product combined with a different market would require a completely different management plan—totally different product development, marketing and sales from what she has been successfully doing to date. Claudia rejected this product-market match as being too far afield from her current business to be successful, but she is now considering offering staffing services to small businesses. Note that for someone else with access to large amounts of cash and the desire to rapidly expand, their decision might have been different yet equally as appropriate.

Adding a new product is a major strategic decision and should not be taken lightly, but if your initial product strategy is working and you can afford to take time and resources to add a new product, then go back to Part Two and start the process again. It will be much easier and faster the second time (and third time, and fourth time).

This is how you grow. Plan for expansion, then do it.

Marketing Plan

1. Who are your current customers? In your original plan, you identified your target market. Are these the people who are actually purchasing your products/services?

If they are you can increase sales by finding more people just like them. Go back to the description of your current customers, in your business plan. Develop a more complete profile of your customers: What characteristics do they share? What are their buying habits? Why do they buy your products/services? Then think about who else fits this profile and go after them.

If your current customers are not the people or companies you expected and planned for, who are they? Frequently businesses develop a different set of customers from those they originally anticipated. Perhaps their image appealed to an unexpected customer group. Perhaps they got unexpected market information when they "opened their doors" that made it logical to target a different customer group. When this happens, don't be afraid to "go with the flow." Your business is an education— you learn by doing. Analyze who your customers are. If they're not who you expected, there may be an opportunity staring you in the face. Don't miss out on it just because it wasn't in your original plan. Rethink your marketing plan and take advantage of it.

If you have no (or few) customers, you need to do more research. Are the benefits you're providing really desired by your target market at your selling price? Is your promotional message getting across? Is your location appropriate? There may be a mismatch between your perception of their needs and their real needs. If you can't generate customers, perhaps you ought to consider another kind of business.

2. Is there another market for your products/services? Is there a new group of customers that you haven't considered yet or a market calling to you that you're not hearing? Be open to this possibility at all times.

3. Who are your competitors? You started your competitive analysis; now it's time to update it. Who do you now feel are your five leading competitors (or whatever number makes sense for your business)? If you don't know, go find out!

Competitive data is critical to evaluating and redeveloping your market strategy. Your customers always have another choice of how to spend their money, and they will want to know the distinctions between you and your competition. Even if you don't yet see the value of competitive information, your banker will. If you want to borrow money, one of the first questions your banker will ask is "Who are your competitors?" You must be prepared to answer.

Last, there is a tremendous amount to be learned from your competitors' mistakes and successes. It is far cheaper to learn it from them than to do it yourself.

You should be reviewing competitive advertising, press releases and promotional materials. You should be getting comments about your competitors from suppliers, customers, employees, friends and business advisors. You should be visiting your competitors yourself and making your own observations. If you're not doing this, now is a good time to start. Keep competitor files up-to-date, view them often and ask: How are my competitors impacting my business? What should I do about them?

4. What do you do better than your competitors? What do your competitors do better than you? Maybe they have a better product, a more motivated sales force or better cost and quality controls which result in a price advantage. Maybe they have a superior location or a better distribution system. Or perhaps they are instituting a strong sales training program. Perhaps they have more financial backing giving them more (or less) flexibility to try new tactics.

Once you know what their strengths are, learn from them. Avoid their weaknesses in your own business, but be ready to attack them with your marketing plans.

The biggest problem for women is setting their prices too low.

5. Is your promotion plan—including your promotional pieces (brochures, publicity, etc.)—still appropriate for your product and target market? As you go through this quarterly review for your business, you may find that your image and promotional plan are no longer in line with the actions you are taking or planning to take. While it is very expensive to regularly change your promotional pieces, at some point it will be more cost effective than continuing to use outdated material.

6. Is your pricing policy helping you or hindering you in your sales efforts? You selected a pricing policy based largely on how you believed your target market would value your product/service. Are you able to sell as many "units" as you expected? The biggest problem for women is setting their prices too low. Not only does this lead to lower sales dollars per unit, but it often leads to lower total sales as people question the value of the purchase. After all, who wants a bargain basement computer consultant?

Look at the contracts you didn't get. Did you lose them because of price? Can you afford (or do you want to afford) to meet the competition? Setting a price for your products/services is one of the hardest things businesses have to do. Review what your competitors are doing, review what your market expects, review your profit objectives, then make a decision.

7. Is your location helping or hindering your efforts? Are you getting the customer traffic you need to generate sufficient sales? Does your location match the image you're trying to portray? Do you have enough space for any anticipated expansion? If not, consider what it would take to change your location. You may not be able to do it immediately. Decide what it would take for you to be able to make a change, set it as a goal and aim for it.

Sales Plan

1. Have you done your quarterly sales checkpoint analysis? If your business has a very long sales cycle, it may be meaningful for you to set up quarterly checkpoints. Do so now (use the weekly and monthly checkpoints as a guide) and monitor them on a quarterly basis. If you haven't set up quarterly checkpoints, then you should evaluate whether they would help you in your business.

2. How are you currently selling your products/services? Your business plan describes how you planned to sell. Is this working for you or have you changed your activities to meet the needs of the marketplace? Identify three activities that have proven very successful (e.g., mailing brochures, giving seminars, attending luncheons, etc.). Then identify three activities that didn't work. Do more of the first and less of the second.

3. Is your follow-up after the sale sufficient to maintain customer loyalty? Your best prospects are your current customers. If you don't provide adequate service after the sale, your customers may start buying from your competition. For 99% of businesses, repeat sales are vitally important (and frequently overlooked in the scramble for new customers).

   Sometimes the most important follow-up is unsolicited. Go back to your customers and ask "How is everything?" Not only does this uncover unexpected needs, but it also allows you to tell them about your new products/services.

4. Are your sales techniques effective? A good indication of this is whether you feel comfortable selling to all parts of your market. There are techniques to selling and you can learn them. Just get the training.

5. Are you comfortable with your salespeople? Do they need training? Salespeople aren't born knowing how to sell, and while you may be able to impart all the product knowledge they need, sales training is a highly specialized field. Also, make sure your salespeople are describing your products/services or company in a way that generates sales. If you can't readily describe your company, chances are they can't either.

Operations Plan

1. Are there any tasks that keep slipping through the cracks? If there are activities that consistently don't get done (or get done late), you may need to consider shifting the responsibilities so that all activities are completed on time. This may necessitate hiring more people.

2. Are you getting complaints about your product or delivery schedule or service or location (or something else)? Or worse yet, are your customers complaining and not telling you? (Are they buying less? Are you having trouble with repeat business? Are you getting a cooler reception?)

   If you suspect there's a problem, there probably is. The best way to find out is to ask your customers. This is hard to do, but it's often the only way to get the information you need. Be open to their suggestions—there's nothing worse than being defensive about customers' complaints—then deal with the complaints. Remember that every complaint is an opportunity for you—it's your way of getting your customers to tell you precisely what they would really like your product (or service or business) to do.

3. Are your costs in line with your projections? Most of your operational issues will be reflected in your financial analysis. Do your budget deviation analysis and make the necessary changes.

Go back to your customers and ask "How is everything?"

Some people get so wrapped up in the marketing end of the business that they spend money without making sure the business can support it. Keep your eye on operations and make sure you are operating as cost-effectively as possible without compromising product/service quality.

Other people get so wrapped up in operations that they don't spend enough time generating sales and supporting the customer. If this describes your business, consider hiring or reassigning people so that all the jobs get done.

4. Is your business operating efficiently? The way work flows through your business can greatly impact your efficiency and, hence, your profit. Especially if you have more than one employee, it is important to look at who does what, when they do it and how everyone interacts with everyone else. Despite the desire many of us have to control every aspect of our business, in my experience the people who know best how to make operations more efficient and productive are the employees who are doing the work. Ask them how they could make their job easier, faster and better for the customer, and they'll be delighted to tell you.

5. Is your business operating effectively? While efficiency involves doing things right, effectiveness means doing the right things. You and your employees may be very efficiently working on wrong things. Do your activities contribute to the long-term profitability of the company? I know many business owners who spend time on committees for non-profit agencies (in the name of networking) while their business desperately needs more of their attention.

Are your departments organized appropriately? I know of a business owner who has two managers for four employees and she still spends much of her time managing operations. Do your employees spend more time competing for your attention than communicating effectively with each other? Are they working on clerical activities which could be done by someone with different skills? Do you (and others in your business) know how to prioritize your activities?

Take a hard, objective look at your business. Pay attention to your intuition. If necessary, take a time management class (or send your employees) or create a mission statement or take a fresh look at your vision. Above all, make sure you are doing those activities that lead you and your business to where you want to go.

Personnel Plan

1. Are your employees supporting the organization effectively? Evaluate the tasks which need to get done and assess whether the people assigned to each task have the skills and interest to do them well.

2. Have you identified talents you're not making use of? People are more productive and creative when they are using their best talents.

3. Are your employees satisfied with working for you? Good employees are hard to find, and satisfied employees take a keen interest in the growth of the business. Employees will often complain about salary, working

conditions, hours and other employees. These are important and should be taken into consideration. But most employees want to feel they make a difference to your company. They'll make suggestions about new products, new markets, new operating techniques. Listen to them. Share your dreams with them and encourage them to share theirs with you.

SEMI-ANNUAL BUSINESS PLAN REVIEW

As with your quarterly review, start by doing your budget deviation analyses and reviewing your dreams, goals and plans. Answer all the quarterly questions, and then also answer the following:

1. Are you on track for meeting your annual personal, quantitative and qualitative goals? At least once a year you should see where you stand. You may even realize your goals are unreasonable or, for some reason, undesirable. If so, this is a good time to make changes so you don't spend another six months aiming for the wrong goals.

2. Are your promotion and pricing objectives still appropriate for your business? Things can change quickly and you may need to change your objectives to match.

3. What is happening technologically, socially and economically that will impact your business? In the U.S.? In the world? In your community? If you're in health care, the threat of AIDS will continue to have a serious impact on your business. Even more significant will be the changes in the health care system dictated by current economic conditions. If you're getting ready to open a new retail store and economists are predicting a recession in your area, you may want to rethink your timing. Yet even more significant is the growth in mail order shopping and, lately, network marketing. You should be reading newspaper articles, trade magazines and general business publications to keep up with what's happening in these arenas. Now is the time to look straight in the eye of this information and see if you need to take action.

4. Have you attended a human relations seminar or workshop? What did you learn? How will you apply it to your business? Most business owners will tell you that getting their employees to do what needs to be done (and do it the "right way," and care about it, and be creative, and . . .) is the most difficult part of running their business. The best business plans can be foiled by employees who don't carry them through. At the same time I believe most employees are people of good will who want to have significance in the world in a positive way and who, deep down, want to achieve this in their jobs. Unfortunately many of us business owners, through our lack of training and lack of understanding of human nature, unintentionally and systematically destroy whatever motivation our employees might have started with. As women we have an edge in this area. We were raised to be good listeners and to work well with people. Despite what you may hear about business, your listening, motivational and even child-rearing skills are directly applicable to managing employees. So get the training you need and then do what comes naturally for you.

5. Have you met with your attorney, your accountant and your banker? You should be meeting with these vital advisors at least twice a year to let them know what you're doing and seek their advice.

6. Should you change your weekly, monthly or quarterly sales checkpoints? You have now had sufficient time to monitor these numbers and see if they're moving closer to meeting your annual sales goals. If they're not working, change them.

7. Do you have the right number of employees? You may evaluate this more often, but as a minimum, every six months or so you should take a hard look at your organization and see if you need more or fewer people. If you do, go through the process outlined in the personnel plan and get the right people on board.

8. Has your business had any personnel turnover in the last six months? How does this compare to your prior experience? If your employees are leaving, make sure you understand why. You may even ask a third party to talk to them and get at the real reasons. I know of a small business owner who has 100% personnel turnover—everyone she hires quits within one to two years. The owner makes excuses about it—the job is difficult, she hired the wrong person for the job, the customers keep screwing up and that makes the employees upset. While all of these excuses may be valid, that doesn't relieve her—or you—of the responsibility to hire, train and *keep* good employees.

If your employees are leaving, make sure you understand why.

ANNUAL BUSINESS PLAN REVIEW

On an annual basis it is important to take a fresh look at your entire business plan. You've made changes along the way. You've dealt with some issues you hadn't anticipated, and there are many issues still hanging. The value of going through the business planning process should be apparent—it provides you with a way to make decisions that take into account all aspects of your business. Now you should take advantage of your valuable learning experiences and go through the process again. Every year you should update your entire business plan.

For the text of the plan, review the quarterly and semi-annual questions and make the changes to the plan that are appropriate. Then modify your financial projections. Your original Year Two projections now become Year One. Update them based on this year's hard-earned experience and spread them out monthly for next year. Then update Year Three to Year Two and add a new Year Three.

Part of the normal operation of any business in each year is to prepare for the next year. This is just another part of managing your business.

## CHAPTER EIGHT

Using Your Business Plan to Get Financing

Many of you have come this far with your business plan for the sole purpose of getting money. I wish I could tell you that getting money for your business is easy, but it's not. It's frustrating, time consuming, and, for some businesses, a never-ending process.

First I'd like to dispel some myths about financing.

• **Myth #1:** I can find a bank to lend me money even though I don't have any of my own money to invest in the business. The chances of this are almost nil. You need to invest a *minimum* of 10% of your desired loan amount for the bank to even talk to you. That money can come out of personal savings or perhaps you've already spent it on your business. You have options on where to get money, but you must have some to get more.

• **Myth #2:** I can get a bank loan for my business even though I have no collateral or a co-signer. You can't. Banks have a responsibility to their depositors which makes risky loans irresponsible and undesirable. Without collateral or a co-signer or some proven way to repay the bank if your business can't meet its loan obligations, you will not get a loan.

• **Myth #3:** I can get a bank loan without signing away my personal assets (such as my house or my car). Not likely. Most lenders require personal guarantees, even from established business owners. This means that if your business fails, the bank can take possession of your personal assets to repay the loan. This may sound very risky to you, but look at it from the bank's perspective. If *you* think the loan is too shaky to take the risk, why should the bank feel any differently?

• **Myth #4:** If I can't get a bank loan, I can probably find venture capital. Unless you are an expert in your field *and* have a business with a very high profit margin and growth rate *and* have a proven market *and* need more than $1 million, forget it. And even if this is your situation, thus far in the 1990s the venture capital industry is virtually dead for start-up businesses.

• **Myth #5:** There are groups of investors out there who are looking for people just like me to invest in. There *are* investors out there—called "angels"—but they do not invest in the kinds of businesses that women (and, actually, most

169

Women-owned businesses are starting at twice the rate of men-owned businesses.

men) tend to start. As with venture capitalists, you must be an expert in your field *and* have a business with a very high profit margin and growth rate *and* have a proven market for an angel to be interested in your business. If this describes your business, look for angels through your accountant or attorney or your local regional development board.

• **Myth #6:** The government will lend me money. The government does not lend money to private citizens to start or build businesses. And contrary to advertisements that occasionally run on television, the government does not have grant money for start-up businesses. The government does administer several lending programs through the Small Business Administration (SBA) in which it helps banks and other organizations lend money to businesses; these programs are described later in this chapter. But you still have to go through a bank or some other lending institution if you want a loan.

• **Myth #7:** I can get a loan even if my credit rating is bad as long as I've already paid off my old loans. No, you can't. If you have defaulted on a loan within the last seven years (even if you later paid it off) or if you have declared bankruptcy in the last ten years, the bank will have good reason to doubt your intention or ability to pay your business loan on time. Except under extraordinary circumstances, you can't get a new loan if your credit rating is bad. If you don't know what your credit rating is, talk to your local consumer credit counseling service. They will be able to assist you, and their services are free.

• **Myth #8:** I can get financing for my business without a business plan. This one is partially true. If you don't need much money, have lots of collateral, and your bank is willing to give you a personal loan, you may not need a complete business plan to get funding. However, you still need a cash flow statement, an income statement, a balance sheet, and a working knowledge of where your business is going. Also, the odds of your getting funding improve dramatically when you have a business plan and present it professionally and with confidence.

• **Myth #9:** If I were a man, it would be easier to get a loan. This one is also partially true. Men often get a better reception from bank loan officers, and there is still discrimination against women. However, you're kidding yourself if you think Myths #1 through #8 don't apply to men as well as women.

• **Myth #10:** Starting a business will give me the immediate cash I need to feed my family and take care of my personal financial obligations. I don't know where this one comes from, and I'm always surprised at how many women believe it. If you've prepared your cash flow projections, you already know how false this is.

In short, there are no magic answers. You must have a business plan. And even if you have one, getting financing for your business, especially if it's a start-up, is very difficult. (One banker I spoke with said that 95% of the businesses that approach him for start-up funds are not bankable.)

Difficult is not impossible. Obviously not, since there are 6.5 million women-owned business in the United States (1992), and women-owned businesses are starting at twice the rate of men-owned businesses.

The remainder of this chapter describes the basics of business financing, ways to get to know your banker (critical if you want a loan), some alternatives for getting financing if none of the conventional ways works out and a brief discussion of discrimination in financing.

THE BASICS OF BUSINESS FINANCING

There are two broad categories of business financing: debt financing and equity financing. These are described below. In addition, I suggest you obtain the following easy-to-read booklets:

- *Consumer Handbook to Credit Protection Laws*, Board of Governors of the Federal Reserve System, June 1980.

- *A Guide to Business Credit and the Equal Credit Opportunity Act*, Board of Governors of the Federal Reserve System.

- *A Venture Capital Primer for Small Business*, U.S. Small Business Administration, Publication FM5.

- *The ABCs of Borrowing*, U.S. Small Business Administration, Publication FM1.

You can get the first two documents by contacting your local bank or writing to Publications Services, Division of Support Services, Board of Governors of the Federal Reserve System, Washington, DC 20551. You can get the second two documents by contacting your local SCORE or SBA office or writing to SBA Publications, P.O. Box 30, Denver, CO 80201-0030.

Debt Financing

When you borrow money, that is debt financing. Most of us think of borrowing from a bank, but you can also borrow money from your father, your Aunt Millie, your best friend, some business acquaintances, your neighbors or anyone who is willing to lend you money.

Regardless of who does the lending, there are four issues of concern to the lender:

1. **Interest**—This is the fee, usually expressed as a percentage, that you pay the lender for lending you money. For example, when you make a purchase with your credit card and you don't pay the balance due immediately, you are charged an interest payment on the unpaid balance of your bill. (In 1993, that interest charge ranged roughly from 11% per year to 20% per year.)

   The amount of interest charged by a lender is dependent upon:

   - The general state of the economy. When interest rates were high, it was common to be charged an interest rate of 21% or more.

   - The terms of the loan. The length of the loan (number of months over which you pay interest), the repayment terms (discussed below), and the amount of money you're willing to personally put into your business all impact the interest rate.

- The collateral (or security). Risky collateral, such as accounts receivable, can drive up the interest rate.

- The internal policies of the lender. Each bank has different policies for how to set interest rates. That's why if you call around to different banks, you'll find their rates vary. Even if you borrow money from a relative, she or he may have an unwritten "policy" of lending at low or no interest to a family member.

- The level of risk. Many lenders charge higher interest rates to compensate for what they perceive as increased risk. In fact, this is one way lenders have used in the past to discriminate against women—they charged them an unreasonably high interest rate.

Surprisingly, there are many different ways of calculating interest even if the percentage of interest is the same. In other words, one 10% loan is not necessarily the same as every other 10% loan. For this reason, the government requires lenders to provide you with information that allows you to make a direct comparison between loan rates. This information includes:

a. *Finance Charges*—the total dollar amount you pay to "use credit" (i.e., to get a loan), including the interest charge, loan fees (which are the fees over and above the interest that the banks charge to give you the loan), credit-related insurance premiums, and so on.

b. *Annual Percentage Rate or APR*—the percentage cost of credit on a yearly basis. The APR is calculated in exactly the same way by all banks.

When you talk to a bank about a loan, make sure you ask for the finance charges and the APR. Then you can compare apples to apples when you look into alternative bank loans. Keep in mind, however, that you may not always want the cheapest loan. There are other factors, such as repayment terms and security (described below) which you must consider before deciding which loan is appropriate for your business.

2. **Repayment Terms**—These are the details of how the loans will be repaid. There are many variations of loan repayments.

- Timing. Every loan, whether from a bank or from your parents, should specify when you will complete repaying the interest plus principal (i.e., the original amount of the loan). Short-term loans are generally repaid in one year or less and are used to finance short-term needs, like working capital. Intermediate-term loans are repaid in one to five years and are used to finance intermediate-term needs, like certain equipment. Long-term loans are repaid in more than five years and are used to finance long-term needs, like land or a building. A line of credit is used like a credit card—you borrow money when you need it and you repay with interest within a year.

- Payment schedule (i.e., when you make payments and how much you pay). There are an infinite number of ways for you to make payments on your loans. The two most common are: a) paying off the loan (interest and principal) in equal monthly installments for the term (length) of the loan; and b) making monthly interest payments and then repaying the principal in a lump sum at the end of the term of the loan.

If you think about your cash flow statement, you can see how the loan payment schedule can significantly affect your cash needs. For example, you may want to make very small payments in the first few months while your business is just getting started and then increase your payments later when you're up and running and your cash flow looks a little better. You may even be willing to pay a little more in interest for this benefit. Your banker can help you determine a payment schedule that's best for you.

3. **Security**—The idea behind a business loan is that it is repaid out of future earnings. Since there is always the possibility that those earnings will not materialize and you will not be able to repay the loan, most lenders will want some security that they will not lose all of their money. The three most common forms of security are collateral, co-signing and other forms of repayment assurances. A fourth form of security is loan guarantees, but they are not so common. Let me be clear—a bank will not lend you money unless you have one or more forms of security.

- Collateral. Collateral is something valuable you own that you promise to give to the lender if you default on (i.e., fail to pay) your loan. (This is also known as giving the lender a "security interest" in your property.) If this unfortunate situation occurs, the bank or other lender sells the property and pockets the proceeds of the sale to recoup some of its losses. If your business has valuable assets like inventory, equipment or property, your lender may accept this as collateral for your loan. Otherwise you will need personal collateral, preferably your home or sometimes your car.

  The thought of losing a home or a car is very frightening for some people, and rightly so. But your banker will question your enthusiasm for your business if you are willing to risk her or his money but unwilling to risk your own. Experience has shown that people who have their own assets on the line work harder to make their business succeed than people who are working with little of their own money at risk. Bankers have no desire to be in the repossession business, but they like to have some recourse in case your business fails.

  By the way, a bank will never think your assets are as valuable as you do. Don't be surprised for the bank to want $20,000 or more worth of collateral for a $5,000 loan.

- Co-signers. Co-signers do just what the word says—they sign their name to the loan just under yours. By doing this, co-signers accept the legal responsibility to make all interest and principal payments

A bank will not lend you money unless you have one or more forms of security.

People who have their own assets on the line work harder to make their business succeed.

you can't make. A valuable co-signer has a good credit rating and a demonstrated ability to repay. It is not uncommon for bankers to ask qualified, bankable women to have their husband or father co-sign a loan—sometimes a form of discrimination (though many men are required to have their wives co-sign their loans). If this happens to you, take a deep breath, stay professional, have your business advisors help you determine if you really are bankable (or really do need a co-signer) and review the section of this chapter entitled A Word About Discrimination (page 188).

- Other Forms of Repayment. If you are looking for a small loan, some banks will accept other sources of repayment in lieu of collateral or a co-signer. Examples include alimony, your husband's salary or your salary (if you are keeping a current job while you start your business). You must show that the source of repayment is stable (e.g., steady employment, regular alimony payments, and so on) and that there is enough money left over to repay the loan after all other household expenses are paid. If the source of repayment is your alimony or your husband's salary, he will probably have to co-sign the loan. The laws on this vary from state to state, so if you are in this situation, check with your attorney.

- Loan Guarantees. A loan guarantee is a promise by a third party to pay off your loan if you default. It is similar to co-signing except the third party is a government or civic organization which has specifically set aside a special fund to guarantee loans to particular groups of people. For example, the Small Business Administration (SBA) has a fund, typically several billion dollars annually, which it uses to guarantee up to 90% of a loan to a small business. Here's an example:

  Let's say you've just been laid off from your position as vice president of a large company and you decide to start a mail order clothing business. You have a lot of strong management and financial experience, but no experience with mail order clothing. You've prepared your business plan, which shows you need $150,000 to start your business. You have a lot of collateral, but you only have $50,000 in cash. You apply to your bank for a bank loan. They think your plan looks great except for one weak link: your lack of experience in the business. Your banker suggests they involve the SBA in the deal. You fill out all of the SBA forms and applications, and your banker sends it to the local SBA office for their review. Within two weeks they agree to guarantee $100,000 (67% of your capital needs). Your bank then finalizes its approval of the loan and within 30 days you have your money.

  In addition to the federal government, there are many towns, cities, counties, states and even private women's organizations that have funds set aside for loan guarantees. In theory, the programs all sound great. Here are the problems: a) Many have requirements which many small businesses, especially women-owned businesses, don't meet. For example, the SBA generally requires you have at least 25% equity in the business. This means that if you need $20,000 to start your business, you must put up at least $5,000 yourself, more if you have sufficient resources. Also, while the SBA has no lower limit for loans, only a few banks will make an SBA-guaranteed loan for less than $100,000. In their favor, the SBA is willing to make loans for working capital and provides generous repayment terms. This is not always true for local programs. b) In most communities, there is no single source for getting the information you need on available loan guarantee programs, their restrictions, their availability, who to talk to, how to fill out the applications, and so on. You must talk to many different agencies, people and banks just to find out what programs are available in your area. Nevertheless, if you can spend the time and if you fit the requirements, this can be an excellent way to get a loan.

4. **Risk**—Every lender, whether it's your banker or your Aunt Millie, will consider the risk that you may not be able to repay the loan and will make decisions on whether to lend you money and on what terms based on their assessment of that risk. A sound business plan helps to mitigate the appearance of risk because it shows you have thought through all of the marketing, management, operational and financial aspects of your business. Your willingness to put up valuable collateral mitigates risk, not only because the lender has something of value to fall back on if you can't repay, but also because she or he knows you will work extremely hard to avoid losing your house or your car. Prior experience in your field of endeavor or as a high-level manager gives added confidence that your projections are meaningful.

A sound business plan helps to mitigate the appearance of risk.

One of the things bankers will check is your credit rating. She or he will call a local credit bureau and check on your record of paying loans, credit card balances, utility bills—anything you routinely pay. If you have a history of being late in paying your bills or your loans or if you have filed for bankruptcy within the last ten years, your chances of getting a bank loan are almost nil.

If you have never had credit in your name, you will also have a problem getting a loan because you have no credit track record (sometimes called a "credit history"). You may even be proud of the fact that you pay for everything promptly and in cash. While this is admirable, it doesn't establish a track record that a bank can have access to, and it is almost impossible to borrow money without that track record. If you are in this situation, remedy it immediately. Put your phone bill or the electric or gas bills in your name. Or get a credit card in your name. Use it regularly to make purchases, even if they are small. Then pay promptly.

As far as lenders are concerned, your ability to make your business a success is a judgment call on their part. The more you have going in your favor, the more likely they are to judge you favorably and give you a loan.

Example: Debbie Helter wanted to borrow $5,000 to expand her business selling fine artwork (she had been in business for three months). She contacted the bank loan officer at the bank at which she had her bank accounts, her IRA and her VISA. The loan officer treated her badly by asking patronizing and inappropriate questions. Debbie was badly shaken; she wrote a letter to the president of the bank, pulled all her accounts from that bank and approached another bank.

Debbie had learned a lot from her first experience and was ready to try again. She put together her books for her first three months in business and laid out her marketing plan. She practiced exactly what she was going to say, requested a female loan officer and confidently asked for her loan. Debbie got a six-month, $5,000 loan—exactly what she needed. In order to get it, she had to put up her van (worth $15,000) and her inventory (also worth $15,000) as collateral.

The first part of this story is frustrating, and occasionally still occurs. Debbie could have used her experience at the first bank to keep her from moving forward with her business, but instead she learned what she could from it and moved on. In Debbie's case, her bad experience added to her confidence that she was doing the right thing.

Equity Financing

Equity refers to the ownership investment in the business. Equity is a hard term to define because its value keeps changing. For example, let's say you put up $5,000 to start your business. During the course of the year, your business earns $2,000. This means the value of the business has increased by the $2,000 it earned. As the sole owner, your equity in the business (i.e., the value of the business to you) is now $7,000 ($5,000 + $2,000), even though you only put up $5,000 in original equity. Conversely, if the business had lost money, your equity would have decreased.

An equity investor in your business puts up money for financing with the expectation of being a part-owner of the business. As part-owner she gets a share of your profit, some responsibility for losses and a say in how you manage your business. For example, if you're one of those one-in-a-thousand people lucky enough to get a venture capitalist to finance you, she or he may have the right to tell you how to run your business. Some business owners refuse venture capital financing for just this reason.

There are three legal forms of equity financing:

1. *General Partner*—Your general partner is involved with day-to-day management decisions and shares in your profit or loss in proportion to her share of the investment. For example, let's say you need $20,000 to start your business. You put up $12,000 (60%) and your partner puts up $8,000 (40%). By the third year your business net profit is $40,000. Assuming you don't reinvest in the business, you would get 60% of the profit ($24,000) and your partner would get 40% of the profit ($16,000). When you think of the typical partnership situation, the two principals (i.e., owners) of the business are called general partners.

    If you plan to have a partner, you would be foolish to put up your money without specifying *in writing* who is responsible for which functions and decisions and how joint decisions will be made. Your partner may be your best friend or even your sister, and you may get along fine when your business is in the planning stage, but things have a way of getting out of hand when the crises hit, and that is no time to be deciding who does what.

2. *Limited Partner*—Limited partners have no say in the day-to-day running of your business, and their liability is limited to the amount of their original investment (in other words, they cannot lose more than they originally invest). The amount of profit a limited partner gets is a complex issue. If you are considering this form of ownership, you should discuss it with your attorney and your accountant.

3. *Stockholder*—If you choose to form a corporation, the owners of your company are called stockholders, and they invest in you by buying small portions of your company which are referred to as shares of stock. (Appendix VI provides a description of the legal forms of business.) Like partners, your stockholders have partial ownership of your company and are entitled to a percent of your profits as well as some say in how the company is managed. However, the mechanics for receiving profits and exercising control are very different.

The stockholders each have voting rights in your company, usually one vote per share of stock. When the corporation is formed (and usually every year thereafter) the stockholders use their voting rights to elect a board of directors, which has the legal responsibility to guide the corporation. The board of directors then elects the officers of the corporation, i.e., the president, vice-president, secretary and treasurer. The officers are full-time employees of the corporation and are responsible for its day-to-day management.

At least once a year the board of directors votes on how to disburse the profits of the corporation. Generally they invest some of the profits back in the business and disburse the rest to the stockholders in the form of dividends.

For most small businesses, the original owners are generally the largest stockholders and, if they're wise, retain a majority of stockholder votes. After all, they (and you) probably don't want to give up control of your company. Then they vote themselves onto the board of directors and elect themselves as officers to run the corporation.

For example, suppose you've been running a printing business part time from your home and have now decided to make it a full-time venture. You already own some equipment and supplies, but you need an additional $20,000 for more equipment and working capital. Since you only have $12,000 in the bank, you decide to raise money by forming a corporation and selling shares of stock. On the advice of your attorney, you set the stock price at $1,000 per share. You then find four friends who are each willing to invest $2,000 in your company; they each buy two shares of stock and you buy 12 shares. At the first stockholder's meeting, you elect yourself, your attorney, your business consultant and one of the stockholders to the board of directors. The board's first act is to elect corporate officers. Since the print shop will initially be run by only one person—you—you are elected to all four officer positions—i.e., you are the company president, vice-president, secretary and treasurer.

For small businesses, the original owners are generally the largest stockholders.

At the end of the first year, your company has a net loss, but in the second year, you reap a net profit of $10,000. The board of directors votes to put $8,000 back into the business and divide the remaining $2,000 among the stockholders. Since the corporation had issued shares of stock, each stockholder receives $100 in dividends for each share he owns, i.e., each of the stockholders gets $200 (2 x 100) and you get $1,200 (100 x 12) in addition to your salary.

You may be familiar with holding stock in large corporations which have thousands of stockholders. These companies are "publicly traded," i.e., they sell shares of their stock to the general public on a major stock exchange. This is not the same as your situation. If you go this route, you will be "privately held" and you will sell shares of stock only to a few of your close friends, relatives and business acquaintances.

Forming a corporation takes time and money. There are many legal as well as some accounting requirements for doing this. If you're interested, speak with your accountant and attorney.

"Angels" and venture capitalists are equity financiers. Generally they require that you form a corporation, and they purchase stock to provide their investment in your business. Most professional equity financiers will not purchase *less* than 51% of your company stock, leaving them—not you—as the majority stockholder. They want to be in a position to step in and manage the company in case the profit levels are not living up to their expectations. As a business owner, you may find this hard to swallow, but in some situations it's the only way to get the money you need to get started.

If you're considering this kind of financing, be aware that professional equity financiers do not invest in conventional companies (e.g., secretarial services, training companies, PR and marketing companies, and so on). They can't afford to. They take huge risks when they invest (after all, you're not bankable), and they expect to be well compensated with huge rewards. This is only probable in high-growth industries, run by experienced managers, and most of us—men and women—don't fall into this category. It is extremely difficult to get this kind of financing.

There is much more to understanding equity financing which is beyond the scope of this book. If you feel you need more information, talk with your business advisors.

Comparing Debt to Equity Financing

Your decision of whether to use debt or equity financing will have tax, ownership and other legal and financial ramifications for your business. However, for most small business owners, the more important issues are time and complexity. It takes much less time and is substantially less complex to raise money by borrowing it. If you're a very small business, you don't need much money (less than $100,000) and you're not yet concerned with very rapid growth, debt financing is easier to understand and more readily available.

If you're planning to grow rapidly, need a lot of money to get started and are prepared to spend time learning the complexities of equity financing, equity financing might be appropriate for you. If you believe you fit this situation, find an accountant and an attorney who have experience in these areas and let them guide you through it.

You must remember, however, that most people do not invest in you simply because they think your idea is great—that is probably secondary. Their primary motivation is to make money. At the very least, they want to make more money than they would investing in a Certificate of Deposit. If your business is risky (most are), they want to be well compensated for taking the risk of losing their entire investment.

Even if your investor is a relative or friend, they will expect to be repaid— at a profit—either with interest or dividends. You should be prepared to specify which option you'd like to offer and what the terms of the deal are.

Whichever way you go, there are three things you must do: Turn your business plan into a financing proposal (both your banker and your investor will want to see one), get to know your banker (she or he can help in more ways than you can imagine) and prepare for presenting your financing proposal. These are discussed below.

TURNING YOUR BUSINESS PLAN INTO A FINANCING PROPOSAL

Some funding sources will have a proposal format they prefer, and they will give you a copy of the format for the asking. It will probably be different from the format of the business plan you've just prepared, but most of the elements will be the same. Check with them before you modify your business plan—they will probably accept what you've already prepared. Just make sure you include everything they ask for, even if it's not already included in your business plan.

Each financing proposal should have its own cover sheet citing the name of the financial institution for whom the proposal has been prepared—go back to the section of this guide describing the cover sheet for guidelines. Some areas of your business plan may be extremely important for you but of little use to your banker. Examples include your dreams and your personal goals. Use judgment when deciding if these personal issues belong in your financial proposal. If in doubt, ask.

If you've been in business for more than six months, add your historical income statement, cash flow statement and balance sheet as well as prior tax returns to your financial section. If you have it, your funding source will want to see three years' worth of financial data. Many people have prior years' tax returns but no other financial statements. If this is your situation, try to reconstruct cash flow statements and balance sheets for this time period. If you can't, you should still include tax returns. Even if you don't have three years of history, include what you do have.

Most funding sources require that you include a personal financial statement with your financing proposal to indicate your ability to repay the loan should your business go sour. A worksheet for this is in the appendix. Your banker may also have a worksheet you can use. In addition, you will need to provide a list of credit references. Bankers are intensely (and justifiably) interested in your prior credit history—both business and personal—and they will check your references.

Your funding source will have some concerns that do not seem like risks to you.

Other than the minor differences described above, the difference between a business plan and a financing proposal is one of emphasis: The main function of your plan is to enable you to understand and master the complexities of your business, while the function of the financing proposal is to show your prospective funding sources that you not only know what you are doing but will also make their investment as risk-free as possible. The same document may serve both purposes; however, it is also possible that your funding source will have some concerns that do not seem like risks to you. Listen to his or her concerns and make sure you address them in your financing proposal. The funding decision will be based on the funding source's perception of the situation, not yours.

Once you have completed your financing proposal, have someone else read it, preferably one of your technical advisors. They should be looking for such things as: Is it complete? Does it hold logically together? Does it have industry jargon that your banker or other funding source won't understand? Does it have typos or misspellings that might jar the reader's attention? The idea is to have someone else critique it so it makes the best possible first impression on the prospective funding source.

More important than the mechanics of preparing the document is that you should know what's in it when the prospective funding source asks questions. Your real power with, say, a banker comes when you demonstrate your understanding of your business and business in general by clearly, succinctly, logically and thoroughly answering her or his questions. Follow these guidelines:

- Complete your business plan before you apply for the loan. This includes the text, the financials and the explanation of the financials.

- Know your business plan thoroughly before you walk in. You want to answer any questions about your business by referring verbally to your plan in a clear and precise manner and without having to fumble through the pages of your plan to find the answer. As a minimum, you should be able to readily answer every question in the checklist in Chapter Six.

- Make sure your financial projections are complete and organized and that you can readily explain your data.

- Be prepared to describe how much money you need to borrow, why you need to borrow it and how you will repay it. If you've done your homework, this should be straightforward.

If you're prepared on these four items, you will speak logically and you will demonstrate your understanding of business in general and your business in particular. This will go further toward establishing credibility with your banker than anything else you can do.

For example, if your banker says: "I don't see where you're going to get ten customers in the first year."

You want to be able to say something like: "I outlined in my marketing plan that there are 150 potential customers I can readily reach through my current contacts. Ten customers out of 150 prospects is only a 7% success rate, which I believe is reasonable."

You may be thinking, "That's a lot of work." It is a lot of work, but no more so than running your business. If you can't answer the questions for your banker,

If you can't answer the questions for your banker, then you don't know them yourself.

then you don't know them yourself, and your problem is bigger than just getting money—you will have a problem managing and growing your business.

- Shake hands firmly—and look the banker straight in the eye.

- Speak directly—don't beat around the bush.

- Speak confidently—eliminate the negative phrases and inflections from your speaking habits ("Well, I *think* this is right" will have the banker questioning if you know what you're talking about).

- Dress professionally—a sexy outfit will almost ensure that you won't get the loan. Dress conservatively, i.e., wear a dark blue or gray suit with a white or light colored blouse. Minimize jewelry. Bankers are a conservative bunch and will have more confidence in you if you dress like them.

Your appearance and presentation won't make up for a poor business plan, but they can substantially enhance a good one. Conversely, a poor presentation style can cause your banker to doubt your ability to carry out your plan. And that's part of what her or his decision is based on.

- Talk about what you're there to talk about—don't get sidetracked into irrelevant conversations.

- Describe how you're going to make things happen rather than what's going to happen to you.

- Take the lead in initiating conversation.

- Talk about what you *will* do and why you *will* be successful, not what you *hope* to accomplish.

You are responsible for what happens to you—you make it happen. The more you speak as if you believe that, the more you *will* believe it. This manner of speaking will not only give your banker more confidence in you, it will give you more confidence in yourself.

- If at first you don't succeed, keep trying. Harder. Persistence is the sign of a true entrepreneur.

     If your first approach for a loan isn't successful, evaluate what worked and what didn't work. Then change the things that didn't work. Be creative in looking for a solution.

- Practice your presentation before you go talk to the banker. Practice with your technical support group, with your moral support group or in front of a mirror. Don't say "Here's what I'm going to say." Present it as if you were in front of the banker.

     Don't let your meeting with your banker be the first time you've described your business plan. You'll be amazed at the improvement in your presentation with just one practice session. With more than one, you'll be way ahead of most people. Your best resource is someone who is willing to challenge your data, give you sound feedback, who knows enough to critique your presentation style, and who will role play with you to get you over the tough parts. If you don't know anyone who fits the bill, ask your technical support group to help you find someone.

Don't let your meeting with your banker be the first time you've described your business plan.

- Spend time with role models. Observe the way professional people speak and appear. What do they say that instills confidence? How do they say it?

If you're not used to dealing with bankers, spend time with people who are. You don't want to change your personality, but you do want to observe first-hand some ways to be an effective businessperson. It may take a little time before you really have the confidence you portray, but the fastest way to get it is to speak and act like a winner.

GETTING TO KNOW YOUR BANKER

The old adage "There are no small business loans; just loans to small business owners" is true. People make loans to people, and your banker is much more likely to loan you money if she or he knows and has confidence in you. Unfortunately for women, we often haven't had the opportunity to get to know our bankers through groups like Rotary or Jaycees, and we haven't been aware enough—either because we didn't know how or didn't realize it would be important—to develop a relationship with a banker on our own. This is compounded by the fact that we often lack the business background to give an unknown banker confidence in our ability to create a successful business and that there is still some outright discrimination against women by bankers. Clearly the best solution is to get to know your banker *before* you need money.

Follow these guidelines:

1. Walk into the branch office of the bank where you have your checking or savings account, introduce yourself and shake hands with the branch manager and describe your business. Even if you don't yet have your business plan, tell him or her what you're planning to do. Be brief, cordial and professional. And talk in terms of what you're *going* to do, not what you're *hoping* to do.

   If you're uncomfortable approaching a banker, try role playing the conversation with your business advisors—they should be able to help you feel more at ease. And remember, branch managers make their money by making business loans. It's their job to get to know people like you.

2. After you've made initial contact, stop in regularly to inform your banker of your business' status. If you are preparing your business plan, ask for some help or advice. Then take it.

   Even if you don't need financing now, stop in every six months and share your business plan and your financial statements. If you limit your visits, you will not be a nuisance. You and your banker may not be able to predict when you will need financing, but you both want the relationship to exist when the need is there.

   By the way, many women put themselves in a Catch 22-type situation in such meetings. They feel like they're being a pest, so they talk in a self-deprecating manner, which causes them to be a pest rather than a professional sharing information. For example, you might be accustomed to saying, "You know more about this than I do," when it's not true. Or you might say, "I know you're busy, but . . . " or "I'll keep this short. I know you have more important things to do." Remember two things: a) You don't have to put yourself down ito make the banker feel good; and b) It's your banker's job to make business loans, and you are someone helping her or him to do that job.

3. The idea here is to develop an ongoing, trusting relationship. Show your excitement about your successes and ask for advice if things aren't going as planned. Be brief, logical and, above all else, professional.

    The more you involve your banker in the solutions to your business problems, the more likely she or he will want to help you. Also remember this relationship is a two-way street. Don't hide your business problems for fear your banker will lose confidence in you. You have a lot to lose if she or he finds out that you've lied. Be straight with your banker and expect your banker to be straight with you.

4. At some point early in the relationship, ask what the bank's philosophy is on business loans. Some banks are more conservative, some more aggressive. Some prefer to make loans (or not make loans) in particular industries; for example, many will not make loans to retailers. Find out where your bank stands in relation to your type of business. Also, ask for the bank's criteria for making business loans. I'm always surprised at the differences in policy and philosophy at different banks. Find out up front what you can expect in the future. If your current bank doesn't match your anticipated needs, find another bank immediately, transfer your current bank accounts and develop a relationship with the branch manager at the new bank.

5. One strategy for getting to know your banker and giving her or him confidence in you is to take out a small, secured loan through your bank. Let's say you need $5,000 to start your business and you have $5,000 in the bank for that purpose. Instead of using your own money, borrow money from the bank using your $5,000 as collateral. Then pay on it regularly. It may cost you a little more in interest charges, but it may be worth it to get to know your banker.

6. If you're not getting positive feedback or response, find another banker. Remember, you're trying to develop a relationship. It's usually not worth it to waste time with people who are not interested in you.

7. When it's time to get a loan, your banker should already be very familiar with your needs and your financial situation. If you've done your homework, she or he will assist you in determining what kind of loan you need and how to fill out the application. Work with your banker and she or he will be more likely to grant you the loan or, if necessary, go to bat for you with the bank loan committee (the group that makes the decisions on who gets the larger loans).

It takes time to develop this relationship. Make the time. It will pay off for you when you really need money.

But, suppose you need money immediately and don't have a relationship with your banker? This is not a good situation to be in, but there are various avenues you can take.

1. Start by asking your network of business acquaintances for the names of two or three bankers who are known for their willingness to work with women in business. Look for people who know about loans, know their institutions and are interested in you. Women loan officers may be a good choice.

2. Take your completed business plan to all of them, tell them what you're trying to do and solicit their advice, information and suggestions on how to get the loan you need. Be open to their ideas, rather than being stubborn about a particular solution. Again, the more you involve your banker in the solution to your problem, the more likely she or he is to want to help you.

This is where your preparation on your business plan can really pay off. The more logical and well-thought-through your plan sounds to your banker, the more likely she or he is to work with you.

Remember bankers are just people who can't afford to take risks with other people's money, and they are more likely to believe in your success if you can come across logically and powerfully.

Again, above all, be professional.

ALTERNATIVES FOR GETTING FINANCING

For many of you, all this discussion of debt, equity and bankers may be a moot point. The credit situation in the U.S. right now is extremely tight and is not likely to change soon, so regardless of gender, it is extremely difficult to get a start-up loan. Furthermore, if you have no track record, collateral or co-signer and if you're not in a high growth, high-tech, "glamour" business, you are probably not in the position to take advantage of these mainstream mechanisms for getting money to start your business.

In this case, your options are slim but growing, and it's not time to give up. Here are some possibilities:

1. Save more money. No one likes to hear this one, but sometimes it's the only possibility. If you have to, get another job or keep the one you have, but discipline yourself to put away a little money each week. You probably don't need to save *all* the money you need for your business, just enough to demonstrate to the bank that you're serious. Figure out how long it will take you to get the money you need and work toward that goal. Even if you go this route, get to know your banker *now* and keep her or him posted on your progress.

2. Start your business part time and keep your current job. This is another unpopular option, but it can work for some people. You will probably have to start your business more slowly, and your days may be excruciatingly long for a while, but there are some advantages: You get to see

what being in business is really like and what your market wants to buy before you commit a huge amount of time and money, and you might be able to get a bank loan if you have a steady income. Depending on your situation, perhaps the biggest advantage is that you're not living hand to mouth with the constant fear of not being able to put food on the table. It's almost impossible to effectively start or run a business when you're under this level of stress.

3. Use your credit cards to purchase what you need to start your business. This is very expensive credit (credit card interest is higher than bank loan interest), but it is certainly one way to get the money you need. A word of caution: Don't do this without factoring this expensive credit into your cash flow projections. The last thing you want to do is miss too many credit card payments and screw up your credit rating for the next seven years.

4. Find friends or relatives to lend you money. I want to reemphasize this option because it's the way many, many small businesses get started. But it can be frightening to ask people for money. What if you fail? How badly will you hurt your personal relationships if your business falls through? These are good questions, and you need to be clear about the answers before you move in this direction. If you have a sound business plan which you share with your investors, if you treat them professionally—just as you would your banker, if you keep them updated on your business progress and if you put your agreement in writing, you will alleviate many of your biggest concerns in this area. By all means, don't borrow from anyone you don't believe can afford to lose the money. But if you know people who can help you and you believe in your business, don't be afraid to ask for help.

If you know people who can help you and you believe in your business, don't be afraid to ask for help.

5. Try to arrange credit with your suppliers or customers. Your suppliers may be willing to provide the raw material you need today and allow you to pay for it with interest over the next six months. Or the computer store might allow you to make a down payment on a $10,000 computer and pay the rest with interest over the next year. Or a customer might be willing to pay half your fee up front—before you do the work—and the remainder when the work is complete. You can even negotiate for things like rent and utilities. It never hurts to ask someone if you can defer payments in exchange for interest (or some other valuable commodity). The worst that can happen is they'll say no. But if they say yes, it's as good as a loan from a bank.

6. Investigate the Small Business Administration's (SBA) Microloan Demonstration Program. In 1991 the Small Business Administration created a new program to help women, low-income and minority entrepreneurs get business loans. Under this program the SBA lends money to what it refers to as "intermediary lenders," and these intermediary lenders use the money to make loans to people in the target groups, which, as you can see, includes women. The business loans typically are for amounts less than $10,000, but under some conditions can be up to $25,000, and they are intended to be used for working capital, inventory, supplies,

furniture, fixtures, machinery and/or equipment—probably just the things you need.

The intermediary lenders are *not banks*; rather they are non-profit agencies created to support the economic development of the target groups, and they have names like "Coalition for Women's Economic Development" and "Self-Help Ventures Fund." In addition to the money they receive for loans, these organizations also get government funding to provide assistance to the borrowers on how to run their businesses, which means free support for you.

There are currently 110 such organizations around the country funded by the SBA, and they are listed in Appendix III, so you can easily check to see if there's one near you. To date, they have made 210 loans, of which more than half went to businesses owned by women.

7. Look for women's economic development groups. In response to the large numbers of women just like you who are starting or expanding a business, there is an increasing number of private organizations being set up around the country to support you. These organizations provide technical help with your business, moral support groups and, in some cases, money. Their requirements for lending money take many of the special needs of women into account. Even if they can't lend you money, they may know who in your area can.

Some of these organizations are part of the SBA Microloan Demonstration Program and are listed in Appendix III, but not all of them. Start by looking under "Women" in the phone book. If you don't see anything, look for business women's groups in your area. Or call your local SBDC or Chamber of Commerce. Or contact the Aspen Institute (see p. 17). Or keep networking until you find a group that can help you.

8. Contact the federal and state Offices of Women's Business Ownership in your area. The Small Business Administration (SBA) has Offices of Women's Business Ownership (OWBO) around the country with responsibility for providing women with information about federally funded programs for small business. The OWBO representatives in each state are listed in Appendix III. Many of them hold regular loan information meetings to describe the loan programs available through the SBA and to outline how you can tap into them. In addition, there are educational and networking programs geared specifically to women-owned businesses. These are described in more detail in Chapter One, and the SBA also has pamphlets about the programs.

Many women assume that because there is an OWBO representative, there must also be a special federal financing source just for women-owned businesses. This is not true. But your OWBO representative can describe the programs that do exist and can explore whether they pertain to your situation.

Some states also have state Offices of Women's Business Ownership, usually within the state office of economic development. Also known as Women's Business Advocates, these people have similar responsibilities to the federal OWBO representatives plus, in some cases, additional responsibility: to assure that women have equal access to state-funded small business programs, to recommend legislation to counteract the institutional bias that many of these programs have against the types of businesses women tend to start and to create or foster new programs for women-owned businesses. The state Women's Business Advocates stay current on the programs, organizations, legislation, educational opportunities, government procurement opportunities, and so on that are available within their states. They are excellent resources and are generally accessible, and it is well worth your time to get to know them. Appendix III lists the addresses and phone numbers of the contact within each state who has responsibility for staying abreast of women's business issues.

9. There are other sources of money for women business owners springing up around the country. For example, the National Association for Female Executives (NAFE) has a venture capital program for its members in which it invests from $5,000 to $50,000 in women-owned businesses. NAFE's program is very creative and is geared to meet the needs of women-owned businesses. You can get information on NAFE by writing them at 127 W. 24th Street, New York, NY 10011 or calling them at (212) 645-0770. But NAFE is not a panacea: Like any venture capital program, it invests in businesses with a very high growth potential so it can recoup its investment plus a high return on investment for risking its money on your business. For example, NAFE recently invested in a company which produces "user-friendly" cleaning kits for sophisticated office and scientific equipment. If you own a one-woman consulting business or a traditional house cleaning business or secretarial services business, or a home-based business manufacturing craft-type products, NAFE is not for you.

   While NAFE's is the program I'm most familiar with, I'm also aware that Seagram's, Avon, and other companies have creative financing programs for women. Check around in your area and keep your ears open for other programs like this. Some of them are long shots, but they all open up possibilities for financing when other options are not available.

10. Be aware of what's happening in your community. There are a variety of state and local programs in almost every community in the United States to provide special financing for small businesses. Check with your banker, your local government offices of economic development (county and city), and your state offices of economic development. The information you seek is not readily available from one source. If you really need the money, be persistent.

11. Network, network, network. There are people out there willing to help you, but you never know who they are or where they'll turn up or how they'll provide the help. You can't count on this help; neither can you afford to stop looking for it. Let people know what you're trying to do. The more excited and enthusiastic you are about your business, the harder you try and the more you take ownership of your success, the more people will want to help you.

There are sources of money for women business owners springing up around the country.

The most remarkable case of this I've seen involved two women, Julie and Karen, who were trying to start a clothing manufacturing business. They have a fabulous product and they both have years of experience in the industry—one as a designer and seamstress, one managing a garment business. They are both single heads of household with several children, no real estate and no savings to speak of. No bank in town would lend them money.

Julie and Karen tried every avenue they could think of. They talked with SCORE, the SBA, the local SBDC and other women's groups. Finally they were "found" by a local woman executive. She gathered a group of women acquaintances together and arranged for them to buy dressmaking services from Julie and Karen in $500 lots. This gave Julie and Karen enough money to go to some trade shows in which they received $18,000 in orders and established relationships with key sales reps.

Again, you can't bank on this kind of support, but you can't afford not to look for it either.

12. Ask yourself a new question. Instead of "How much money do I want (or need)?" ask "What can I successfully do given the cash I'm likely to get?" You may need to downsize your start up, but that's far better than never getting off the ground. Besides, you can always grow later after you've achieved some measure of success and are more bankable.

Those are the alternatives. Be patient, but be persistent and professional. You'll find money somewhere.

A WORD ABOUT DISCRIMINATION

Discrimination against women in the banking and credit industries used to be overt, and horror stories abounded. For many years bankers would literally try to talk women out of starting a business (using phrases like "You don't need to live with those headaches" or "Why go to all this trouble? It would be much easier for you to teach instead") or would reject our loan requests specifically because we were women or would treat us in a disgustingly condescending manner (saying things like "Honey, you should be at home taking care of your husband and kids" or "This is much too complicated for your pretty little head").

Today, these situations are rare, and there are even some women business owners who believe that discrimination in the banking and credit industries has ceased to exist. It is exciting to observe this shift, yet I would not go so far as to agree that there is no discrimination. Rather, I believe the nature of discrimination is rapidly changing and may even be lessening. Here are some of the varying beliefs about discrimination today:

1. *It is so difficult for anyone to get a loan right now that it's hard to tell whether or not there's discrimination against women.* It is well recognized that the credit market is tight. (In English, this means it is extremely difficult to get a loan from a bank today.) In my community, the head of small business lending for a sizeable bank told me recently that 95% of the start-

up requests "don't have a chance" of getting funding. Given this environment, there is little difference between the experiences of men and of women at banks, and discrimination is less evident.

2. *Discrimination against women starting small companies has dramatically lessened; the problem has shifted to growth capital, where there are few capital funds women can tap for money.* Traditionally women have started small companies and bankers have become accustomed to seeing us in that capacity. For women who want to start or purchase large companies, there is still a strong bias in the lending industry. Bankers ask questions like: "Can she really run a business that size?" a question they rarely consider with men. Also, the venture capital or "angel" networks which exist in most cities are not used to funding women-owned businesses and still don't do it. In some communities there is even special funding available for minorities, but nothing specifically targeted to women.

3. *Discrimination against women is institutionalized.* Since women tend to start smaller businesses and since they typically do not have pre-existing banking relationships, they are often relegated to the more junior bankers. These lenders do not have the sophistication to help with loan packaging, do not have the authority or experience to make exceptions to bank rules and may not be able to effectively make the woman's case before the bank's loan review committees.

   Also, banks and other money sources traditionally fund manufacturing businesses with plans for growth. Since women tend to start small retail and service businesses, there is a mismatch between the kinds of businesses women start and the kinds of businesses these funding sources understand and feel comfortable with. Bankers will say that small retail and service businesses are very risky because they're so dependent on one person, have no real collateral (meaning manufacturing equipment or large, long-lead contracts) and are too small for them to make money on. This is all true, yet there are many who believe bankers and other money sources could be far more creative in evaluating loan requests from women and, if they wanted to, could develop workable loan packages. To date, some banks have shown a willingness to negotiate with groups of women business owners to create the climate—and set aside funds—for "unusual" deals. In the near term, this may be the only hope for getting business loans for our businesses.

4. *Women do not understand banks, and we don't behave in a powerful way.* When you put these two concepts together, we look like victims and tend to be "victimized." Most small business owners do not understand bankers' needs nor how bankers look at loan proposals, and women are no different. But women are less likely to get the benefit of the doubt and have it explained to them. With regard to our power, I admit to feeling ambivalent. Many women discount their knowledge, their intuitition, their experience and themselves. This causes them to come across in a powerless way, giving bankers reason to doubt their ability to build a business. But is it right to blame the victim for being discriminated against?

There are some women who say that we are reaching the point where women will be able to enter the funding mainstream, and I see evidence of this:

1. Bankers are beginning to see women business owners as a viable—and necessary—market segment. Our explosive growth (we are starting businesses at twice the rate of men and will comprise roughly 40% of all businesses in the U.S. by the year 2000) and the publicity of statistics about our contribution to the U.S. economy are shifting their perspective. Increasingly bankers are putting on loan seminars for women and, in isolated cases, are considering unique financing schemes. Some of this shift is due to changes in federal regulations, but much of it comes from a recognition that if they do not learn to work with women, they will be missing out on a sizeable portion of the small business marketplace.

2. Venture capital pools for women are beginning to meet with success in raising funds. In the past, women tried to create pools of venture money specifically for women business owners, but all attempts were unsuccessful. Now there seem to be some well-to-do women business owners who are willing to invest money so other women can benefit. The jury is still out as to whether these new efforts to establish venture funds for women will meet with success, but there are those who believe that "now's the time."

Clearly, the situation regarding discrimination is in a state of flux. Regardless, if you think you are bankable, here are some actions you can take to make your case to the bank stronger:

Be professional and know your stuff. Know it as well as—or better than—a man. This means:

- Be prepared

- Be thorough and organized

- Be confident

- Be persistent

- Look and act professional

Bankers have to know certain information—the information in your business plan—to determine whether or not to make the loan. They must also have confidence in your ability to personally carry out the plan. The more thorough, complete and accurate your business plan is, the more confidence your banker will have in you. Conversely, the more questions your banker has to ask to fill in the gaps in your plan, the more he or she will doubt that you know what you're doing. As a woman, you're less likely to get the benefit of the doubt for any holes or errors, so your best option is to be as knowledgeable, prepared and persistent as possible.

I recently heard of two women who wanted to start a saddle shop. They had shopped around for a location, had done the market research and had thought through their plan—but in their financing proposal, their financial projections were written by hand and some of the pages were upside down. These women were turned down from a number of banks for their loan and are saying they were discriminated against. I believe they sabotaged themselves. You can do better.

Undoubtedly some of you are saying "I've tried to do all this stuff and I'm tired of it because it doesn't make a difference." Unfortunately, though the world is changing, the change is not as fast as we'd like. As I've referred to several times, there are some women who have met with success by banding together and cutting a joint deal with a bank or banks who have agreed to evaluate loans in a different way. It's not the ideal solution, but perhaps it could work for you.

Despite all this discussion about things being better than they used to be, there may be some of you who have been the victim of outright discrimination. The key to fighting discrimination is: *Don't let your anger get in the way of achieving your goal.* Your objective is to get money to start your business. If you allow your anger to get in the way, you will be stooping to the level of the people discriminating against you and will probably meet their expectations: you won't get a loan. Redirect energy and actions with a focus on starting your business, not being angry.

If you find yourself in this situation, there are several actions you can take:

- *You can remain calm and try to use the situation to your benefit.* Start by assuming the problem is a lack of information. Maybe it isn't, but this assumption keeps the conversation on a business level and focused toward your goal of getting a loan. Ask the banker such questions as: "What questions haven't I answered?" "What else would you like to see?" "Am I missing some information?" "How could I have represented this information more favorably?" As a minimum, you will get some sound advice you can use in a meeting with another bank. At best you may still be able to get a loan with this bank.

- *You can move your bank accounts to another bank and apply to the new bank for a loan.* If the situation with the first bank is really untenable, don't keep banging your head against the wall. Learn what you can and then use this information to your advantage at another bank.

  If you select this option, consider writing a letter to the bank president describing your situation and experiences. The poor judgments and actions of an individual bank loan officer are typically *not* an accurate reflection of bank policy and the beliefs of the bank executives. I know of a similar situation in which the bank president personally called the woman whose loan had been rejected and saw to it that she got her loan.

- *You can (and should) write to the bank and get a formal, written reason for their rejection of your loan.* Banks are required to provide a written reason if you are rejected for a business loan—but only if you ask.

- *You can file a complaint with the bank's regulator.* The government has set up federal enforcement agencies which monitor and police banks and other financial institutions to ensure they do not discriminate based on gender (among other things). If you believe you've been the subject of discrimination, write to the regulator (names and addresses are in Appendix VII) with your specific complaint.

- *You can file a lawsuit against the bank or other funding source.* Filing a lawsuit might give you some personal satisfaction and, if the court rules in your favor, it might cause some long-term beneficial changes to the system, but it has its drawbacks: Court proceedings are expensive and

The key to fighting discrimination is: Don't let your anger get in the way of achieving your goal.

take a long time (not a benefit if you want your loan quickly). Also the business community will probably not look favorably on you for suing your banker. All in all, you may have some excellent reasons for selecting this option, but you will pay a very high personal price for it. You may even be sacrificing your business. You need to carefully weigh the costs and the benefits in your particular situation before you make your decision.

The last four years have brought about some rather dramatic changes with regard to discrimination. The funding world is not yet gender-blind, but it is at least moving in the right direction.

SUMMARY

There is a wealth of information and advice about business that you can gain from reading this and other books and from attending business classes, workshops and seminars. Much of this information may be new to you, but you will learn it over time as you have learned many, many other things in your life.

The important thing is to keep in mind the principles of building a successful business.

Zuckerman's Principles of Business Success

- Commit to your vision of success. The key to achieving success in your business (and your life) is to be clear about and committed to your personal definition of success. You may fit into the traditional definition of small business success, but you certainly don't have to. For you, success may look like a personal income of $100,000 and enough time to play with your Mercedes and your yacht. Or it may look like a billion-dollar business and your picture on the cover of *TIME* magazine. Or it may be a modest income and more time to spend with your family. What's important is to establish *your* vision of success and commit to it.

- Use the business planning process to manage your business. You can choose to let the day-to-day crises of the business determine your daily activities or you can choose to plan your time and resources to meet your vision of success. I recommend the latter. And the best way to do that is with a business plan that you continually use and update to manage your business.

- Keep your customers happy. All of business boils down to meeting customers' wants and needs at a profit. The better you understand your customers and gear your business to satisfy their wants or meet their needs, the more likely you are to be successful. Stay in touch with your customers. Ask them what they like, survey them, talk to them, explore ideas with them, then follow through and you will be successful.

- Network, network, network. There are many people out there who will gladly help you if you will let them. They will provide you with information, support, contacts, references, ideas, advice and guidance. You can network with your customers, your competitors, your suppliers, other business people, and on and on. Networking may be the single most valuable activity for achieving business success.

- Persevere. Of all the qualities that make a small business owner successful, perseverance is at the top of the list. Talk to any successful business woman and she'll tell you: "I never lost sight of my goal," or "I kept going in the face of all obstacles" or "I was determined to make my business a success." Sometimes when the going gets tough (and it will), it's hard to find the energy or the drive or the will to keep moving forward. But it's at those times that perseverance really pays off. Many other women have done it, and you can too.

Good Luck!

Glossary of
Financial Terms

Accounts Payable (also called Payables): Money you owe to an individual or business for goods or services you have received but not yet paid for. If you buy on credit, you record the purchase on your balance sheet under Accounts Payable until you pay your bill.

Accounts Receivable (also called Receivables): Money owed to a business for goods or services which have been delivered but not yet paid for. If people buy from you on credit, you record the purchase on your balance sheet under Accounts Receivable until they pay you in cash.

Accrued Expenses: Expenses that result from the passage of time. For example, salaries and interest accrue as time passes, and they show up on your financial statements as something you owe until they are paid.

Accumulated Depreciation: The total amount of depreciation which has accrued over time on your capital equipment.

Administrative Costs: See Overhead.

Amortization: The process of gradually paying off a liability over a period of time. For example, your home mortgage is amortized by periodically paying off part of the face amount of the mortgage.

Annual Percentage Rate: See APR.

APR (also called Annual Percentage Rate): The interest charged by a bank, which accounts for all fees associated with the loan, including basic interest charges and all service charges. The APR allows you to directly compare different bank loans. For personal loans, banks are required by law to tell you the APR. For business loans, they'll tell you if you ask.

Assets: The valuable resources or properties owned by an individual or business enterprise. Assets may consist of claims against others.

Balance Sheet: An itemized statement which lists the total assets, liabilities and net worth of a business to reflect its financial condition at a given moment in time.

Bookkeeping (also called Recordkeeping): The systematic recording of the transactions affecting a business, including all sales and expenses. The "books" are the documents in which the records of transactions are kept.

Bottom Line: The figure that reflects company profitability on the income statement. The bottom line is the profit after all expenses and taxes have been paid.

Break-even: In a business, the point of activity when total revenue equals total expenses. Above break-even, you are making a profit. Below breakeven, you are incurring a loss.

Capital: Funds necessary to start or expand your business. Capital is usually put into the business in a fairly permanent form such as in fixed assets, plant and equipment or in other ways which are not recoverable in the short run unless the entire business is sold.

Capital Equipment: Equipment used to manufacture a product, provide a service, or to sell, store and deliver merchandise. Such equipment will not be sold in the normal course of business, but will be used and worn out or be consumed over time as business is conducted.

Cash Flow: The actual movement of cash within a business: Cash inflow minus cash outflow. An analysis of cash flow is used to determine whether a business has enough cash on hand to pay its bills when they come due.

Collateral: An asset pledged to a lender to support a loan. If the borrower cannot repay, the lender has the right to repossess or sell the collateral to recoup her or his money.

Contribution Margin: see Gross Profit.

Cooperative: A business in which the employees own, operate and manage the business. The distinguishing feature of a cooperative is that profits are distributed based on the amount of time each owner-employee has invested in the business rather than on the amount of capital each has invested in the business.

Cost of Goods Sold: The direct cost to the business owner of those items which will then be sold to her or his customers. Cost of goods sold does *not* include other costs of being in business, such as rent, utilities, and so on.

Credit: Another word for debt. You can give credit to your customers by allowing them to make a purchase now with the promise to pay later. Large department stores often give credit through the use of store credit cards. A bank gives you credit when it allows you to borrow money.

Current Assets: Valuable resources or properties owned by a firm that will be turned into cash within one year or used up in the operations of a firm within one year. Generally includes cash, accounts receivable, inventory and prepaid expenses.

Current Liabilities: Amounts owned that will ordinarily be paid by a firm within one year. Generally includes accounts payable, the current portion of long term debt and interest and dividends payable.

Current Ratio: Current assets divided by current liabilities; a measure of the firm's liquidity.

Debt: Debt refers to borrowed funds, whether from your own coffers or from individuals, banks or institutions. It is generally secured by collateral or a co-signer (i.e., the collateral or cosigner provides security to the lender that some money is still recoverable even if the borrower cannot repay the loan).

Depreciation: Business expenses which account for the wear and tear of your capital equipment. Depreciation is a bookkeeping entry and does not represent any cash outlay.

Distribution Channel (also called Channel of Distribution): The route a product follows as it moves from the original grower, producer or importer to the ultimate consumer. Often a middleman is used (i.e., clothing manufacturers sell to retail clothing stores, who sell to consumers).

Equity: Equity refers to an investment in the business. An equity investment carries with it a share of ownership of the business, a stake in its profits and a say in how its managed. Since an equity investment is repaid out of profits, the value of the original investment could grow tremendously, shrink dramatically or be lost altogether depending on how profitable the firm is. Equity is calculated at any time by subtracting the liabilities of the business (what it owes) from the assets of the business (what it owns) at that point in time.

G&A: see Overhead.

General & Administrative Costs: see Overhead.

Going Concern: A business that is currently in operation.

Gross Margin: see Gross Profit.

Gross Profit (also called Gross Margin or Contribution Margin): The difference between the selling price and the cost of an item. Gross profit is calculated by subtracting cost of goods sold from net sales.

Guarantee: A pledge by a third party to repay a loan in the event the borrower cannot. For example, the Small Business Administration provides loan guarantees in which it promises the bank that it will repay your small business loan in the event your business fails.

Income Statement (also called Profit and Loss Statement or P&L Statement): A useful business form that shows your income and expenses for a given period of time.

Inventory: The materials owned and held by a business intended either for internal consumption or for sale. Inventory includes new material, intermediate products and parts, work-in-progress and finished goods.

License: Formal permission to do something. In business, licenses are granted for such things as producing and selling items with someone else's logo or trademark or design. For example, shirts, dolls or trinkets with cartoon characters on them are usually produced and sold by a company which has gotten a license from Warner Brothers or Walt Disney Studios, not by the studios themselves.

Liquidity: Ability of a business to meet its financial responsibilities. The degree of readiness with which assets can be converted into cash without a loss. If a firm's current assets cannot be converted into cash to meet its current liabilities, the firm is said to be illiquid.

Loan Agreement: A document which states what a business can and cannot do as long as it owes money to the lender (usually a bank). A loan agreement may place restrictions on the owner's salary, on dividends, on amount of other debt, on working capital limits, on sales or on the number of additional personnel.

Loan: A business agreement between two legal entities whereby one party (the lender) agrees to lend money to a second party (the borrower). A secured loan is one which is backed by a claim against personal assets or the assets of a business. An unsecured loan is backed by the faith the bank has in the borrower's ability to pay back the money.

Long-Term Liabilities: The liabilities (expenses) which will not mature within the next year. For example, most mortgages are long-term liabilities until the year in which they will be totally paid off.

Market Niche: A group of customers for which what you have to offer is particularly suitable.

Microbusiness: An owner-operated business with few employees and less than $250,000 in annual sales.

Net Worth (also called Owner's Equity): The total value of an entity in financial terms. Net worth is calculated by subtracting your total liabilities (what you owe) from your total assets (what you own). Net worth can be calculated for a business or an individual.

Note: A document that is the recognized legal evidence of a debt. A note is signed by the borrower, promising to pay a certain sum of money on a specified date at a certain place of business to a certain business, individual or bank. In financial jargon, sometimes a "loan" is referred to as a "note."

Operating Costs: see Overhead.

Overhead (also called Administrative Costs, General and Administrative Costs, G&A, Operating Costs): A general term for costs of materials and services not directly adding to or readily identifiable with the product or service being sold. Examples include rent, utilities, insurance, and so on.

P&L (also called Profit and Loss): see Income Statement.

Partnership: A legal relationship created by the voluntary association of two or more persons as co-owners of a business for profit.

Payables: see Accounts Payable.

Prepaid Expenses: Expenditures that are paid in advance for items not yet received. For example, insurance is often paid for in advance for future months.

Principal:

(1) The amount of money borrowed in a debt agreement. Principal is that amount of money on which interest is calculated; it must be repaid with interest on an agreed-upon schedule.

(2) The owner of a business is a principal in that business.

Pro Forma: A projection or an estimate of what may result in the future from actions in the present. A pro forma financial statement is one that shows how the actual operations of a business will turn out if certain assumptions are realized.

Profit: The excess of the selling price over all costs and expenses incurred in making a sale. Also, the reward to the entrepreneur for the risks assumed by her or him in the establishment, operations, and management of a given enterprise or undertaking.

Profit and Loss (also called P & L): See Income Statement.

Quick Ratio: Current assets minus inventory divided by current liabilities. A measure of a firm's ability to meet its current financial obligations.

Receivables: see Accounts Receivable.

Recordkeeping: see Bookkeeping.

Revenue: Total sales during a stated period.

Sales Representative (also called Sales Rep): An independent salesperson who directs her or his efforts to selling your products/service to others but is not an employee of your company. Sales reps often represent more than one product line from more than one company and usually work on commission. Larger businesses do have staff sales reps.

Security:

(1) General: That which is promised to a lender to protect her or him in case the borrower defaults on a loan. Includes collateral, a co-signer (who promises to pay) or a loan guarantee from a third party.

(2) Financial: A stock, bond or mutual fund which is sold by a stockbroker or other securities dealer.

Short-Term Notes: Loans that come due in one year or less.

Sole Proprietorship: A type of business organization in which one individual owns the business. Legally the owner *is* the business and personal assets are typically exposed to liabilities of the business.

Spreadsheets: Generic term for a type of computer program which allows you to easily record and manipulate numeric data. In business, spreadsheets are used for such things as bookkeeping, preparing financial statements and forecasting sales.

Sub-Chapter S Corporation: A corporation which has elected under Sub-Chapter S of the IRS Code (by unanimous consent of its stockholders) not to pay any corporate tax on its income and, instead, to have the shareholders pay personal taxes on it, even though it may not have been distributed to them.

Target Market: The specific individuals, distinguished by socioeconomic, demographic and/or interest characteristics, who are the most likely potential customers for the goods and/or services of a business.

Term Loan: A loan which matures in more than one year. In financial jargon, a term loan often matures in up to ten years. Term loans are paid off like a mortgage: so many dollars per month for so many years. The most common uses of term loans are for equipment and other fixed asset purposes, for working capital and for real estate.

Trade Associations: A nonprofit organization, usually made up of people or businesses in the same industry, that serves the common interest of its membership. Trade associations generally hold regular meetings for their members, host trade shows, publish industry-related magazines and serve as an information clearinghouse.

Trade Credit: Credit is given you by a supplier. Trade credit is generally accompanied by a trade discount, which is a discount from the agreed-upon price which you receive if you pay your bill early. By paying later you forego the price discount, but you get use of the funds for a longer period of time.

Venture Capital: Money invested in enterprises that do not have access to traditional sources of capital (banks, stock market, etc.). Venture capital is usually associated with very-high-risk, very-high-payoff businesses. A venture capitalist is the investor who provides this money.

Working Capital: The cash needed to keep the business running from day to day. This is in contrast with plain old capital, which is a more permanent use of funds. (See Capital.) Working capital is used to fund such things as inventory, accounts and notes receivable and cash and securities. In financial jargon, working capital is calculated by subtracting current liabilities from current assets.

APPENDIX II

Sample Business Plans

This appendix contains a sample business plan and a sample financing proposal.

The business plan is for a consulting business, Miracle Consultants, that wants to get organized and grow. Miracle Consultants is actually a composite of several different companies and I created the plan for illustrative purposes.

The financing proposal is for a real business named PEABODY'S—Toys That Teach, Inc. owned by a woman whom I have called Jennifer Michaels (see p. 242). Ms. Michaels started PEABODY'S so she would have more time to spend with her three children, and she operates out of the basement of her home.

In my discussions with her, she, like many of us, finds balancing business and family to be more difficult than expected. She sometimes heads for her basement office at 5:00 A.M. in order to get her work done, though she has become more disciplined about closing the basement door in the evenings rather than going downstairs to do yet more work. PEABODY'S is growing more slowly than it might if Ms. Michaels had unlimited time and energy for the business, but it is growing nonetheless.

A version of this plan was used to obtain a $50,000 SBA-guaranteed loan. I have re-organized the plan to make it more closely follow the format I prefer, but the relevant non-financial facts of the business are as stated in the original financing proposal. All financial data in the body of the plan has been adjusted and the financial statements and projections have been excluded in order to protect the interests of PEABODY'S investors. As you might imagine, Ms. Michaels had to submit financial statements and projections in order to get bank approval of her loan. A few other items of interest:

1) While this plan did receive funding, that funding was from a particular bank (with its own lending philosophy) at a particular location and a particular point in time. In your own situation, this same proposal might not work for you—or it might work faster.

2) More importantly, in order to get this $50,000 loan of which 90% is guaranteed by the federal government, Ms. Michaels had to put up the business inventory, receivables, and all business assets (i.e., the computer, fax machine, etc.) as collateral *and* sign a personal guarantee (meaning all of her furniture, jewelry, car, etc. could be collected in case of default) *and* accept a lien on her house *and* agree that she would get permission from the bank before spending money she might receive from a personal lawsuit and from the sale of other family-owned real estate. In total, she had to put up $211,000 in collateral for a $50,000 loan for which the bank is only at risk for $5,000. Welcome to today's world of business financing!

Please note that the financial data for Miracle Consultants was developed on a computer using a spreadsheet program. I highly recommend that you somehow access a computer and spreadsheet software prior to doing your own plan. If you do not have them readily available, contact your local college or university or call some of the local government support agencies described in Chapter One and get the help you need.

BUSINESS PLAN

FOR

Miracle Consultants

Owner: Suzanne Miracle

Address: 200 Chamber St.
Anytown, USA 12345

Phone: (101) 555-1234

STATEMENT OF PURPOSE

The purpose of this plan is to serve as an operating tool to guide Miracle Consultants in expanding services, dramatically increasing sales and doubling profits.

TABLE OF CONTENTS

Section One: The Business

Section Two: Financial Statements

Notes: We did not prepare a Balance Sheet nor a Sources and Uses of Cash Statement as they are not relevant for a small consulting business.

SECTION ONE: THE BUSINESS

A. DESCRIPTION OF BUSINESS

Miracle Consultants guides moderately sized businesses in Anytown to become more successful through:

- Helping owners and managers visualize the future of their business and prepare plans for reaching that future

- Building effective, energetic management teams that are committed to the plans

We typically work with companies that are dissatisfied with sales and/or profits and are unable to prioritize activities to improve operations. Unlike other consulting firms that focus on one or two specific areas of business, we tie together our thorough understanding of running a business with our knowledge and training in how people behave so our work creates real and lasting change within the companies we serve.

At present 30% of our business is from companies with under $1 million in sales, 50% is from companies with between $1 million and $10 million in sales, and 20% is from non-profit agencies. We intend to shift our marketing focus toward larger companies so that within three years 80% of our business will be from companies with sales between $1 million and $10 million. We will continue to work with non-profit agencies as a way to support Anytown as well as promote our name in the community.

Miracle Consultants was started six years ago by Suzanne Miracle and continues to be a sole proprietorship. Other than part-time clerical help, Ms. Miracle has been and continues to be the sole employee of the business. We are typically open Monday through Friday from 9:30am to 4:30pm in order to accommodate Ms. Miracle's desire to spend time with her children. We are available at other times (early mornings, evenings and weekends) as needed by our clients. Our business tends not to be seasonal, except that November through January are occasionally slow—people spend time preparing for the holidays and prefer not to meet with a consultant.

The growth of moderately sized businesses in Anytown is increasing the demand for consulting services. Miracle Consultants should readily be able to tap into this demand because of its sound and growing reputation in the community, its excellent public relations exposure stemming largely from Ms. Miracle's volunteer activities and its growing referral base of successful clients and others. Miracle Consultants will continue to capitalize on these factors by routinely asking clients for referrals, continuing to expand its network of other professional referral sources (accountants, bankers, attorneys, other consultants) and creating public relations opportunities.

B. SERVICE DESCRIPTION

Miracle Consultants offers the following services:

1. **We help our clients envision the future and create strategies for achieving it.**

   It is increasingly recognized that in order to create long-term business success, it is necessary to have a clear vision of the future that is understood and shared by all employees. Miracle Consultants works with business owners, managers and employees to facilitate the creation of *their* future business vision including:

   - The values which drive the business' decisions

   - The business' mission

   - A clear description of how people want the business to be in the long term

   - Specific, measurable goals to which staff is willing to commit

   We also support our clients in creating effective business strategies and detailed tactical plans for reaching the vision.
   Specific activities for creating this vision include:

   - Tailoring the visioning process to the client with help from either the owner or a steering committee

   - Facilitating management meetings and/or retreats

   - Leading the data gathering process to obtain market, financial and employee data

   - Planning appropriate communication with all employees regarding the vision and training managers and others to conduct such communication

2. **We assist our clients in reaching their desired future by helping them resolve the communication issues that stand in their way.**

   It has been our experience that in most businesses people do not communicate well enough, either interpersonally or in a group, for the organization to reach its potential (or even its goals). This leads to one or more of the following:

   - Long, boring, unproductive meetings in which nothing of substance is decided

   - Inability to envision anything, much less the future

   - Frustrated, unmotivated employees

   - In some of the worst cases, unconscious sabotage of business strategies

Miracle Consultants works with business owners, managers and employees to create an organizational climate in which effective communication takes place. We developed this capability in order to ensure that the visions developed by our clients could be carried out. An offshoot of this work is that employees in our client companies become more creative, more productive and more motivated with a far greater likelihood of living up to their individual potentials.

Specific activities for creating a climate for effective communication include:

- Facilitating management and employee meetings and/or retreats

- Individual counseling of owners, managers and employees

- Training in the process of effective communication (interpersonal and group)

- Training and coaching in how to hold effective meetings

3. **We also help our clients put in place some of the systems necessary to reach their desired future.**

    In order to work together effectively, people must know what is expected of them, how they stack up against these expectations and how their jobs impact the organization. To achieve this state, we help our clients put in place the following systems:

- Role clarification and job descriptions for all employees and groups

- Performance evaluation systems

- Budgeting systems, including analysis of budget deviations

Specific activities for putting these systems in place include:

- Tailoring forms, computer programs/templates and manuals to the organization

- Training people to use them in their work environment

- Coaching people in the value of these systems so they will follow through with them

C. MARKET DESCRIPTION

Miracle Consultants presently defines its market in terms of revenues and geography:

- Our clients are companies within a 50-mile radius of Anytown

- 30% of our clients have annual sales of roughly $300,000 to $1 million, 50% of our clients have annual sales of roughly $1 million to $10 million and 20% of our clients are non-profit agencies.

Within these parameters, our clients include retailers, manufacturers, distributors and professionals in a variety of industries. Typical characteristics include:

- Have been in operation for at least ten years. (While we know we could be of service to start-up businesses, they normally cannot afford a consultant.)

- Owner is still the primary driver of the business. His or her values dominate.

- Have some managers in addition to the owner, but have not yet created a cohesive management team.

- Do not yet have experienced marketing and human resource professionals on staff (e.g., the VP of Operations also handles Human Resources, the VP of Sales also handles Marketing).

- Desire to grow.

While we do not specifically target male-owned businesses, business demographics have dictated that the purchaser of our services (the owner or company president) is typically a man. Other typical characteristics of the actual purchaser include:

- Between the ages of 40 and 55

- Wife is involved in the business and is a decisionmaker in our being hired

- Well-educated (college degree)

- Earns more than $40,000 per year

- Involved with a trade association

- Tends to listen to self-improvement tapes

In the past, we have been hired for the following stated reasons:

- "To help us increase sales"

- "To help us set goals that we are committed to"

- "To help us create a long-range plan"

- "To help us work together effectively"

(4)

We believe we are actually hired because we are honest, sincere and excellent listeners and because we convey a unique combination of our strong business expertise plus credibility in resolving people and organizational issues. (Consultants are typically trained in one or the other of these areas, but not both.)

While all companies could benefit from our services, not all will buy them. Typically, a client will only buy when "ready." Signs of readiness include:

- Sales are stagnating or down

- Profits are stagnating or down

- Employee morale is terrible

  AND EITHER:
- The owner or president believes in effective planning and communication

- The owner or president is enlightened about the benefits we provide and able to admit that someone outside the company could help

  OR:
- The owner or president feels concerned about her or his lack of future vision

- The management team is not making decisions or is in conflict

- The owner or president is in sufficient pain over her or his lack of ability to solve the organization's problems and doesn't know where to turn for help (rare to find someone who will admit to this)

Surprisingly our sales tend to increase in a down economy: People are more concerned about declining sales and are willing to spend what little cash they have on a consultant.

Over the next three years we intend to shift our client base as a way of increasing sales. We will eliminate our work with clients under $1 million in annual sales and focus solely on companies with annual sales of $1 to 10 million. We will take on work with non-profit agencies on a case-by-case basis if it supports our cash flow or provides a valuable marketing side benefit (e.g., prospective business clients on the agency Board of Trustees) or if we believe strongly in the agency and have a personal desire to support it that supersedes our desire for additional revenues.

Demographic data was obtained using the Dun's *Million Dollar Directory* available on disk at the public library. Within a 50-mile radius of Anytown:

Companies with sales between $1/2 and $1 million 8,438

Companies with sales between $1 and $10 million 6,075

Miracle Consultants can currently handle a maximum of 15 to 25 clients at any time and is projected to handle a maximum of 22 clients in the plan period, so we anticipate that the market for our services is available and growing.

D. COMPETITION

Direct competition includes: other planning consultants, other organizational development consultants and other training consultants. Currently we do not have an analysis of these competitors; however, the Yellow Pages lists roughly 70 different firms in Anytown under the headings "Business Consultants" and "Management Consultants." Eliminating the 5 CPA firms, the 11 firms that we know are not competitors, and the 3 counseling agencies for start-up businesses leaves 52 possible competitors based on Yellow Pages data. We know there are other consultants not listed there. In fact, the ranks of consultants continue to grow as local corporations downsize and laid-off employees try their hand at consulting.

Despite this, we rarely have been in head-to-head competition with another consultant for the same job. However, we see this coming in the future and plan to do a more rigorous assessment of our competition.

Indirect competition includes CPA firms. Their work often overlaps with ours in terms of business strategy. While they are typically not trained to do the visioning and counseling work we do, many business owners rely on their CPA for business advice and are not interested in other outside help.

Our major competition seems to be the feeling by the business owner or management team that they can do the work themselves. We routinely lose work when business owners decide to facilitate visioning or goalsetting sessions themselves or when they decide that even though they want what we have to offer, they are unwilling to pay for it. (We once lost a job because the owner decided to spend the money on a new forklift truck—an understandable decision!).

Our competitive advantages are:

- Well-publicized successes with our clients

- Ms. Miracle's ability to connect with people

- Unique combination of business, interpersonal and organization development skills

- Longevity—we've been around for six years, longer than many consultants, and people know we're here to stay

- Ms. Miracle's gender: male business owners are more likely to open up to her than to another man, thus enhancing the valuable counseling portion of our work

- Wide (and growing) network in the Anytown community

Our competitive disadvantages are:

- Lack of prior "line" experience, i.e., experience managing the major operation of a business. (This hurts us both in marketing our services and in helping clients create effective strategies and action plans.)

- Ms. Miracle's gender: it is more difficult for us to establish technical credibility

- Lack of a "needed product" to help us expand our client base and to carry us through slow periods (e.g., accountants have traditional tax work to help them in this regard)

- One-person organization: hurts our image, no one to delegate administrative jobs to, not enough time available to grow the business, difficult balancing act between business and family that impacts business growth

We believe our strengths, especially our longevity and our strong public relations exposure, will enable us to overcome our weaknesses.

E. MANAGEMENT PLANS

1. PRODUCT DEVELOPMENT PLAN

Within the first year of the plan period we will begin to offer a wider scope of marketing and human resource services. We will accomplish this by developing relationships with other marketing and human resource professionals (herein referred to as "associates") who offer more in-depth expertise than ours. We will bring them in on jobs as our clients and prospects perceive a need for their services.

This concept evolved from listening to our clients and prospects: as they grow, they have an increasing need for marketing and human resource services, and they are not yet large enough to afford these services in house. Furthermore, the very nature of our work literally drives their perception of need for these services. Thus, this is a natural fit for us: the target market is the same as our current target market and links directly to the work we do.

Initially, we will provide the following:

- Marketing Focus Groups

- Market Surveys

- Compensation Plans

- Employee Handbooks

As the concept becomes more successful, we will consider adding other services.

We consider the biggest stumbling blocks to be:

a. Establishing sound working relationships with quality associates. While we know a number of people who can provide these support services, we must develop a fee-based relationship that will provide enough incentive for them to do quality work while at the same time provide us with a reasonable income in exchange for doing the marketing and putting our reputation on the line.

b. Maintaining quality, especially in areas that are not our expertise. We will develop systems to carefully screen and monitor our associates.

2. MARKETING PLAN

Our marketing strategies are:

a) Increase our visibility to our target markets in Anytown. Companies generally cannot be convinced to buy our consulting services nor do they routinely need them. They buy them *at the time* they perceive they have a need. We need to increase visibility so that they think of us when they need us.

b) Increase our credibility to our target markets in Anytown. Companies hire us because they trust and connect with us. Many of the typical methods of reaching markets (direct mail, advertising) actually reduce credibility and trust. We need to find ways to increase credibility and visibility at the same time.

c) Rigorously expand and work our referral base to generate new clients. Accountants, attorneys, bankers and other consultants are usually the first to know when companies have a need for our services. Furthermore, their clients tend to follow their advice. We will work to build our reputation with these sources. Also, we will routinely request referrals from our current satisfied clients.

The specific tactics we have used so far include: join boards of non-profit agencies, attend business networking functions, public speaking, writing for local business newspaper and lunch meetings with bankers, accountants and other consultants.

While we have not been as successful as expected to date, we believe that the strategy and tactics are still appropriate, but our follow-through has been lacking. The reasons for this are: 1) lack of organized systems for follow-through, 2) difficulty in establishing credibility because of Ms. Miracle's gender and because she represents a one-person company, and 3) Ms. Miracle's fears of success and of not being taken seriously which have stood in her way.

Ms. Miracle has spent much energy dealing with her fears and is tired of being disorganized and unfocused. Furthermore, recent publicity has elevated our credibility in Anytown. We are determined to create a marketing focus and consistently follow through on tactics. Our tactics for the plan period are:

Promotion Tactics

1. Public speaking engagements to business organizations minimum once a month.

2. Involvement on planning committee for Anytown Chamber of Commerce.

3. Regular contacts with minimum of 20 strong referral sources.

   a. Semi-annual meetings: stress work accomplished, especially with their referrals, and nature of work/client desired

   b. Monthly contact (send clipped article of interest or note)

   c. Semi-annual newsletter

   d. *Regular referrals to them*: this is crucial, must be a give-and-take

   e. Join an organization to which they tend to belong (e.g., Rotary, Kiwanis)

4. Monthly contact with "hot" prospects: either send clipped articles of interest or a newsletter; then call them quarterly.

5. Monthly contact with "warm" prospects: either send clipped articles of interest or a newsletter; then call them semi-annually.

(9)

6. Semi-annual request for referrals from current clients: must be specific as to what we want.

7. Creation of flexible brochure to provide to prospects and referral sources that will allow us to spotlight different associates as appropriate.

Pricing Strategy/Tactics

At the outset, we priced low ($50 to $75 per hour) because we worked with smaller businesses and that was all they could afford. We have been slowly increasing prices to increase our revenues and to bring them in line with fees consultants typically charge larger companies. Current fees range from $75 to $100 per hour for short assignments and $1000 to $1500 per day for facilitating a group meeting. When appropriate, we propose a fixed price for a long-term project. In truth, we rarely invoice for all the time spent on a project because we don't think our clients understand or find value for that magnitude of money. This makes invoicing a tense time as we struggle to determine what a client will think is billable. In discussions with other consultants, we find that we are not alone in this. To date, we have not found a viable solution.

Our current pricing strategy is to increase revenues by maintaining our higher prices. We also plan to do additional pricing research and stay flexible.

Our expenses average $2,000 per month. Consequently, we need 20 to 27 hours per month of consulting or two days of facilitating to break even. We have been exceeding break-even for the last two years. The difficult part is bringing in enough work to cover Ms. Miracle's desired personal income. This is discussed in the Sales Plan.

With regard to our new product line, our intent is to work out an arrangement where we receive a percentage of the associate's fee. We will collect fees from the client, pay the associate and keep a percentage in exchange for our doing the marketing. We expect this to range from 15 to 25%.

Location

Many consultants work from their home to keep overhead down. We did this for a while, but found that: a) much of our consulting work was being done in restaurants which seemed tacky and b) it was difficult to establish credibility because we appeared to not be a "real business." We recently relocated to an attractive, moderately priced office building near the local expressway, and this has proved valuable.

3. SALES PLAN

Sales Cycle

Miracle Consultants' sales cycle (time from initial sales-type contact to closing a sale) ranges from one month to two years, with the average being roughly 6 to 12 months. Smaller companies (less than $1 million in sales) tend to be shorter: 1 to 2 months. Typical scenario is:

1. Initial contact: either from a networking meeting, a referral or a response to an article about us in the newspaper.

2. Initial sales meeting with company owner or president. Discuss his/her needs and describe what we do.

2a. Sometimes we meet again with the company owner or president to gain a clearer understanding of his/her needs.

3. Prepare a proposal. Depending on its complexity, we either mail the proposal or present it in person.

4. Wait! If the proposal is on target, there is generally a brief waiting period (roughly one month) for the owner/president to make up his/her mind. If the owner/president gets cold feet (more money than expected, management team rejected the idea, "we can do this ourselves" syndrome), the waiting period can be one year or more. Depending on the time and nature of the waiting period, we stay in contact through a combination of phone calls, letters, handwritten notes or sending pertinent magazine articles.

5. When the decision is made to move forward, we work out the details of our simple contract.

6. Begin the work.

7. Invoice either immediately (for a portion of the work) or by month, or at a pre-determined point in the contract.

Rate of Success in Closing Sales

Our success rate is skewed by our ability to close sales with very small clients. We no longer want these clients and will refer them to free business support services (e.g., SCORE) in Anytown. For our target market, our success rate to date has been:

- 60% of prospects request a proposal after the initial "sales" meeting.

Of those that request a proposal:

- 45% become contracts within one year (i.e., 27% of prospects)

- 45% reject the proposal (also 27% of prospects)

- 10% keep us hanging for longer than a year (6% of prospects). Thus far, a small number of these have turned into contracts.

Value of Average Sale

In terms of revenues to us, our clients currently fall into three categories:

1. Revenues less than $1,000 per year per client. We had taken on these clients as a way to increase cash flow, but they distract from our focus. We will keep our two current clients in this category, but we will not take on more. We will also continue to do pro bono work for non-profit agencies on an occasional basis as a way of building our reputation in Anytown.

2. Revenues between $1,000 and $10,000 per year. These are either clients who request one short-term project or clients who thought they would use our service longer term but we did not meet their expectations. We will continue to take on short-term projects as they arise because they are good "filler" work. With regard to not meeting expectations, we will: a) work on getting far more clear about their expectations so we can either meet them or, if we are unable, not take on the work in the first place and b) work on describing our business more effectively so that our customers are not surprised by it.

3. Revenues of about $8,000 in Year 1 followed by revenues between $10,000 and $20,000 for 2 to 3 years, before dropping off to between $3,000 and $8,000 on an ongoing basis. Once we have helped a company create a vision and get its management team and employees working together effectively, the need for our services drops off. Clearly these are our best clients and we need more of them. To date, only 12% of our clients have fallen into this category.

Based on our research, we expect our new product line to generate sales of between $1,000 and $10,000 with an average of $2,500. Unlike our traditional services, there will be a Cost of Sales to us of doing this business. We will assume that we can incur revenues at an average of 20% of the associates' fee.

Sales Goals

During the three-year plan period, Ms. Miracle will continue to work shorter hours (35 to 40 hours per week) in order to spend valuable time with her young children. We believe we can still achieve a 30% - 40% annual increase in sales. Resulting sales figures are as follows:

Year 1: $61,000 - 66,000

Year 2: $79,000 - 92,000

Year 3: $103,000 - 128,000

While we know this will be difficult and will require a substantial amount of effort, we believe:

1. The market is there; we must creatively find a way to tap it.

2. Our name has been around in Anytown for six years and is finally being recognized. In addition, we have had clients for a long enough period that they are seeing the permanent results of our work, and we, therefore, are gaining an increasing amount of publicity. We believe that we are on the upturn of reaping the rewards of our past hard effort.

3. Our new product line will increase our sales potential.

4. Simply writing down our goals, however large, will increase our chances of achieving them.

Feasibility: Required Number of Clients

From experience and research and using conservative assumptions, we project the following:

- 30% of sales will come from current clients (avg sale = $5,000/yr)
  $66,000 x .3 = $19,800 in sales needed from current clients
  $19,800/$5,000 per client = 4 current clients needed (we have them)

- 30% of sales will come from new high-value clients (avg sale = $8,000/yr in Year 1)
  $66,000 x .3 = $19,800 in sales needed from new high-value clients
  $19,800/$8,000 per client = 2.4, say 3 new high-value clients needed

- 20% of sales will come from contracts with "associates" (avg sale = $2,500/contract)
  $66,000 x .2 = $13,200 in sales needed from new product line
  $13,200/$2,500 per client = 5.3, say 6 new contracts with "associates" needed

- 20% of sales will come from projects (avg sale = $5,000/project)
  $66,000 x .2 = $13,200 in sales needed from new product line
  $13,200/$5,000 per client = 2.6, say 3 new projects needed

Barring unforeseen circumstances, the work from current clients should be readily available as we have excellent relationships with them.

The numbers above show the need to generate 12 new clients in Year 1 of the plan period (3 high-value clients + 6 contracts with associates + 3 projects). If we continue with our current sales closing rate of 27%, we will have to generate 12/0.27 or 44 new prospects (roughly one per week) *and* convert them into sales quickly. While we do not have past data regarding prospect generation, we know it hasn't been this good. We will have to solidly work our marketing plan to achieve this.

In addition, if we continue with our current proposal generation rate of 60%, we will have to prepare 26 proposals (44 prospects x .6) to get this work. Currently proposal work is very time consuming.

From this analysis, we need to do the following:

a. Solidly work our marketing plan

b. Screen prospects more effectively

c. Improve our selling techniques

d. Develop a system to mechanize as much of proposal generation as possible

We will re-evaluate our success in these areas semi-annually to make sure that we can meet our desired sales growth of 30 to 40% annually.

(13)

4. Operations and Personnel Plans

Except for the new work with associates, Ms. Miracle will perform the majority of the work for the business. Not only will this meet Ms. Miracle's interest in doing the work herself, it will also meet her desire to hold off hiring personnel for as long as possible to save the expenses of paperwork, taxes,\ and employee benefits.

As a worst-case sanity check on time available:

Year 1: $66,000/12 months = $5,500 per month average sales
$5,500 per month/$75 per hour = 73 hours of work per month

Even if one month was double the average *and* at the minimum hourly rate, Ms. Miracle would have the time available to do the work.

Year 3: $128,000/12 months = $10,667 per month average sales
$10,667/$75 per hour = 142 hours of work per month

These data show that if all work in Year 3 came from our lower value hourly rate efforts, we would have to hire someone. However, we expect that much of the work will come from our higher value efforts and do not anticipate hiring employees until after Year 3.

In order to increase the quality of her work, Ms. Miracle will attend between two and three seminars per year in visioning, planning, coaching or group development.

Our landlord provides centralized clerical and telephone support in our office building. Although the hourly rates are high, it is currently more cost effective than hiring someone. We will continually monitor this expense and will be prepared to hire part-time clerical staff when appropriate.

With regard to our new product line, we will develop quality monitoring systems to assure that clients are satisfied with the services of our associates. Ms. Miracle will need to allocate time to providing feedback to the associates.

With regard to equipment, we purchased a new computer system last year and do not anticipate needing a new one during the plan period. Note that this would change if we hire clerical support staff.

5. Financial Administration Plan

We currently use Intuit's *Quickbooks*™ to maintain financial records and produce financial statements and invoices. Our clerical support person can input our records and generate Profit & Loss Statements as well as a budget deviation analysis in roughly one hour per month. We typically have financial statements in hand by the tenth day of the following month.

(14)

F. DESCRIPTION OF MANAGEMENT

Ms. Miracle was born in Anytown and has lived there all her life. She has a BA in Business Administration and an MBA from The University of Anytown. In addition, she has taken short courses in Group Facilitation and Business Planning from Consultant College. Prior to starting Miracle Consultants, she held jobs as a business planner and a marketing manager for a Fortune 500 Company.

Ms. Miracle has owned Miracle Consultants for six years and has built it to $50,000 in sales. During this time, she had two children, cared for an elderly parent in her home and served as president of a local non-profit agency. This demonstrates her high energy and her ability to deal with multiple high-priority tasks, critical traits for a consultant. She loves the flexibility of working for herself and is partially driven by her desire to forever be her own employer.

Ms. Miracle's husband earns roughly 80% of what they need to support their family. In addition to the remaining 20%, Ms. Miracle must bring in enough money to pay for child care for two children. (Ms. Miracle's brother is now caring for their mother.) Her husband and family are very supportive of the business and help her with child care when necessary.

Miracle Consultants has been at the same sales level for two years. In order to enhance her ability to meet her growth goals, Ms. Miracle has created a Board of Advisors comprised of Larry Katz (extremely successful independent consultant—he'll be a role model), Dave Craney (a consultant with a large consulting firm—he'll know how to put management systems in place), Robert Veneer (owner of an industrial distribution firm—he fits in our target market) and Donna Bradley (accountant—she'll keep us focused on the numbers).

G. APPLICATION AND EXPECTED EFFECT OF LOAN

To date Ms. Miracle has invested $12,000 in the business. We anticipate all future funding to be paid from cash flow or from personal savings. The only exception is an auto loan. We do not expect to have any difficulty obtaining this loan.

H. SUMMARY

Miracle Consultants is a consulting firm that addresses an important need for small but growing businesses: that of creating a vision and putting in place the people and systems needed to reach it. As this need gains increasing recognition and acceptance in the business world, the demand for Miracle's services will continue to grow.

Suzanne Miracle, the owner and sole employee of the business, has been moderately successful in her six years in business. However, she has been held back by her own fears: the fear that she will be unable to juggle the needs of her family with a rapidly growing business and the fear that she might fail. Now that she is finished bearing children *and* after much soul searching, she is determined to do what it takes to make this business grow while still providing love and nurturing to her family. She has set as her goal to increase sales by 30 to 40% annually during the three-year plan period with a corresponding tripling of profits.

Ms. Miracle has had great success with past clients and has received much publicity for her work. She expects this, combined with rigorous follow-through with contacts and referral sources, to propel her sales over the next three years. Furthermore, with only a minimum of additional expenses, she has the capability to take on this additional work, so revenues will largely fall to the bottom line. Thus she believes her goals are achievable.

Ms. Miracle has long considered creating an Advisory Board and has finally started one. She is confident in their ability to support her through this transition in her business.

SECTION TWO: FINANCIAL STATEMENTS

Capital Equipment List

Equipment List	Purchase	
	Date	Cost
Adler Satellite III Typewriter/Printer	May-87	$350
Computer Furniture (2 tables, 2 chairs)	May-87	$850
Four Drawer File Cabinet	Jul-88	$95
Used Office Furniture (desk, credenza,	Aug-90	$1,000
chair, file, bookcase)		
Gateway 2000 25 MHz 386 Computer	Jan-92	$1,990
w/14" 1024NI VGA color monitor and modem		
Brother Fax-400 Fax Machine	May-92	$450
Additional 4 MB RAM	Apr-93	$185
TOTAL HARDWARE AND EQUIP		**$4,920**
Computer Software:		
Microsoft Windows	Jan-92	*
Microsoft DOS	Jan-92	*
Qmodem	Jan-92	*
Wordperfect for Windows	Jan-92	$385
Intuit Quickbooks	Jan-92	$55
Microsoft Excel	Jun-92	**
Polaris PackRat	Feb-93	$105
CompuServe	May-93	$125
* Included with computer		
** Offered for free as a special deal from hardware supplier		
TOTAL SOFTWARE		**$670**
Automobile		
1990 Honda Accord LX	May-91	$15,700
(Note: On average, the car is used 60%		
for business purposes)		
TOTAL CAPITAL EQUIP AND SOFTWARE		**$21,290**

Miracle Consultants Sales Projections by Month, Year One (Likely Case)

		JAN	FEB	MAR	APR	MAY	JUN	JUL	AUG	SEP	OCT	NOV	DEC	TOTAL
1	**CONSULTING FEES - SM**													0
2	Current Client #1	300	1200	300	300	900	300	300	300	900	300	300	300	5700
3	Current Client #2	1000	400	400	400	400	400	400	1000	400	1000	400	400	6600
4	Current Client #3	600	600	600	600	600	600	600	600	600	600	600	600	7200
5	Current Client #4	300	300	300	300	1500	1500	750	300	750	300	300	300	6300
6	**Total Current Clients**	2200	2500	1600	1600	3400	2800	2050	2200	2650	2200	1300	1300	25800
7	New Client #1					2500	2500					1500	1500	8000
8	New Client #2							1000	1000	3000	3000			8000
9	**Total New Clients**	0	0	0	0	2500	2500	1000	1000	3000	3000	1500	1500	16000
10	Project #1		2500	2500										5000
11	Project #2				2500	2500								5000
12	Project #3						2500	2500						5000
13	**Total Projects**	0	2500	2500	2500	2500	2500	2500	0	0	0	0	0	15000
14	**TOTAL FEES - SM**	2200	5000	4100	5900	7800	5550	3200	5150	7700	4600	2800	2800	56800
15														
16	**CONSULTING FEES - ASSOC**													0
17	Associate Contract #1			1000	1000									2000
18	Associate Contract #2					1000	1000							2000
19	Associate Contract #3							1000	1000					2000
20	Associate Contract #4									1000	1000			2000
21	Associate Contract #5													0
22	Associate Contract #6													0
23	**TOTAL FEES - ASSOC**	0	0	1000	1000	1000	1000	1000	1000	1000	1000	0	0	8000
24														
25	**TOTAL SALES**	$2,200	$5,000	$5,100	$6,900	$8,800	$6,550	$4,200	$6,150	$8,700	$5,600	$2,800	$2,800	$64,800

(20)

Miracle Consultants Sales Projections by Quarter, Year Two (Likely Case)

		1ST QTR	2ND QTR	3RD QTR	4TH QTR	TOTAL
1	CONSULTING FEES - SM					
2	Current Client #1	1800	1500	1500	900	5700
3	Current Client #2	1800	1200	2400	1200	6600
4	Current Client #3	1800	1800	1800	1800	7200
5	Current Client #4	1500	3000	750	750	6000
6	Current Client #5	3000	3000	3000	3000	12000
7	Current Client #6	3000	3000	3000	3000	12000
8	Total Current Clients	12900	13500	12450	10650	49500
9	New Client #1	2000	2000	2000	2000	8000
10	New Client #2	2000	2000	2000	2000	8000
11	New Client #3	2000	2000	2000	2000	8000
12	New Client #4	2000	2000	2000	2000	8000
13	Total New Clients	8000	8000	8000	8000	32000
14	New Project #1					0
15	New Project #2					0
16	New Project #3					0
17	New Project #4					0
18	Total New Projects					0
19	TOTAL FEES - SM	20900	21500	20450	18650	81500
20						
21	CONSULTING FEES - ASSOC					
22	Associate Contract #1	1500	1500			3000
23	Associate Contract #2	1500	1500			3000
24	Associate Contract #3		1500	1500		3000
25	Associate Contract #4		1500	1500		3000
26	Associate Contract #5			1500	1500	3000
27	Associate Contract #6			1500	1500	3000
28	TOTAL FEES - ASSOC	3000	6000	6000	3000	18000
29						
30	TOTAL SALES	$23,900	$27,500	$26,450	$21,650	$99,500

(21)

Miracle Consultants Sales Projections by Quarter, Year Three (Likely Case)

#		1ST QTR	2ND QTR	3RD QTR	4TH QTR	TOTAL
1	CONSULTING FEES - SM					
2	Current Client #1	1800	1500	1500	900	5700
3	Current Client #2	1800	1200	2400	1200	6600
4	Current Client #3	1800	1800	1800	1800	7200
5	Current Client #4	1500	3000	750	750	6000
6	Current Client #5	1500	1500	1500	1500	6000
7	Current Client #6	1500	1500	1500	1500	6000
8	Current Client #7	3000	3000	3000	3000	12000
9	Current Client #8	3000	3000	3000	3000	12000
	Current Client #9	3000	3000	3000	3000	12000
	Current Client #10	3000	3000	3000	3000	12000
10	Total Current Clients	21900	22500	21450	19650	85500
11	New Client #1	2000	2000	2000	2000	8000
12	New Client #2	2000	2000	2000	2000	8000
13	New Client #3	2000	2000	2000	2000	8000
14	New Client #4	2000	2000	2000	2000	8000
15	Total New Clients	8000	8000	8000	8000	32000
16	New Project #1					0
17	New Project #2					0
18	New Project #3					0
19	New Project #4					0
20	Total New Projects					0
21	TOTAL FEES - SM	29900	30500	29450	27650	117500
22						
23	CONSULTING FEES - ASSOC					
24	Associate Contract #1	1500	1500			3000
25	Associate Contract #2	1500	1500			3000
26	Associate Contract #3	1500	1500			
27	Associate Contract #4		1500	1500		
28	Associate Contract #5		1500	1500		3000
29	Associate Contract #6		1500	1500		3000
30	Associate Contract #7			1500	1500	3000
31	Associate Contract #8			1500	1500	3000
32	TOTAL FEES - ASSOC	4500	9000	7500	3000	24000
33						
34	TOTAL SALES	$34,400	$39,500	$36,950	$30,650	$141,500

NOTES TO
MIRACLE CONSULTANTS SALES FORECASTS:

CURRENT CLIENTS

Sales estimates are Likely Case scenarios based on historical revenues tempered with our knowledge of the clients' current situations.

NEW CLIENTS

Best Case: Five new clients per year @ $15,000 per year starting Year 1

Worst Case: No new clients until Year 2; then one per year @ $8000

Likely Case: The revenue stream for each new client will be $8000 in Year 1, $12,000 in Year 2 and $6,000 in Year 3. We estimate:

                     Two new clients in Year 1

                     Four new clients in Year 2

                     Four additional clients in Year 3

Our justification for this optimistic scenario is:

- We have four warm prospects right now
- We have three current jobs with non-profit agencies that will provide solid exposure to our target market
- We have been accepted into a training program that will put us squarely in touch with excellent referral sources

PROJECTS

Projects imply short term business. Sales estimates for Year 1 are Likely Case scenarios based on historical experience. For years 2 and 3 we will not accept projects because we intend to fill out time with long term clients.

CONSULTING FEES - ASSOC

We must actively work on this immediately if we are to meet these estimates.

Best Case: Six projects in Year 1 @ $5,000 per project; eight projects in Year 2 @ $7,500 per project; Ten in Year 3 @ $7,500 per project

Worst Case: Doesn't pan out at all

Likely Case: Four projects in Year 1 @ $2,000

                   Six projects in Year 2 @ $3,000

                   Eight projects in Year 3 @ $3,000

Miracle Consultants Pro Forma Income Statement by Month - Year One

	JAN	FEB	MAR	APR	MAY	JUN	JUL	AUG	SEP	OCT	NOV	DEC	TOTAL
SALES													
Consulting Fees - SM	$2,200	$5,000	$4,100	$5,900	$7,800	$5,550	$3,200	$5,150	$7,700	$4,600	$2,800	$2,800	$56,800
Consulting Fees - Assoc	$0	$0	$1,000	$1,000	$1,000	$1,000	$1,000	$1,000	$1,000	$1,000	$0	$0	$8,000
TOTAL SALES	$2,200	$5,000	$5,100	$6,900	$8,800	$6,550	$4,200	$6,150	$8,700	$5,600	$2,800	$2,800	$64,800
COST OF SALES	$0	$0	$800	$800	$800	$800	$800	$800	$800	$800	$0	$0	$6,400
GROSS PROFIT	$2,200	$5,000	$4,300	$6,100	$8,000	$5,750	$3,400	$5,350	$7,900	$4,800	$2,800	$2,800	$58,400
OPERATING EXPENSES													
Advertising/Promotion	$75	$75	$75	$75	$75	$75	$75	$75	$75	$75	$75	$75	$900
Auto Expense	$65	$65	$65	$400	$65	$65	$65	$65	$65	$400	$65	$65	$1,450
Auto Loan	$365	$365	$365	$365	$365	$365	$365	$365	$365	$365	$365	$365	$4,380
Bank/Credit Card Charges	$5	$5	$5	$5	$5	$5	$5	$5	$5	$5	$5	$5	$60
Books/Subscrips/Software	$80	$80	$80	$80	$80	$80	$80	$80	$80	$80	$80	$80	$960
Copies/Postage	$100	$100	$100	$100	$100	$100	$100	$100	$100	$100	$100	$100	$1,200
Dues	$85	$85	$85	$85	$85	$85	$85	$85	$85	$85	$85	$85	$1,020
Education		$1,000				$1,000				$1,000			$3,000
Entertainment	$100	$100	$100	$100	$100	$100	$100	$100	$100	$100	$100	$100	$1,200
Equipment			$800			$600							$1,400
Gifts	$10	$10	$10	$10	$10	$10	$10	$10	$10	$10	$10	$10	$120
Insurance	$15	$15	$15	$15	$15	$15	$15	$15	$15	$15	$15	$15	$180
Legal/Accounting	$350				$250		$350						$950
Miscellaneous	$10	$10	$10	$10	$10	$10	$10	$10	$10	$10	$10	$10	$120
Office Services	$200	$200	$200	$200	$200	$200	$200	$200	$200	$200	$200	$200	$2,400
Rent	$365	$365	$365	$365	$365	$365	$365	$365	$365	$365	$365	$365	$4,380
Supplies	$45	$45	$45	$45	$45	$45	$45	$45	$45	$45	$45	$45	$540
Telephone	$235	$235	$235	$235	$235	$235	$235	$235	$235	$235	$235	$235	$2,820
Travel		$350				$350				$350			$1,050
TOTAL OPERATING EXP	$2,105	$3,105	$2,555	$2,090	$2,005	$3,705	$2,105	$1,755	$1,755	$3,440	$1,755	$1,755	$28,130
PROFIT (LOSS) PRE-TAX	$95	$1,895	$1,745	$4,010	$5,995	$2,045	$1,295	$3,595	$6,145	$1,360	$1,045	$1,045	$30,270
TAXES	$31	$625	$576	$1,323	$1,978	$675	$427	$1,186	$2,028	$449	$345	$345	$9,989
NET PROFIT (LOSS)	$64	$1,270	$1,169	$2,687	$4,017	$1,370	$868	$2,409	$4,117	$911	$700	$700	$20,281

Miracle Consultants Pro Forma Income Statement by Quarter - Year Two

		1ST QTR	2ND QTR	3RD QTR	4TH QTR	TOTAL
1	**SALES**					
2	Consulting Fees - SM	$20,900	$21,500	$20,450	$18,650	$81,500
3	Consulting Fees - Others	$3,000	$6,000	$6,000	$3,000	$18,000
4	**TOTAL SALES**	**$23,900**	**$27,500**	**$26,450**	**$21,650**	**$99,500**
5						
6	**COST OF SALES**	**$2,400**	**$4,800**	**$4,800**	**$2,400**	**$14,400**
7						
8	**GROSS PROFIT**	**$21,500**	**$22,700**	**$21,650**	**$19,250**	**$85,100**
9						
10	**OPERATING EXPENSES**					
11	Advertising/Promotion	$236	$236	$236	$236	$944
12	Auto Expense	$150	$535	$150	$535	$1,370
13	Auto Loan	$1,050	$1,050	$1,050	$1,050	$4,200
14	Bank/Credit Card Charges	$15	$15	$15	$15	$60
15	Books/Subscrips/Software	$252	$252	$252	$252	$1,008
16	Copies/Postage	$300	$300	$300	$300	$1,200
17	Dues	$255	$255	$255	$255	$1,020
18	Education	$1,000	$1,000	$1,000		$3,000
19	Entertainment	$315	$315	$315	$315	$1,260
20	Equipment					$0
21	Gifts	$30	$30	$30	$30	$120
22	Insurance	$48	$48	$48	$48	$192
23	Legal/Accounting	$350	$240	$350		$940
24	Miscellaneous	$60	$60	$60	$60	$240
25	Office Services	$660	$660	$660	$660	$2,640
26	Rent	$1,200	$1,200	$1,200	$1,200	$4,800
27	Supplies	$145	$145	$145	$145	$580
28	Telephone	$705	$705	$705	$705	$2,820
29	Travel	$350	$350	$350		$1,050
30	**TOTAL OPERATING EXP**	**$7,121**	**$7,396**	**$7,121**	**$5,806**	**$27,444**
31						
32	**PROFIT (LOSS) PRE-TAX**	**$14,379**	**$15,304**	**$14,529**	**$13,444**	**$57,656**
33						
34	**TAXES**	$4,745	$5,050	$4,795	$4,437	$19,026
35						
36	**NET PROFIT (LOSS)**	**$9,634**	**$10,254**	**$9,734**	**$9,007**	**$38,630**

(25)

Miracle Consultants Pro Forma Income Statement
by Quarter - Year Three

		1ST QTR	2ND QTR	3RD QTR	4TH QTR	TOTAL
1	**SALES**					
2	Consulting Fees - SM	$29,900	$30,500	$29,450	$27,650	**$117,500**
3	Consulting Fees - Others	$4,500	$9,000	$7,500	$3,000	**$24,000**
4	**TOTAL SALES**	**$34,400**	**$39,500**	**$36,950**	**$30,650**	**$141,500**
5						
6	**COST OF SALES**	**$3,600**	**$7,200**	**$6,000**	**$2,400**	**$19,200**
7						
8	**GROSS PROFIT**	**$30,800**	**$32,300**	**$30,950**	**$28,250**	**$122,300**
9						
10	**OPERATING EXPENSES**					
11	Advertising/Promotion	$248	$248	$248	$248	**$992**
12	Auto Expense	$150	$535	$150	$535	**$1,370**
13	Auto Loan	$1,050	$1,050	$1,050	$1,050	**$4,200**
14	Bank/Credit Card Charges	$15	$15	$15	$15	**$60**
15	Books/Subscrips/Software	$265	$265	$265	$265	**$1,060**
16	Copies/Postage	$315	$315	$315	$315	**$1,260**
17	Dues	$270	$270	$270	$270	**$1,080**
18	Education	$1,000	$1,000	$1,000		**$3,000**
19	Entertainment	$330	$330	$330	$330	**$1,320**
20	Equipment					**$0**
21	Gifts	$30	$30	$30	$30	**$120**
22	Insurance	$50	$50	$50	$50	**$200**
23	Legal/Accounting	$350	$240	$350		**$940**
24	Miscellaneous	$120	$120	$120	$120	**$480**
25	Office Services	$800	$800	$800	$800	**$3,200**
26	Rent	$1,200	$1,200	$1,200	$1,200	**$4,800**
27	Supplies	$155	$155	$155	$155	**$620**
28	Telephone	$740	$740	$740	$740	**$2,960**
29	Travel	$385	$385	$385		**$1,155**
30	**TOTAL OPERATING EXP**	**$7,473**	**$7,748**	**$7,473**	**$6,123**	**$28,817**
31						
32	**PROFIT (LOSS) PRE-TAX**	**$23,327**	**$24,552**	**$23,477**	**$22,127**	**$93,483**
33						
34	**TAXES**	$7,698	$8,102	$7,747	$7,302	$30,849
35						
36	**NET PROFIT (LOSS)**	**$15,629**	**$16,450**	**$15,730**	**$14,825**	**$62,634**

Miracle Consultants Pro Forma Income Statement
Three Year Summary

		YEAR ONE	YEAR TWO	YEAR THREE
1	SALES			
2	Consulting Fees - SM	$56,800	$81,500	$117,500
3	Consulting Fees - Assoc	$8,000	$18,000	$24,000
4	TOTAL SALES	$64,800	$99,500	$141,500
5				
6	COST OF SALES	$6,400	$14,400	$19,200
7				
8	GROSS PROFIT	$58,400	$85,100	$122,300
9				
10	OPERATING EXPENSES			
11	Advertising/Promotion	$900	$944	$992
12	Auto Expense	$1,450	$1,370	$1,370
13	Auto Loan	$4,380	$4,200	$4,200
14	Bank/Credit Card Charges	$60	$60	$60
15	Books/Subscrips/Software	$960	$1,008	$1,060
16	Copies/Postage	$1,200	$1,200	$1,260
17	Dues	$1,020	$1,020	$1,080
18	Education	$3,000	$3,000	$3,000
19	Entertainment	$1,200	$1,260	$1,320
20	Equipment	$1,400	$0	$0
21	Gifts	$120	$120	$120
22	Insurance	$180	$192	$200
23	Legal/Accounting	$950	$940	$940
24	Miscellaneous	$120	$240	$480
25	Office Services	$2,400	$2,640	$3,200
26	Rent	$4,380	$4,800	$4,800
27	Supplies	$540	$580	$620
28	Telephone	$2,820	$2,820	$2,960
29	Travel	$1,050	$1,050	$1,155
30	TOTAL OPERATING EXP	$28,130	$27,444	$28,817
31				
32	PROFIT (LOSS) PRE-TAX	$30,270	$57,656	$93,483
33				
34	TAXES	$9,989	$19,026	$30,849
35				
36	NET PROFIT (LOSS)	$20,281	$38,630	$62,634

NOTES TO MIRACLE CONSULTANTS
PRO FORMA INCOME STATEMENT

Lines 2,3   Taken from Sales Forecasts

Line 6   Cost of Sales represents the payment to the associates (i.e., other consultants) who actually do the work. We assume we can set up an agreement with our associates whereby we pay them 80% of the cost of their services and we retain 20%. Therefore, the Cost of Sales is 80% of Consulting Fees - Assoc. There are no Cost of Sales associated with our own consulting.

Line 11   Advertising/Promotion consists primarily of stationery and brochures and occasional hiring of a public relations consultant. Historically $50 per month, we will increase it by 50% to promote associates.

Line 12   Auto expense includes gas, maintenance and car repairs. Historically $65/mo (includes gas), except Apr and Oct, when car insurance is due.

Line 13   Auto loan is $365/mo. It will be paid off at the end of Year 1. At the start of Year 2 we will purchase another car and intend to put no money down. Since interest rates are down, we expect we can hold our car payments even. If necessary, we will finance over a longer time span to keep payments down.

Line 14   Since we pay off our credit card on a monthly basis, this includes only the annual credit card fee, cost of checks and cost of a local bank card.

Line 15   Information is our business, and we read many books and magazines to keep up with what's going on in the business world. Also, we anticipate the need to upgrade some of our software during the plan period to keep up with technology. $80/month is our historical average; we increased it by 5% in Years 2 and 3.

Line 16   We stay in touch with our clients and prospects through mailing of letters and magazine articles, so this is an important expense for us. Copies are made at a central office copier in our office building: it's expensive but it saves precious time because it has an automatic feeder and the office building secretary can make the copies. Historically this has run $55 per month. We intend to increase it dramatically as we follow through rigorously on our contacts. We show a 5% increase in Year 3 for expected increases in copying costs and stamps.

Line 17   We belong to numerous organizations as one way of networking (a cornerstone of our marketing plan). In the past, we have averaged $35 per month on dues; we plan to join two new organizations that each cost roughly $300 per year. Also, we allowed for modest inflation in Year 3.

Line 18   We intend to attend three seminars per year at $1,000 per seminar to improve our consulting skills.

(28)

Line 19   It is difficult to pay for entertainment because men (clients, prospects, networkers) want to pay for Ms. Miracle. However, we intend to do a better job of picking up the tab to avoid looking as if we have to be taken care of.

Line 20   In Year 1, we intend to buy the following:

- Bookcase $150
  (We're out of space)

- Table/4 Chairs $650
  (Ours are used and quite grungy)

- Tape Backup $295
  (We're terrible at remembering to back up our disk, and we're afraid we could lose everything)

- 120 Mb Hard Drive $200
  (It doesn't take long to run out of disk space)

Since the equipment expenses are so small, we will expense them all in the year they are incurred and will not incur depreciation. We do not anticipate additional equipment expenses in Years 2 and 3.

Line 21   We occasionally buy gifts for our clients if something seems appropriate and generally give them something around Christmas. This is an historical average.

Line 22   We carry office insurance on the contents of our office; it typically increases 5% per year. As we grow, we will consider Errors and Omissions Insurance. We'd like to carry it now, but it's simply too expensive.

Line 23   We meet with our attorney twice a year to review our business and get her perspective. We have an accountant prepare our tax returns. She also serves on our Advisory Board, but does not charge for this service.

Line 24   The miscellaneous category is included in case we've forgotten something. We doubled it each year to reflect the unknown.

Line 25   Office Services includes clerical and telephone answering support from the centrally located secretary in the office building. Historically, we have spent an average of $150 per month. We expect to utilize her services more frequently to free us up to work with clients.

Line 26   We intend to stay in this office building during the plan period. We are on a month-to-month lease; typically rent is increased 10% every other year. We will begin to look for new space, however, as the landlord seems interested in selling the building.

Line 27   Office supplies include paper, pens, markers, flip chart paper, etc. We average $45 per year, which we increased by 5% in Years 2 and 3.

Line 28   We have two telephone lines to accommodate telephone conversations, our fax and our modem. We will continue to operate with two lines during the plan period. In addition, Ms. Miracle has a carphone to increase the availability of billable time while in the office. The figures in the income statement are based on historical data and increased by 5% in Year 3.

Line 29   Our only traveling expense is for seminar attendance. We've assumed five days at $75 per day, with a 5% increase for inflation in Year 3.

Line 30   This is the sum of all Operating Expenses (Lines 11 through 28). Although the auto loan and equipment costs could be considered non-operating expenses, we have a simple business and separating them out would needlessly complicate this Income Statement. Also, note that Ms. Miracle's personal draw is not included under operating expenses. According to tax law, personal draw is not considered an expense of the business since Miracle Consultants is a sole proprietorship. Of course, it is a very real need for Suzanne Miracle.

Line 32   The difference between Gross Profit (8) and Operating Expenses (30). We realize that while sales are increasing rapidly, profit is not keeping pace. This is because for each sales dollar of Consulting Fees - Associates, we only gain $0.20 of gross profit. The value here is that we get paid for marketing while someone else does the work. This increases our potential sales beyond what Ms. Miracle can accomplish herself, and, if the concept proves viable, will enable us to build a much larger business, perhaps even a saleable asset.

As we look at the dramatic increase in both sales and profit from year to year, we realize that the numbers look quite optimistic. As stated in the text, this points to our strong need to rigorously follow through on our marketing plan. We will continually monitor both sales and profits so we can cut back on expenses if necessary. In addition, we will utilize our Advisory Board to assist us in setting up internal systems to be able to handle the large number of clients projected in Year 3.

(NOTE: Miracle Consultants shows reasonable profits for all three years of the plan period. This was not the case during the start-up years.)

Line 34   Based on prior history, Ms. Miracle anticipates paying 33% of her pre-tax profit in taxes, including Federal Tax (13%), State Tax (4%), Local Tax (2%), and Self-Employment Tax (14%). (Note that sole proprietors must pay this hefty tax.)

Line 36   Pre-tax profit (32) minus taxes (34).

(30)

Miracle Consultants Pro Forma Cash Flow Statement by Month - Year One

#		JAN	FEB	MAR	APR	MAY	JUN	JUL	AUG	SEP	OCT	NOV	DEC	TOTAL
1	**CASH FROM SALES**													
2	Cash From Up Front Fees	$330	$750	$765	$1,035	$1,320	$983	$630	$923	$1,305	$840	$420	$420	$9,721
3	Cash From Receivables	$2,430	$1,870	$3,580	$4,065	$5,250	$6,755	$5,578	$3,713	$4,628	$6,578	$4,945	$2,660	$52,052
4	**TOTAL**	$2,760	$2,620	$4,345	$5,100	$6,570	$7,738	$6,208	$4,636	$5,933	$7,418	$5,365	$3,080	$61,773
5														
6	**CASH FROM FUNDING SOURCES**													
7	Cash From Owners													$0
8	Cash From Loans													$0
9	**TOTAL**	$0	$0	$0	$0	$0	$0	$0	$0	$0	$0	$0	$0	$0
10														
11	**TOTAL CASH INFLOW**	$2,760	$2,620	$4,345	$5,100	$6,570	$7,738	$6,208	$4,636	$5,933	$7,418	$5,365	$3,080	$61,773
12	**EXPANSION EXPENSES**													
13	Capital Equipment				$800			$600						$1,400
14														
15	**OPERATING EXPENSES**													
16	Advertising/Promotion			$600					$300					$900
17	Auto Expense	$65	$65	$65	$400	$65	$65	$65	$65	$65	$400	$65	$65	$1,450
18	Bank/Credit Card Charges			$30				$30						$60
19	Books/Subscrips/Software	$45	$145	$45	$115	$45	$45	$295	$45	$45	$45	$45	$45	$960
20	Copies/Postage	$100	$100	$100	$100	$100	$100	$100	$100	$100	$100	$100	$100	$1,200
21	Dues		$135		$135			$600			$150			$1,020
22	Education				$1,000				$1,000				$1,000	$3,000
23	Entertainment	$100	$100	$100	$100	$100	$100	$100	$100	$100	$100	$100	$100	$1,200
24	Gifts		$120											$120
25	Insurance	$15	$15	$15	$15	$15	$15	$15	$15	$15	$15	$15	$15	$180
26	Legal/Accounting	$350				$250		$350						$950
27	Miscellaneous	$10	$10	$10	$10	$10	$10	$10	$10	$10	$10	$10	$10	$120
28	Office Services	$200	$200	$200	$200	$200	$200	$200	$200	$200	$200	$200	$200	$2,400
29	Rent	$365	$365	$365	$365	$365	$365	$365	$365	$365	$365	$365	$365	$4,380
30	Subcontract Services				$800	$800	$800	$800	$800	$800	$800	$800		$6,400
31	Supplies	$45	$45	$45	$45	$45	$45	$45	$45	$45	$45	$45	$45	$540
32	Telephone	$235	$235	$235	$235	$235	$235	$235	$235	$235	$235	$235	$235	$2,820
33	Travel				$350				$350				$350	$1,050
34	**TOTAL**	$1,530	$1,535	$1,810	$3,870	$2,230	$1,980	$3,180	$3,660	$1,980	$2,465	$1,980	$2,530	$28,750
35														
36	**LOANS**													
37	Principal Plus Interest Payment	$365	$365	$365	$365	$365	$365	$365	$365	$365	$365	$365	$365	$4,380
38	**TAXES**	$1,200			$4,000			$1,816			$1,816			$8,832
39														
40	**TOTAL CASH OUTFLOW**	$3,095	$1,900	$2,175	$9,035	$2,595	$2,345	$5,961	$4,025	$2,345	$4,646	$2,345	$2,895	$43,362
41	**NET CASH FLOW**	($335)	$720	$2,170	($3,935)	$3,975	$5,393	$247	$611	$3,588	$2,772	$3,020	$185	$18,411
42	**CUMULATIVE CASH FLOW**	($335)	$385	$2,555	($1,380)	$2,595	$7,988	$8,235	$8,846	$12,434	$15,206	$18,226	$18,411	$36,822
43	**OPENING BALANCE**	$1,500	$1,165	$1,885	$4,055	$120	$4,095	$9,488	$9,735	$10,346	$13,934	$16,706	$19,726	
44	Plus Cash Inflow	$2,760	$2,620	$4,345	$5,100	$6,570	$7,738	$6,208	$4,636	$5,933	$7,418	$5,365	$3,080	
45	Minus Cash Outflow	$3,095	$1,900	$2,175	$9,035	$2,595	$2,345	$5,961	$4,025	$2,345	$4,646	$2,345	$2,895	
46	**CLOSING BALANCE**	$1,165	$1,885	$4,055	$120	$4,095	$9,488	$9,735	$10,346	$13,934	$16,706	$19,726	$19,911	

Miracle Consultants Pro Forma Cash Flow Statement
by Quarter - Year Two

		1ST QTR	2ND QTR	3RD QTR	4TH QTR	TOTAL
1	**CASH FROM SALES**					
2	Cash From Up Front Fees	$3,585	$4,125	$3,968	$3,248	$14,925
3	Cash From Receivables	$14,890	$22,115	$22,850	$20,083	$79,938
4	**TOTAL**	**$18,475**	**$26,240**	**$26,818**	**$23,330**	**$94,863**
5						
6	**CASH FROM FUNDING SOURCES**					$0
7	Cash From Owners					$0
8	Cash From Loans					$0
9	**TOTAL**	**$0**	**$0**	**$0**	**$0**	$0
10						
11	**TOTAL CASH INFLOW**	**$18,475**	**$26,240**	**$26,818**	**$23,330**	**$94,863**
12	**EXPANSION EXPENSES**					
13	Capital Equipment					$0
14						
15	**OPERATING EXPENSES**					
16	Advertising/Promotion	$630		$314		$944
17	Auto Expense	$150	$535	$150	$535	$1,370
18	Bank/Credit Card Charges	$30		$30		$60
19	Books/Subscrips/Software	$245	$215	$400	$148	$1,008
20	Copies/Postage	$300	$300	$300	$300	$1,200
21	Dues	$135	$135	$600	$150	$1,020
22	Education		$1,000	$1,000	$1,000	$3,000
23	Entertainment	$315	$315	$315	$315	$1,260
24	Gifts	$120				$120
25	Insurance	$48	$48	$48	$48	$192
26	Legal/Accounting	$350	$240	$350		$940
27	Miscellaneous	$60	$60	$60	$60	$240
28	Office Services	$660	$660	$660	$660	$2,640
29	Rent	$1,200	$1,200	$1,200	$1,200	$4,800
30	Subcontract Services	$1,600	$4,000	$4,800	$3,200	$13,600
31	Supplies	$145	$145	$145	$145	$580
32	Telephone	$705	$705	$705	$705	$2,820
33	Travel		$350	$350	$350	$1,050
34	**TOTAL**	**$6,693**	**$9,908**	**$11,427**	**$8,816**	**$36,844**
35						
36	**LOANS**					
37	Principal Plus Interest Payment	$1,050	$1,050	$1,050	$1,050	$4,200
38	**TAXES**	$1,816	$6,054	$3,459	$3,459	$14,788
39						
40	**TOTAL CASH OUTFLOW**	**$9,559**	**$17,012**	**$15,936**	**$13,325**	**$55,832**
41	**NET CASH FLOW**	$8,916	$9,228	$10,882	$10,005	$39,031
42	**CUMULATIVE CASH FLOW**	$8,916	$18,144	$29,026	$39,031	$95,116
43	**OPENING BALANCE**	**$19,908**	**$28,824**	**$38,052**	**$48,934**	
44	Plus Cash Inflow	$18,475	$26,240	$26,818	$23,330	
45	Minus Cash Inflow	$9,559	$17,012	$15,936	$13,325	
46	**CLOSING BALANCE**	$28,824	$38,052	$48,934	$58,939	

(32)

Miracle Consultants Pro Forma Cash Flow Statement by Quarter - Year Three

		1ST QTR	2ND QTR	3RD QTR	4TH QTR	TOTAL
1	**CASH FROM SALES**					
2	Cash From Up Front Fees	$5,160	$5,925	$5,543	$4,598	$21,225
3	Cash From Receivables	$24,778	$31,790	$32,300	$28,258	$117,125
4	**TOTAL**	**$29,938**	**$37,715**	**$37,843**	**$32,855**	**$138,350**
5						
6	**CASH FROM FUNDING SOURCES**					$0
7	Cash From Owners					$0
8	Cash From Loans					$0
9	**TOTAL**	**$0**	**$0**	**$0**	**$0**	$0
10						
11	**TOTAL CASH INFLOW**	**$29,938**	**$37,715**	**$37,843**	**$32,855**	$138,350
12	**EXPANSION EXPENSES**					
13	Capital Equipment					$0
14						
15	**OPERATING EXPENSES**					
16	Advertising/Promotion	$662		$330		$992
17	Auto Expense	$150	$535	$150	$535	$1,370
18	Bank/Credit Card Charges	$30		$30		$60
19	Books/Subscrips/Software	$260	$225	$425	$150	$1,060
20	Copies/Postage	$315	$315	$315	$315	$1,260
21	Dues	$140	$140	$630	$170	$1,080
22	Education		$1,000	$1,000	$1,000	$3,000
23	Entertainment	$330	$330	$330	$330	$1,320
24	Gifts	$120				$120
25	Insurance	$50	$50	$50	$50	$200
26	Legal/Accounting	$350	$240	$350		$940
27	Miscellaneous	$120	$120	$120	$120	$480
28	Office Services	$800	$800	$800	$800	$3,200
29	Rent	$1,200	$1,200	$1,200	$1,200	$4,800
30	Subcontract Services	$3,200	$6,000	$6,400	$3,600	$19,200
31	Supplies	$155	$155	$155	$155	$620
32	Telephone	$740	$740	$740	$740	$2,960
33	Travel		$385	$385	$385	$1,155
34	**TOTAL**	**$8,622**	**$12,235**	**$13,410**	**$9,550**	**$43,817**
35						
36	**LOANS**					
37	Principal Plus Interest Payment	$1,050	$1,050	$1,050	$1,050	$4,200
38	**TAXES**	$3,459	$11,531	$5,609	$5,609	$26,208
39						
40	**TOTAL CASH OUTFLOW**	**$13,131**	**$24,816**	**$20,069**	**$16,209**	$74,225
41	**NET CASH FLOW**	$16,807	$12,899	$17,774	$16,646	$64,125
42	**CUMULATIVE CASH FLOW**	$16,807	$29,706	$47,479	$64,125	$158,116
43	**OPENING BALANCE**	**$58,939**	**$75,745**	**$88,644**	**$106,418**	
44	Plus Cash Inflow	$29,938	$37,715	$37,843	$32,855	
45	Minus Cash Inflow	$13,131	$24,816	$20,069	$16,209	
46	**CLOSING BALANCE**	$75,745	$88,644	$106,418	$123,064	

NOTES TO MIRACLE CONSULTANTS
PRO FORMA CASH FLOW STATEMENTS

Lines 2, 3   When possible we collect a percent of our fee prior to the work being performed. More typically we invoice our clients at the start of the month following performance of the work. Most clients pay within that month. However, some wait a month or more before paying their bill, despite our stated 20-day terms. For these calculations, we assumed that 15% of fees are paid up front, 65% are paid the month following performance of the work and 20% are paid one month after that. These assumptions are loosely—and very conservatively—taken from historical data. The same assumptions were made regardless of whether the work will be performed by Ms. Miracle or an associate.

Sample calculation (for March):

Cash from Up-Front Fees = .15 x $5,100 (Total Sales for March)
= $765

Cash from Receivables = .65 x $5,000 (Total Sales for Feb)
+ .15 x $2,200 (Total Sales for Jan)
= $3,580

Total Cash From Sales in March = $765 + $3,580 = $4,345

In order to calculate Cash From Sales in January and February, the following data was gathered from the *prior year*:

Nov. Sales = $5,000   Dec. Sales = $2,200

Lines 7, 8   Ms. Miracle does not intend to borrow money for the business; she expects it to be self supporting. Therefore these line items are left blank.

Line 13   Although Miracle Consultants' Capital Equipment purchases happen to be small enough to be expensed in the year they are incurred, they are included in this section of the Cash Flow Statement for illustrative purposes. Capital Expenses are listed in the Income Statement as "Equipment," an Operating Expense. Since Ms. Miracle typically pays with a credit card, the cash outflow is delayed to the month following when the expense was incurred.

Line 16   Of the total $900 expenditure in Year 1, we anticipate spending $600 in the first quarter for a new brochure and $300 in the third quarter for a reprint of our stationery.

Line 17   These expenses are paid in the same month as recorded on the Income Statement.

Line 18   We anticipate buying checks in March; our VISA card comes due in July and we pay the bill in August.

Line 19   We estimate that we will buy one computer program in January ($100) and one in June ($250); we will pay by credit card and checks

(34)

will be written on succeeding months. Subscription for a $70 newsletter comes due in April. The rest of the expenses can be assumed to be spread evenly over the year.

Line 20 Copies/Postage can be assumed to be spread evenly over the year.

Line 21 Organization A: $135 payable in February
Organization B: $135 payable in April
Organization C: $300 payable in July
Organization D: $300 payable in July
Organization E: $150 payable in October

Line 22 Education expenses are paid by credit card. The educational institutions are terrible at submitting data, so we typically write out the check two months following the seminar.

Line 23 Entertainment expenses are spread evenly over the year.

Line 24 Most gifts are for Christmas. They show up on the January VISA bill, which is paid in February.

Line 25 Insurance is paid monthly.

Line 26 The timing of the payment for these services is as shown on the Income Statement.

Lines 27-9 The expenses are spread evenly across the year.

Line 30 This line item represents the fees paid to our associates. We anticipate having to pay them in the month following performance of the work, even though we may not get paid the full amount of their work until after that time. This line item is the same as the Cost of Sales on the Income Statement, but shifted by one month.

Lines 31-2 These expenses are spread evenly across the year.

Line 33 Travel is paid for by credit card and is typically paid two months following the incurring of the expense.

Line 34 The total of the Operating Expenses (Lines 16 through 33).

Line 37 From the Auto Loan line item on the Income Statement. This could have been included in the Operating Expenses on the Cash Flow Statement since it is a simple expense. It was put here to illustrate how you might handle a more complex loan.

Line 38 State and local taxes (6%) are paid quarterly in Jan, Apr, Jul, and Oct. Federal taxes are paid by Ms. Miracle's husband as a withholding from his wages, so it is not a cash expense for Miracle Consultants. Self-employment tax is paid in April. Note that the January and April tax figures are calculated as a percentage of Miracle Consultants' prior year pre-tax income of $20,000. The July and October figures are a percentage of this year's estimated income of $30,270. This is different from the income statement, which shows taxes as if they were incurred in the current month. A similar calculation is performed for Years 2 and 3.

Line 40   Capital Equipment Expenses (13) plus Operating Expenses (34) plus Loan Payment (37) plus Tax Payments (38).

Line 41   Total Cash Inflow minus Total Cash Outflow. Note that cash flow is negative in January and April, i.e., we pay out more cash than we take in, and it is very low in February, July, August and December. Our December through February cash flow is typically low because of slow sales in November through January (people are either preparing for or recovering from the holidays and our cash crunch is delayed by a month due to our billing cycle. April and July are difficult because taxes must be paid. August is tight because we have a seminar scheduled.

Note that these figures do not include Ms. Miracle's personal draw from the business. For impact, see Line 46 below.

Line 42   Net Cash Flow (41) this month plus Cumulative Cash Flow (42) last month. This represents the ongoing cash flow in the business. It is negative in January and April and quite low in February, indicating a potential cash problem.

Line 43   The January figure of $1,500 is Ms. Miracle's estimate of what will be in her checking account at the start of January. Beginning in Feb, the current month's Opening Balance (43) equals the prior month's Closing Balance (46).

Line 44   Cash inflow from all sources; same as Line 11.

Line 45   Total cash outflow; same as Line 40.

Line 46   Opening Balance (43) plus Cash Inflow (44) minus Cash Outflow (45). This represents an estimate of Miracle Consultants' checking account balance. It is consistently positive, despite negative cumulative cash flow in January and April, because Ms. Miracle assumes she will start the year with $1500 in her checking account. Also, *note that these figures do not include Ms. Miracle's personal draw. Clearly, she will have to draw from savings to meet her personal expenses in January and April, and probably in February as well. Furthermore, the large closing balances in May through December are highly dependent on meeting very ambitious sales projections. She will have to carefully monitor her situation as the year progresses and, if necessary, rethink her current strategy and tactics in order to assure sufficient income to meet her personal needs.*

On the following page is Ms. Miracle's cash flow projection *including $2000 per month of Owner's Draw.* Her checking account is now consistently negative. She will have to invest almost $8000 in the business (the largest negative number in her checking account - incurred in April) over the first four months of the year in order to be able to pay her bills. In other words, she will *not* be able to draw a salary. Ms. Miracle has sufficient savings to be able to live without drawing a salary, but her savings will run out in Year 1 if she continues to operate at a deficit.

Miracle Consultants Pro Forma Cash Flow Statement (with Owner's Draw) - Year One

#		JAN	FEB	MAR	APR	MAY	JUN	JUL	AUG	SEP	OCT	NOV	DEC	TOTAL
1	**CASH FROM SALES**													
2	Cash From Up Front Fees	$330	$750	$765	$1,035	$1,320	$983	$630	$923	$1,305	$840	$420	$420	$9,721
3	Cash From Receivables	$2,430	$1,870	$3,580	$4,065	$5,250	$6,755	$5,578	$3,713	$4,628	$6,578	$4,945	$2,660	$52,052
4	TOTAL	$2,760	$2,620	$4,345	$5,100	$6,570	$7,738	$6,208	$4,636	$5,933	$7,418	$5,365	$3,080	$61,773
5														
6	**CASH FROM FUNDING SOURCES**													
7	Cash From Owners													$0
8	Cash From Loans													$0
9														$0
10	TOTAL	$0	$0	$0	$0	$0	$0	$0	$0	$0	$0	$0	$0	$0
11	**TOTAL CASH INFLOW**	$2,760	$2,620	$4,345	$5,100	$6,570	$7,738	$6,208	$4,636	$5,933	$7,418	$5,365	$3,080	$61,773
12	**EXPANSION EXPENSES**													
13	Capital Equipment				$800			$600						$1,400
14														
15	**OPERATING EXPENSES**													
16	Advertising/Promotion			$600					$300					$900
17	Auto Expense	$65	$65	$65	$400	$65	$65	$65	$65	$65	$400	$65	$65	$1,450
18	Bank/Credit Card Charges			$30					$30					$60
19	Books/Subscrips/Software	$45	$145	$45		$160	$45	$295	$45	$45	$45	$45	$45	$960
20	Copies/Postage	$100	$100	$100	$100	$100	$100	$100	$100	$100	$100	$100	$100	$1,200
21	Dues		$135			$135		$600			$150			$1,020
22	Education				$1,000				$1,000				$1,000	$3,000
23	Entertainment	$100	$100	$100	$100	$100	$100	$100	$100	$100	$100	$100	$100	$1,200
24	Gifts		$120											$120
25	Insurance	$15	$15	$15	$15	$15	$15	$15	$15	$15	$15	$15	$15	$180
26	Legal/Accounting	$350			$250			$350						$950
27	Miscellaneous	$10	$10	$10	$10	$10	$10	$10	$10	$10	$10	$10	$10	$120
28	Office Services	$200	$200	$200	$200	$200	$200	$200	$200	$200	$200	$200	$200	$2,400
29	Rent	$365	$365	$365	$365	$365	$365	$365	$365	$365	$365	$365	$365	$4,380
30	Subcontract Services				$800	$800	$800	$800	$800	$800	$800	$800		$6,400
31	Supplies	$45	$45	$45	$45	$45	$45	$45	$45	$45	$45	$45	$45	$540
32	Telephone	$235	$235	$235	$235	$235	$235	$235	$235	$235	$235	$235	$235	$2,820
33	Travel				$350				$350				$350	$1,050
34	TOTAL	$1,530	$1,535	$1,810	$3,870	$2,230	$1,980	$3,180	$3,660	$1,980	$2,465	$1,980	$2,530	$28,750
35														
36	**LOANS**													
37	Principal Plus Interest Payment	$365	$365	$365	$365	$365	$365	$365	$365	$365	$365	$365	$365	$4,380
38	**TAXES**	$1,200			$4,000			$1,816			$1,816			$8,832
39														
40	**OWNER'S DRAW**	$2,000	$2,000	$2,000	$2,000	$2,000	$2,000	$2,000	$2,000	$2,000	$2,000	$2,000	$2,000	$24,000
41														
42	**TOTAL CASH OUTFLOW**	$5,095	$3,900	$4,175	$11,035	$4,595	$4,345	$7,961	$6,025	$4,345	$6,646	$4,345	$4,895	$67,362
43	**NET CASH FLOW**	($2,335)	($1,280)	$170	($5,935)	$1,975	$3,393	($1,753)	($1,389)	$1,588	$772	$1,020	($1,815)	($5,589)
44	**CUMULATIVE CASH FLOW**	($2,335)	($3,615)	($3,445)	($9,380)	($7,405)	($4,012)	($5,765)	($7,154)	($5,566)	($4,794)	($3,774)	($5,589)	($11,178)
45	**OPENING BALANCE**	$1,500	($835)	($2,115)	($1,945)	($7,880)	($5,905)	($2,512)	($4,265)	($5,654)	($4,066)	($3,294)	($2,274)	$1,500
46	Plus Cash Inflow	$2,760	$2,620	$4,345	$5,100	$6,570	$7,738	$6,208	$4,636	$5,933	$7,418	$5,365	$3,080	$61,773
47	Minus Cash Outflow	$5,095	$3,900	$4,175	$11,035	$4,595	$4,345	$7,961	$6,025	$4,345	$6,646	$4,345	$4,895	$67,362
48	**CLOSING BALANCE**	($835)	($2,115)	($1,945)	($7,880)	($5,905)	($2,512)	($4,265)	($5,654)	($4,066)	($3,294)	($2,274)	($4,089)	($4,089)

FINANCING PROPOSAL

FOR

PEABODY'S—*Toys That Teach, Inc.*

To be Submitted to
Third National Bank and Trust Co.
August 15, 19—

President: Jennifer Michaels

Address: 1000 Main St.
             Anytown, USA 12345

Phone: (101) 555-5678

OUR MISSION

PEABODY'S develops, manufactures and markets high quality products for children that are enjoyable for the child, that have educational benefits for the child, and are a good value for the purchaser.

(Please see the notes about this plan on page 201.)

STATEMENT OF PURPOSE

PEABODY'S seeks loans totaling $50,000 in order to finance our current rapid growth. We will use this money to hire a sales manager and an administrator, develop and inventory three new products, attend three trade shows, reprint our catalog, and re-instate Ms. Michaels' $30,000 per year salary (which was reduced to $15,000 last year).

This sum is requested to add to prior investment and loans by Ms. Michaels, her family, and outside investors, totalling $88,000.[1]

[1] Ms. Michaels' loan was granted once the bank obtained a guarantee from the SBA. This loan was in addition to the investment stated above as well as a prior home equity loan and line of credit.

TABLE OF CONTENTS

Section One: The Business

Section Two: Financial Data

Financial documents are not provided in this book to protect PEABODY'S investors. You would of course provide them in a plan sent to a prospective lender.

SECTION ONE: THE BUSINESS

A. DESCRIPTION OF BUSINESS

PEABODY'S develops, manufactures, and markets high quality products for children that are enjoyable for the child, have educational benefits for the child, and are a good value for the purchaser.

Our product lines include more than fifty different "Card Kits", each of which contains everything children need to make their own greeting cards, collector cards, or postcards. A Card Kit typically consists of a variety of ready-to-color line drawings on white stock, colored pencils, a pencil sharpener, and stickers. In addition to our standard lines of cards, we also customize cards to tourist attractions. (For example, our largest retail account is Kennedy Space Center.)

PEABODY'S was founded six years ago by Jennifer Michaels, a mother of three young children, whose personal experiences helped her to identify PEABODY's product opportunities. In our first six years, we have grown from a privately financed sole proprietorship to a corporation with five investors and an outside board of directors. During this time, our sales have increased from $10,000 in Year 1 to more than $175,000 last year.

We believe strongly in market research. We hold focus groups, test market our product ideas, and gather data from the field about what is and is not selling. This has enabled us to modify products as necessary to increase sales. In addition, we make it a policy to maintain high product quality so that the parents who purchase our products for their children feel they are getting value for their money.

Our other distinctive competencies include our ability to respond quickly to new product opportunities (thus, we can profitably serve smaller niche markets) and our policy of hiring retirees and moms with school age children (this minimizes our overhead and leaves much room for growth).

B. PRODUCT DESCRIPTION

Products currently in production and being distributed nationwide include:

KARD KIT™ GREETING CARDS

Description: KARD KITS contain everything children need to make their own greeting cards. Packed in a self-contained plastic travel case, each kit contains six cards with outline drawings to color, six mailable envelopes, six coordinated stickers for decorating, six colored pencils and a pencil sharpener. We have seven products for general distribution (see catalog) as well as three private label KARD KITS: Our Clown Birthday KARD KIT for Ringling Bros. and Barnum & Bailey retail stores and museum, and two special versions for First Foto.

Background: Ms. Michaels noticed that her children and their friends enjoyed making things and giving their creations to friends and family. At birthdays and holidays they spent a great deal of time creating that "special card." The only one who dreaded these artistic sessions was Mom, who would hear: "Mom, where are the scissors?" "Mom, what should I draw?" "Mom, I'm done. Do you have an envelope?" One day the thought came to her that it would be nice to have everything in one place for children to make their own cards. Maybe some kind of a kit . . . thus, the KARD KIT was born.

Parameters: All KARD KITs meet the following parameters:

1. We include drawings for the child to color. We recognize the different skill levels of children by having pictures with varying degrees of detail. We include plenty of open spaces for children to add their own words and decorations.

2. We include colored pencils. Children enjoy them much more than crayons and the finished products are nicer. Also, colored pencils are not as subject to breakage in shipping as crayons, and they are not as sensitive to temperatures in storage. Including a pencil sharpener makes the kit self-contained while giving added value to the kit and added color to the packaged product.

3. We include stickers. They are very popular with children and they add more color to the product, thus making it more attractive and eye-catching to the purchaser.

4. We include an envelope for each card. They must be mailable and of high enough quality that the children can color and decorate them as well.

5. The target price to the end user must be less than one dollar per card. Most purchasers realize that regular greeting cards cost at least one dollar, so this price assures the perception of value to the buyer.

FACT PACK™ COLLECTOR CARDS

Description: FACT PACKS consist of six collector cards with pictures to color on the front. On the back are six questions about the subject depicted on the front. The answers are provided at the bottom, in small print, upside down. Once the child has mastered all the facts and has completed coloring the picture with the colored pencils provided in the package, he/she can affix a blue ribbon sticker that says "I Know My Facts." We currently have 18 FACT PACKS available for general distribution (see catalog) as well as customized FACT PACKS for the following customers:

Ellis Island	Henry Doorly Zoo
Chicago Zoo	Minnesota Zoo
Montreal Museum of Fine Art	Montgomery Place
The National Aquarium	B & O Railroad Museum
Lake Farmpark	Jamestown Settlement
Plimouth Plantation	New England Aquarium

Background: During family outings with her three small children, Ms. Michaels was amazed at the high prices of the souvenirs which were also of poor quality and little value. She continually asked: "Why don't they offer something that the children will enjoy and at the same time get benefit from? Then I wouldn't mind buying."

In the meantime, during the search for customers for KARD KIT, Ms. Michaels contacted Sea World with an offer to do a customized kit using their characters. The buyer was interested and requested a prototype. However, several problems arose:

1. Should the cards be birthday, thank you, or non-specific?

2. Ms. Michaels' children were excited about the prospect of a Sea World Kit, but after coloring Shamu, they did not want to send him to anyone. They wanted to keep the card for themselves, which defeated the purpose of a greeting card.

3. A custom sticker would raise the per unit cost of the KARD KITS because of low volume runs.

Then, one night on the way home from seeing a movie with her children, Ms. Michaels was asking them questions about the story and characters. When they got an answer correct, her daughter gave them a pretend sticker. The FACT PACK concept fell into place.

Parameters: All FACT PACKS meet the following parameters:

1. We include six different cards, and each card has six questions. The questions must teach basic facts about the subject, but in a fun way. To present it as a "school lesson" would discourage children from wanting to complete it and from wanting to do other FACT PACKS.

2. We include six standard Blue Ribbon stickers. The stickers are printed on clear material so the picture shows through regardless of where the child places it. The stickers simulate prizes such as given at a fair.

(3)

3. We package FACT PACKS in the same manner as KARD KITS to increase brand recognition.

4. We print cards on heavy stock to be durable. We use rounded corners to give them a finished look and keep them from fraying while children complete and store them.

POSTABLES™ STATIONERY KITS

Description: POSTABLES kits contain everything a child needs to make a post-card-like mailer. Each kit has six cards with outline drawings to color, six colored pencils, a pencil sharpener, and six stickers in the design of a mailbox.

The postcard is actually a tri-fold self-mailing letter. When folded, the back is a line drawing of the tourist area and the front is for the address. When opened, there is plenty of room for the child to write a message. The mailbox stickers are used for sealing. Each kit contains guidelines for how to use POSTABLES.

We are currently in production on three POSTABLES: Hawaii, Key West (FL), and Florida Wild Life. These subjects were chosen because: 1) We have strong sales reps in these areas and 2) the tourist season there falls during our normal slower periods, which will help to even out our production schedule.

Background: We had several inquiries about doing a product with postcards to serve the tourist markets. True postcards, however, presented us with several problems:

1. The side for the address and message is not very large and would be difficult for most children to appropriately use.

2. All our products come with stickers and our package has a compartment for them. We believed that it would be more economical to find something to put in this area rather than re-tool our package and carry inventory of two different clamshell packages.

As we considered this situation, the idea of POSTABLES came to us.

Parameters: This product is still new and in test marketing, so parameters have not yet been developed.

(4)

C. MARKET DESCRIPTION

1. OUR TARGET MARKETS

KARD KITS fall into the greeting card market which has annual U.S. sales of $3.6 billion. However, many of the sales outlets carrying our KARD KITS serve the toy market, which has annual U.S. sales of $12.5 billion. Our sales projections are only a fraction of 1% of this market. Such a low level of penetration means that even if the total market declines, we could likely meet our forecasted sales and even gain market share because we are a very small piece of a very large market.

The end-users of our products are children ages four to 12 years old. However, it would take resources far beyond our current abilities to develop product awareness in children to the point that they would request that our products be bought for them. Consequently, our products are usually purchased by adults for their own children or as gifts for other children.

We sell directly to wholesale distributors and to retail stores (who, in turn sell to parents). Our products are presented to them in a manner that conveys our dedication to quality, in an attractive display and at a price that allows them their customary mark-up. We have found that we must also supply our customers with a regular flow of new products.

The general gift and toy market is so vast that our limited resources would not be able to make much impact. We have therefore identified the following niche markets where we can have an impact:

- Souvenir Market
- Zoos (208 nationwide)
- Museums (5,226 nationwide)
- Amusement Parks (6,385 nationwide)

We have already had a great deal of success—orders and re-orders—in each of these markets, both with our standard products and our customized products.

2. MARKET RESEARCH

Research for KARD KITS was conducted by a team of students from Anytown University. They conducted focus groups and did personal interviews. Their major findings confirmed our product viability and market direction, which are shown below:

1. Mothers encourage their children to make their own cards, but do not like to help their children step-by-step through the process.

2. Children do not like writing thank you notes. A picture to color was much more interesting for the child.

3. Reaction to our products was "enthusiastic," "think it's cute."

4. Thought packaging should be more colorful, but did like the clear plastic bag so they could see what was inside. (A package re-design program was completed in early 1990 that resolved this issue.)

5. Cards were thought to be of good quality and designs were not faddish and will hold the child's attention.

6. There was some concern that the upper end of the retail price range was too high and that a price of over $4.00 would keep people from buying it.

Research for FACT PACKS was done in-house by showing prototypes to prospective buyers, customers, distributors and reps. General comments received were:

1. Package very colorful and professional.

2. The possible subjects for additional FACT PACKS were endless. Most people immediately had one or two ideas for a new FACT PACK.

3. Sales reps and distributors were very interested in the potential for customized FACT PACKS.

We recently asked Anytown University to work with us again to find out why our re-order rate in the general gift and toy channel is low. (This project was done for free.)

The final report did not address our original question. However, it confirmed that a major portion of our business comes from the zoo and museum channels, and it recommends that we continue to concentrate on these markets.

D. COMPETITION

COMPETITIVE ANALYSIS - GREETING CARDS

1. *Creative Art Company*. This is a Christmas card kit sold mail order through Abbey Press. Each kit contains 12 cards (two each of five different designs and two blank cards), 12 envelopes, six small tubs of paint and one paint brush.

> *Cost:* $9.95 per kit ($0.829 per card) including shipping and handling.

> *Comments:* Card designs are poor. Package stated 12 cards, but the kit we received only had ten.

2. *Create-A-Card*. Purchased at Imagination Toys in St. Louis, MO. Contains eight cards, eight envelopes and five markers. Available in either party invitations (four different versions), Christmas cards, or assorted all occasion cards that include two blank cards.

> *Cost:* $5.00 ($0.625 per card)

> *Comments:* Card designs are very simple. Packaged in a very large sectioned plastic bag so that the whole package is about 16" by 12."

3. *Kards for Kids*. Distributed in gift shops, mass merchandise stores, and some mail order catalogs. Cards come with child-like pictures already drawn and colored. Inside are blank spaces for children to fill in, such as: "Dear _____, Thank you for my _____. Love, _____" There is no room for the child to add any personal message or picture.

> *Cost:* Birthday cards and Get Well cards (eight to a pack, include envelopes) wholesale for $2.25 a pack. Thank You Notes, Invitations, Birth Announcements and Moving Announcements (fold-over type cards that seal with a Kards for Kids sticker) wholesale for $2.00 per pack. The end-user cost has been seen at prices ranging from $3.99 per pack to over $5.00 per pack via mail order.

> *Comments:* We do not feel that these are truly competitive to our products because they do not allow the child any opportunity for creativity of their own, nor do they come with markers or decorative stickers. However, buyers who are familiar with this line do compare us to it and this is usually a negative for us since we have not found any stores that have done well with this line.

4. *Hallmark Make-Your-Own Greeting Cards*. Several years ago, Hallmark introduced a line of "do-it-yourself" cards. The entire line took up the end of an aisle display. A kit included four cards with printed messages but no pictures, four envelopes and a piece of red foil to cut apart and use for decorating. The card stock was very good and the cards were a little larger than ours. The display also had Crayola crayons and markers that could be purchased to go along with the cards.

Cost: $4.50 ($1.125 per card) plus $.10 per crayon and $.50 per marker.

Comments: It has been over two years since we have seen a display in a store, so we are not sure if it was just a trial and has since been discontinued.

5. *Color Cards for Kids*. We have received literature on this line but have not seen actual product, and we do not know how they are distributing. The company is Fullmoon Creations. Each kit contains six card designs, six envelopes and four crayons. They are available in Thank You, Everyday, Christmas, Valentines Day and Easter.

Cost: $5.00 ($.833 per card)

Comments: Drawings are rather detailed to complete with crayons. Packaging is very simple.

These competitive products will not hinder our sales. Rather, they will help promote the concept of creating individualized cards. Our quality is equalled only by the Hallmark products where we have a large cost advantage. We feel confident that we have the best value available for this product.

COMPETITIVE ANALYSIS - FACT PACKS

We have found nothing on the market that combines all the elements in our FACT PACKS. The closest has been several card quiz games on dinosaurs that ranged in price from $3.50 to $8.95. Our FACT PACKS retail between $4.50 and $5.99.

COMPETITIVE ANALYSIS - POSTABLES

The only product we have seen on the market was purchased at the Smithsonian Air & Space Museum. The product consisted of very large post cards in a book along with a bag of markers to do the artwork. It retailed for $4.00.

With our product presented as a stationery kit, we expect to convey that it is easier for a child to use. The pencils, sharpener and stickers are all added values for the purchaser.

E. MANAGEMENT PLAN

1. PRODUCT DEVELOPMENT PLAN

KARD KITS: We are currently pursuing the rights to use drawings of well-known characters on our products. If these licenses are obtained, we will incorporate some of the characters into our existing product families. Others will open up new product opportunities for us. Due to the early stages of negotiation and the confidentiality of some of the potential products, identification of the characters is being withheld from this plan.

First Foto Company, which already buys a great deal of our "I Have A New Brother (or Sister)" KARD KITS has recently talked to us about doing these two kits in Spanish. If they decide to purchase these items, we will also be able to sell them through our normal distribution channels.

Other KARD KITS under consideration are Ethnic Birthday (Hispanic and African-American), Ethnic Thank You (Hispanic and African-American), and religious Christmas Cards. No funds are currently committed to these products.

FACT PACKS: With additional funding, we plan to develop the following new FACT PACKS: Endangered Species, Rain Forest Animals, and Aquarium Life. We are getting many inquiries for products on these subjects.

In addition, we have the following subjects under consideration when funding permits: a) American Indians. Our western reps have accounts that are interested. Also, the Smithsonian Institution, one of our customers, is constructing a new American Indian Museum; and b) Pond Pals, Interesting Insects. These both fit in well with the park, zoo and museum channels as well as with educational distributors.

2. MARKETING PLAN

Promotion

In February through November, 1987, we did the following Market Test Program:

1. **Mail Order:** We advertised on three levels. **Results: Poor**
   Local   *Township Times*
   City   *Anytown Gazette*
   National   *Family Circle*

2. **Direct Mail:** Mailings were done on three levels. **Results: Poor**
   Local   Sent to Anytown School District
   Regional   Sent to Anytown suburbs
   National   Co-op mailing done to 1,500 craft and hobby stores

3. **Wholesale:** Sales calls were made in three locations. **Results: Very Good**
   Anytown
   Anycity
   Anyburb

(9)

The decision was made to concentrate on wholesale sales using sales reps, and this decision has resulted in our rapid sales growth.

Our use of sales reps is discussed in the Sales Plan section of this plan. Other current promotion approaches are as follows:

1. **Free Publicity.** Trade journals as well as consumer publications are always looking for new items to tell their readers about. So far, we have had many free write-ups, including:

Redbook	*Hospital Gift Shop Management*
The Spotlight	*Potentials in Marketing*
Greetings	*Souvenir & Novelty*
Souvenir and Card	*Educational Dealer*
Giftware News	*Cleveland Plain Dealer*
Wall Street Journal	*Crain's Cleveland Business*

When a trade journal runs one of our press releases, we receive numerous inquiries, many of which lead to orders. It was from such a reply to a press release that we started doing business with Spaceport USA at Kennedy Space Center. They have become our largest retail account.

Continuous efforts are made to get as much free publicity as possible.

2. **Trade Shows.** In 1992, we exhibited at the following shows:

American International Toy Fair (New York)
International Stationery Show (New York)
Chicago Gift Show (Chicago)

At each of these shows, we wrote enough orders to cover expenses. In addition, we received additional orders from our contacts, found new reps to carry our products, and made contacts which generated free publicity.

Next year we plan to be more selective about the shows we attend. Since our market penetration and higher re-order rate is in specialty channels like zoos and museums, we plan to concentrate our trade show activities in those markets. We will exhibit at the national conference of the American Museum Store Association so we get maximum exposure to this market. In addition, we are planning to exhibit at the New York Premium Show to try to capture some of this market. (See discussion below.)

Some of our sales reps also exhibit at the regional toy and gift shows. For a small fee ($50 to $150) and a display of samples, our reps include our products in their booths. Results have been fair to good, and we will continue to support them.

3. **Response to Inquiries.** We continually receive inquiries about our products, both from the few ads we have run and from free publicity. All inquiries are answered promptly with a catalog, and in some cases, a sample. The leads are then passed to the appropriate sales rep for follow-up.

4. **"One-on-One" Campaign.** Since FACT PACKS were first developed, we have saved articles from newspapers and trade journals about potential customers for this product. These articles often give the buyer's name and detail their goals and objectives. We use this information to write a "one-on-one" letter to that buyer stating how our products can help fill their needs. We also send a sample of a product and a catalog. For less than $10, we make a direct "sales pitch" to the person who can take action.

   So far, we have been successful with the Smithsonian Institution and First Foto Co. from this campaign. These two accounts have provided orders for thousands of dollars.

5. **Direct Mail.** While our original unsuccessful attempt at direct mail was to the end-user, we feel there is an opportunity to do more direct mail at the wholesale level. Many of our channels are niche markets that can be covered well by direct mail. A four-color postcard mailing to zoo and pertinent museums was extremely successful.

   We plan another direct mail campaign to zoos and museums in the coming year.

In addition, based on inquiries and some successes in other potential markets, we are considering the following markets and promotion ideas:

1. **Hospital Gift Shops ($1 billion per year).** We have advertised in and had several free write-ups in *Hospital Gift Shop Management*, and the results have been good. We exhibited at a hospital gift shop show in Anyburb and wrote orders for 33% of the hospitals attending.

   We recently participated in a card deck mailed out to the 7000+ recipients of *Hospital Gift Shop Management*, and a fair number of our many inquiries converted to orders.

   While this market is easy to identify, it is difficult to serve. Many reps do not like to call on hospital accounts because the gift shops buy through committees of volunteers, making it difficult to get anyone to make decisions. However, we are finding the larger hospitals are getting more sophisticated and this makes it more attractive for reps to call on them. We also write a lot of hospital orders at their trade shows.

2. **Premium Market.** We had an inquiry from a large manufacturing company, which wanted us to develop a new product for them to use in a promotion. We developed a prototype, but the project died a natural death. It did, however, pique our interest in the premium channel since quantities are so large. We have therefore been researching this market.

   We have found a sales representative who specializes in this market; we have participated in two trade shows with him; we have learned that there is a long lead time from the time a customer sees our product until they call for a quote and then again until a final decision is made by the end-customer; we have learned that the customers will typically be ad agencies looking for a promotional product for one of their accounts. Although we have been asked for four different quotations, we have not yet received an order.

(11)

Because the volumes are so attractive, we are going to exhibit at the National Premium Show in May. However, due to the distortion such quantities would have on our forecasts, none of these amounts has been included in our financial projections.

3. **School Supply Wholesalers (414 nationwide).** While exhibiting at various gift shows, we were approached about using FACT PACKS in schools. We, therefore, identified a group of sales reps who specialize in the school supply market, and we are working with some of them to get our products placed in their retail outlets as well as in catalogs distributed to schools.

We have developed a catalog page "ad" for placement in these catalogs; thus far, we have been included in one catalog which is distributed to 75,000 schools nationwide.

If our products do well in this channel, we will consider adding one of the educational distributor channel trade shows to our schedule next year and will target this market segment for more attention.

4. **Military Exchanges.** Since our products are ideal for children away from family and friends and who have idle time, we feel there is a place for them in the military exchanges around the world.

We have met with the Small Business Specialist of the local Defense Logistics Agency who has given us help in getting on the correct mailing lists and taking the other actions necessary to try to serve this market.

Packaging

Our original plan was to be a mail order business where packaging is unimportant because the product is purchased before it is shipped. Once we decided to concentrate on wholesale channels, packaging became an important issue.

When FACT PACKS were first introduced, we used a nationally known design firm to create the FACT PACK package, and feedback from reps and buyers was very positive. We then converted the KARD KIT line to similar packaging. However, within six months our re-order rate fell below an acceptable level. By interviewing buyers, reps, outside consultants, and even other toy manufacturers, we learned that our package was too compact. While reps and buyers liked it and we continually received positive letters from people who purchased our products, the packages were getting lost on the store shelves.

In response, we developed a new package and introduced it at the International Stationery Show in New York. That was three years ago, and the re-order rate has returned to and even surpassed its original levels. In addition, we routinely get feedback on the high level of quality in our packaging.

3. SALES PLAN

We are developing a network of manufacturers reps and wholesale distributors across the country to supplement our home office activity. Most reps carry all of our lines and call on gift shops, card shops, drug stores, toy shops, zoos, museums and hospital gift shops. Some rep organizations have showrooms at the major gift marts. We have found that being displayed in showrooms does not generate many orders. Rather, we need rep organizations that are out on the road calling on stores and telling them about our products.

Initially, we hired reps primarily from the gift industry. Since adding the FACT PACK product lines, we have added many reps in the toy channel. While the majority of their orders are for FACT PACKS, they do write some KARD KITS orders.

We continually evaluate the rep organizations, looking for additional coverage and replacing unproductive reps. We find that as we grow and gain more exposure with premium accounts, we are able to work with a better level of sales reps. Some of our newer agencies are doing a tremendous job and know how to concentrate on the specialty accounts where we do so well.

To assure that we maintain a good flow of communication with this increasing family of reps, we have established a newsletter called *The Peabody Press*. We send it out as needed to keep the reps up-to-date on our products and activities.

4. OPERATIONS PLAN

We have located vendors throughout the country to supply us with the various components of our products. All components arrive at PEABODY's for assembly into finished product.

We routinely investigate new suppliers to assure we are getting the best possible quality, price, terms, and service. Many of our key suppliers now give us 60 day terms which has been a tremendous boost to our cash flow.

Prior to placing an order, we review cost trade-offs to evaluate the advantages of larger run sizes vs. the larger cash outlay and cost to carry the extra inventory. Since so many of our items are printed materials, the cost per unit varies greatly depending on the size of the production run. Our pricing structure was established using existing costs so future cost reductions due to larger volume runs will greatly enhance our profit level. As our volume increases and our ordering rate for components goes up, we can achieve as much as 20 cents per unit cost decrease.

Assembly is done by a part time staff which draws on two pools of workers: 1) Mothers of school age children and 2) retired workers. Some are actual employees while others work on a casual labor basis.

Currently we ship orders within 48 hours of receipt. The response by reps and buyers that "Everything is in stock, ready to ship" has been excellent. They usually mark on their orders to ship complete, backorders will not be accepted. Current staffing levels can handle this volume with room for a lot of growth before additional personnel are needed. When order rates are particularly heavy, three temporary staff people are identified and trained to fill orders.

5. PERSONNEL PLAN

Sherry Callido currently works 20 to 24 hours per week in customer service. She handles all the order packing and shipping activities and helps in assembly as needed. She has extensive background in service and is available for increased hours as our volume builds.

Laurel Risert currently works 15 to 20 hours per week in the assembly area and takes over the order fulfillment duties when necessary.

We have other part time personnel to help fill orders. They are trained and available on an as-needed basis.

In the coming year, we plan to add a part time administrator/bookkeeper (15 to 20 hours per week) to handle office tasks, such as order-entry, billing, receivables, etc. We have interviewed one candidate and are talking to others at this time.

We will also add a full time person with responsibility to increase sales through his/her own efforts and by managing the sales reps. We are looking for someone with strong sales abilities, and intend to pay a base salary of $1000 per month plus a commission. We expect a three month training period before this person is making enough sales to cover their cost. Therefore, we intend to make the hire after we have built up sufficient sales volume to cover their expenses. We expect to have someone in place by the end of the first quarter.

(14)

F. DESCRIPTION OF MANAGEMENT PERSONNEL

Ms. Michaels, the company founder and president, has a Bachelor's Degree in Business Administration from Anytown State University with a specialty in marketing. In addition, she has done graduate work in the MBA program at the University of Anycity.

She has more than fifteen years of experience with A Fortune 100 Company where she held various positions in product planning and program management. Her specific duties included such things as sales support, price and contract negotiations, packaging, customer contact, identifying new products,and establishing development plans. In addition, she spent 1-1/2 years with A Small Business where she did extensive work in advertising, public relations, trade show planning, product sourcing and supplier negotiation.

In order to augment her skills, Ms. Michaels has enlisted the help of the following people who are on her Board of Directors: Mitchell Cinders, Vice President of Global Bank, Dorothy Farmett, Owner of A Kampground, Joan Lucky, Controller for A Machine Tool Co. and John Night, Marketing Manager for A Distributorship. The Board meets quarterly to discuss current issues and to make plans for the future.

G. COMPANY OWNERSHIP AND FUNDING

PEABODY's was started in February 1987 as a sole proprietorship. In May, 1988, it was incorporated in Anystate, and 100 shares of stock were issued. In 1991, 35 shares of stock were sold to five outside investors, raising $40,000. Ms. Michaels is working with a broker to sell an additional 14 shares of stock. She will retain 51 shares (and control of the company) for herself. The annual stockholder's meeting is held the Sunday before Thanksgiving each year.

The company was originally funded through personal funds of the Michaels family, a line of credit at Our Local Bank, a home equity loan from Our Other Local Bank, and extended terms by many of the suppliers. By 1991, our growth rate required additional cash, which we raised through the sale of stock. Since that time, our investors have also loaned us an additional $18,000. The $58,000 raised through stock sales and loans has been used to fund daily operations as well as the following:

- Postcard mailing to zoos and museums
- Participation in the 1992 Toy Fair
- Participation in the Las Vegas Premium Show
- Participation in the International Stationery Show
- Development and printing of new catalog
- Point of purchase display
- Development and introduction of Whales of the World FACT PACK
- Development and introduction of Beautiful Butterflies FACT PACK
- Three press releases (including photography)
- Increase in inventory (purchased large amount of pencils at a close-out price)
- Investment in new software for order-entry and accounting programs

H. APPLICATION AND EXPECTED EFFECT OF LOAN OR INVESTMENT

The $50,000 will be used as follows:

Develop and inventory new products .... $ 3,600
Rain Forest Animals
Aquarium Life
Endangered Species

Attend additional trade shows 11,500
February Toy Fair
American Museum Store Association
National Premium Show

Direct mailing to zoos and museums 1,700

Reprint catalog 3,000

Salary - New Sales Manager ($1000/mo. base starting March) 10,000

Salary - Administrator ($100/wk. starting January) 5,200

Salary Increase - Ms. Michaels (re-instate to $30,000/yr; 15,000
was reduced to $15,000 April, 92)

Total **$50,000**

The new products have been requested by many customers and we believe they will sell well. In addition, they will address our customers' desire for a continuing supply of new products.

The trade shows will increase our visibility and our customer base. We expect that they will pay for themselves, as they have in the past.

The mailing to zoos and museums will continue to put our name and products in front of our niche customers. In the past, mailings to these customers have generated many inquiries which have converted to orders.

We require additional catalogs in order to respond to the many inquiries we receive.

Hiring a new sales manager with a sales track record will greatly increase sales. We expect that the additional profits incurred by this person will exceed their cost to us within 3 months. In addition, Ms. Michaels will have more time to devote to product development, operations and planning.

Hiring an administrator will also free up much of Ms. Michael's time, which can be better spent on product development, operations and planning.

I. SUMMARY

PEABODY'S - Toys That Teach, Inc. develops, manufactures and markets high quality products for children that are enjoyable for the child, that have educational benefits for the child, and are a good value for the purchaser. PEABODY'S is owned by Janice Michaels and five outside investors; Ms. Michaels has majority ownerhship.

PEABODY'S is seeking $50,000 to help finance our rapid growth. The money will support new product development and marketing efforts, enable us to hire an administrator and a sales manager, and re-instate Ms. Michaels' full salary which was cut in half last year to add cash to the business.

PEABODY'S sells primarily to the souvenir market, zoos, museums and amusement parks. Among our customers are such well known organizations as Kennedy Space Center (largest retail account), The Smithsonian Institution, Ellis Island and The National Aquarium. Our studies show that there is much room for growth in our niche markets and our repeat business from large, reputable customers demonstrates our ability to tap these markets.

PEABODY'S sales have grown from $10,000 to over $175,000 in our six years of operation, and we expect this new funding to allow our growth to continue.

Resources

SBA Office of Women's Business Ownership (OWBO) Representatives are employees of the federal government who are responsible for helping you tap into federal programs for women business owners or for all business owners. The codes are as follows:

(R) - Regional
(D) - District
(B) - Branch
(P) - Post-of-Duty

The SBA Demonstration Project participants have been funded by the federal government to provide you with free (or very low cost) training and one-on-one counseling on how to start and run your business.

The SBA Microloan Participants have been funded by the federal government to make small business loans (average of $7500) to women, minority and low income business owners.

Your State Office Administering Programs of Women Business Owners is funded by your state government to help you tap into state programs targeted to you. State programs vary. In some states these offices are literally designated as Women's Business Advocates (see asterisks).

State	SBA Offices of Women's Business Ownership	SBA Demonstration Projects Participants	SBA Microloan Program Participants	State Offices Administering Programs of Women Business Owners
Alabama	Ms. Susan D. Dunham (D) Business Development Specialist Small Business Administration 2121 8th Avenue, Suite 200 Birmingham, AL 35203-2398 (205) 731-1338 (205) 731-1404 FAX	Ms. Kathryn Cariglino, President Women's Yellow Pages of Greater Mobile, Inc. 1420 Government St. PO Box 6021 Mobile, AL 36660 (205) 473-5320 To assist women business owners in Mobile, AL	Elmore Community Action Committee, Inc. 1011 West Tallahassee PO Drawer H Wetumpka, AL 36092 Contact: Marion D. Dunlap (205) 567-4361 Service area: Autauga, Elmore and Montgomery counties	Jack Crittenden Alabama Center for Commerce 401 Adams Ave. Montgomery, AL 36130 (205) 242-0400
Alaska	Ms. Joyce Jansen (D) Business Development Specialist Small Business Administration Federal Building, #67 222 West 8th Avenue Anchorage, AK 99513 (907) 271-4022 (907) 271-4545 FAX	N/A	Community Enterprise Development Corporation of Alaska 1577 C Street Plaza, Suite 304 Anchorage, AK 99501 Contact: Perry R. Eaton (907) 274-5400 Service Area: Statewide	Bill Paulick Small Business Advocate Division of Economic Dev. Box 110804 Juneau, AK 99811 (907) 465-2017
Arizona	Ms. Gail Gesell (D) Business Development Small Business Administration 2828 N. Center Ave., Sta. 800 Phoenix, AZ 85004-1025 (602) 640-2325	N/A	Chicanos Por La Causa, Inc. 1112 E. Buckeye Road Phoenix, AZ 85034 Contact: Pete Garcia (602) 257-0700 Service Area: Urban areas of the counties of Maricopa and Pima	Harriet Barnes Governor's Office for Women 1700 W. Washington, #420 Phoenix, AZ 85007 (602) 542-1755

| Arizona, cont. | | PREP Housing Development Corp/Micro Industry Credit Rural Organization 802 East 46th St. Tuscon, AZ 85713 Contact: John D. Arnold (602) 622-3553 Service Area: Cochise, Santa Cruz, rural Maricopa, rural Pinal and rural Yuma counties | Berthenia Gill Minority Business Development Arkansas Industrial Development Comm. One State Capitol Mall, Room 4C300 Little Rock, AR 72201 (501) 682-1060 |
| Arkansas | Ms. Valerie Coleman (D) Business Opportunity Specialist Small Business Administration 2120 Riverfront Suite 100 Little Rock, AR 72202 (501) 324-5871 Arkansas Enterprise Group 605 Main Street, Suite 203 Arkadelphia, AR 71923 (501) 246-9739 Service Area: Southern half of state including counties of Arkansas, Ashley, Bradley, Calhoun, Chicot, Clark, Cleveland, Columbia, Dallas, Desha, Drew, Garland, Grant, Hempstead, Hot Spring, Howard, Jefferson, Lafayette, Lee, Lincoln, Little River, Miller, Monroe, Montgomery, Nevada, Ouachita, Phillips, Pike, Polk, Saline, Sevier and Union. | N/A | Delta Community Development Corp. 675 Eaton Rd. PO Box 852 Forrest City, AR 72335 Contact: Michael Jackson (501) 633-9113 Service Area: Cross, Crittenden, Monroe, Lee and St. Francis counties White River Planning and Development District, Inc. 1652 White Drive PO Box 2396 Batesville, AR 72503 Contact: Van C. Thomas (501) 793-5233 Service Area: Cleburne, Fulton, Independence, Izard, Jackson, Sharp, Stone, Van Buren, White and Wodruff counties |

State	SBA Representatives	Demonstration Projects	Microloan Program	State Offices
California	Gloria Minarik (R) ADD/Business Development Small Business Administration 71 Stevenson St. 20th Floor San Francisco, CA 94105-2939 (415) 744-8491 (415) 744-6812 FAX Ms. Nancy Gilbertson (D) Business Development Specialist Small Business Administration 2719 N. Air Fresno Dr., Suite 107 Fresno, CA 93727 (209) 487-5605 ext. 445 VACANT (D) Business Development Officer Small Business Administration 800 Front Street, Room 4-S-29 San Diego, CA 92188-0270 (619) 557-7269 Ms. Rachel Baranick (D) Business Development Specialist Small Business Administration 901 W. Civic Center Dr., Sta.160 Santa Ana, CA 92703-2352 (714) 836-2494 ext. 3102 Ms. Maria D. Teple (D) Business Development Officer Small Business Administration 330 N. Brand Blvd., Suite 1200 Glendale, CA 91203-2304 (213) 894-4894	American Woman's Economic Development Corp. Judith Luther Wilder Regional Director 301 E. Ocean Blvd. Suite 1010 Long Beach, CA 90802 (310) 983-3747 She will have two sites, one in Long Beach and the other in Orange County. WEST Company A Women's Economic Self- Sufficiency Training Program Director: Maggie Watson 340 North Main Street Fort Bragg, CA 95437 (707) 964-7571 Ms. Etienne LeGrand Executive Director Women's Initiative for Self Employment 450 Mission St., Suite 402 San Francisco, CA 94102 (415) 247-9473 To establish a site in Oakland, CA	Arcata Economic Development Corporation 100 Ericson Court, Suite 100 Arcata, CA 95521 (707) 822-4616 Contact: Cindy Copple Service Area: Del Norte, Humboldt, Mendocino and Siskiyou counties Center for Southeast Asian Refugee Resettlement 675 O'Farrell Street San Francisco, CA 94109 (415) 885-2743 Contact: Vu-Duc Vuong Service Area: Ten-county area including counties of Alameda, Contra Costa, Marin, Merced, Sacramento, San Francisco, San Joaquin, San Mateo, Santa Clara and Stanislaus Coalition for Women's Eco- nomic Development 315 West Ninth Street, Suite 705 Los Angeles, CA 90015 Contact: Forescee Hogan-Rowles (213) 489-4995 Service Area: Los Angeles County	Charmaine Sonnier Office of Small and Minority Business 1808 14th St., Suite 100 Sacramento, CA 95814 (916) 322-5060

California, cont.	Ms. Lisa Zuffi (D)
	Business Development Specialist
	Small Business Administration
	211 Main Street, 4th Floor
	San Francisco, CA 94105-1988
	(415) 744-8490
	
	Ms. Bobby Conner (D)
	Branch Manager
	Small Business Administration
	660 J Street, Suite 215
	Sacramento, CA 95814-2413
	(916) 551-1426
			Valley Rural Development
			  Corporation
			dba Valley Small Business
			  Development Corp.
			955 N Street
			Fresno, CA 93721
			Contact: Michael E. Foley
			(209) 268-0166
			Service Area: Counties of
			  Fresno, Kings, Kern, Stanislaus,
			  Madera, Mariposa, Merced,
			  Tuolumne and Tulare.	

Colorado	Ms. Nancy McCray (R)
	Surety Bond Guarantee Specialist
	Small Business Administration
	999 18th Street, Suite 701
	Denver, CO 80202
	(303) 294-7067
	(303) 294-7153 FAX
	
	Ms. Evelyn Gross (D)
	ADD/Business Development
	  Specialist
	Small Business Administration
	721 19th Street
	Denver, CO 80202
	(303) 844-3984
	(303) 844-6490 FAX
		Mi Casa
		Business Center for Women
		  (BCW)
		Elsa Holguin
		Project Director
		571 Galapago Street
		Denver, CO 80204
		(303) 573-1302
		FAX: (303) 595-0422
		Judy Patrick, Associate Director
		Eileen Donlin, Assistant Project
		  Director
			Greater Denver Local Develop-
			  ment Corporation
			1981 Blake Street, Suite 406
			Denver, CO 80206
			Contact: Cecilia H. Prinster
			(303) 296-9535
			Service Area: City of Denver,
			  counties of Adams, Arapahoe,
			  Boulder, Denver and Jefferson.
			
			Region 10 LEAP, Inc.
			P.O. Box 849
			Montrose, CO 81402
			Contact: Stan Broome
			(303) 249-2436
			Service Area: West Central area
			  including Delta, Gunnison,
			  Hinsdale, Montrose, Ouray and
			  San Miguel counties.
				Dr. Charlotte Redden
				Women's Busines Program
				1625 Broadway, Suite 1710
				Denver, CO 80202
				(303) 892-3840

State	SBA Representatives	Demonstration Projects	Microloan Program	State Offices
Connecticut	Ms. Kathleen Duncan (D) Business Management Specialist Small Business Administration 330 Main Street, 2nd Floor Hartford, CT 06106 (203) 240-4642 (203) 240-4659 FAX	Ms. Rosalind Paaswell Chief Executive Officer American Women's Economic Development Corporation 641 Lexington Ave., 9th Floor New York, NY 10022 (212) 688-1900 To establish a site in Southern Connecticut.	New Haven Community Investment Corp. 770 Chapel St., Suite 4B New Haven, CT 06510 Contact: Salvatore J. Brancati, Jr. (203) 787-6023 Service Area: New Haven County	Patricia Koch Department of Economic Development 865 Brook St. Rocky Hill, CT 06067-3405 (203) 258-4360
Delaware	Ms. Carlotta Catullo Program Assistant Small Business Administration One Rodney Square, Suite 412 920 North King Street Wilmington, DE 19801 (302) 573-6295	N/A	N/A	Gary Smith Small Business Advocate Delaware Development Office 99 Kings Hwy Box 1401 Dover, DE 19903 (302) 739-4271
District of Columbia	Ms. Jeanna Alexander (D) Business Development Specialist Small Business Administration 1111 - 18th Street, NW Washington, DC 20036 (202) 634-1500 ext. 258 Main Number (202) 634-1500	American Woman's Economic Development Corp. (AWED) Susan Phillips Bari Regional Director 1250 24th Street, N.W. Room 120 Washington, DC 20037 (202) 857-0091 (202) 223-2775 FAX	ARCH Development Corporation 2208 Martin Luther King Ave., SE Washington, DC 20020 Contact: Duane Gautier (202) 872-3589 Service Area: Portions of DC referred to as Adams Morgan, Mt. Pleasant and Anacostia, Congress Heights, Columbia Heights and 14th St. Corridor.	Charles Countee Director Office of Business and Economic Dev. 717 14th St., NW Washington, DC 20036 (202) 727-6600

District of Columbia cont.			Laurice Thompson Florida Dept. of Commerce Small and Minority Business Advocacy Office 102 W. Gaines St. Collins Bldg., Room 501C Tallahassee, FL 32399-2000 (904) 487-4698
	H Street Development Corporation 611 H St., N.E. Washington, DC 20002 Contact: William J. Barrow (202) 544-8353 Service Area: Portions of DC including specific areas of the NE, SE and NW quadrants. Technical Assistance Only: American Women's Economic Development Corp. Washington, DC Regional Training Center 1250 24th St., NW, Suite 120 Washington, DC 20037 Contact: Rosalind Paaswell (212) 692-9100 (NY) Service Area: District of Columbia		
Florida	Community Equity Investments Inc. 302 North Barcelona Street Pensacola FL 32501 Contact: Daniel R. Horvath (904) 433-5619 Service Area: Western Florida Panhandle. United Gainesville Community Development Corp., Inc. 214 West University Ave, Suite D PO Box 2518 Gainesville, FL 32602 Contact: Vian M. Cockerham (904) 376-8891 Service Area: North Central Fla.	Ms. Hedy Ratner, Co-Director Women's Business Development Center 8 South Michigan Ave., Suite 400 Chicago, IL 60603 (312) 853-3477 To establish a site in Miami, FL	Ms. Kim Lucas (D) Business Development Specialist Small Business Administration 7825 Bay Meadows Way Suite 100B Jacksonville, FL 32256-7504 (904) 443-1900 (904) 433-1980 FAX Mr. Kurt Fabian (D) Business Development Specialist Small Business Administration 1320 S. Dixie Hwy., Suite 501 Miami, FL 33146 (305) 536-5521 (305) 536-5058 FAX

State	SBA Representatives	Demonstration Projects	Microloan Program	State Offices
Georgia	Ms. Edith Fuller (R) Surety Bond Guarantee Specialist Small Business Administration 1375 Peachtree Street, NE Atlanta, GA 30367 (404) 347-2386 (404) 347-2355 FAX Ms. Paula Hill (D) Business Development Specialist Small Business Administration 1720 Peachtree Street, NW, 6th Fl. Atlanta, GA 30309 (404) 347-2356 (404) 347-4745 FAX	Women's Entrepreneurial Center Leah Creque-Harris Project Director The Candler Building 127 Peachtree St, NE Suite 700 Atlanta, GA 30303 (404) 659-4008	Small Business Assistance Corp. 31 West Congress Street, Suite 100 Savannah, GA 31401 Contact: Tony O'Reily (912) 232-4700 Service Area: Counties of Bryan, Chatham, Effingham, Bulloch and Liberty Fulton County Development Corp. dba Greater Atlanta Small Business Project 10 Park Place South, Suite 305 Atlanta, GA 30303 Contact: Maurice S. Coakley (404) 659-5955 Service Area: Fulton, Dekalb, Cobb, Gwinnett, Fayette, Clayton, Henry, Douglas and Rockdale counties.	Hooper Wesley Small and Minority Business Program 200 Piedmont Ave. Suite 1302 Atlanta, GA 30334 (404) 656-6315
Hawaii	Small Business Administration 30 Ala Moana, Room 2213 P.O. Box 50207 Honolulu, HI 96850-4981 (808) 541-2974	N/A	N/A	Sandra Cirie Business Advocate Economic Develop & Tourism PO Box 2359 Honolulu, HI 96804 (808) 586-2594
Idaho	Mr. Rod Grzadzieleski (D) Business Development Specialist Small Business Administration 1020 Main Street, Suite 290 Boise, ID 83720 (208) 334-9079 (208) 334-9353 FAX	N/A	Panhandle Area Council 11100 Airport Drive Hayden, ID 83835-9743 Contact: Jim Deffenbaugh (208) 772-0584 Service Area: Northern Pan- handle of Idaho	Tammy Dickenson Administrator Div. Community Development State Department of Commerce 700 W. State Street Boise, ID 83720 (208) 334-2470

| Illinois | Ms. Nancy Smith (R)
Regional Manager, Women's
Business Program
Small Business Administration
300 South Riverside Plaza
Suite 1975 South
Chicago, IL 60606
(312) 353-5000 ext. 764
(312) 353-3426 FAX

Mr. Sam McGrier (D)
ADD/Business Development
Small Business Administration
500 West Madison St, Sta. 1250
Chicago, IL 60606
(312) 353-5429 EXT. 6243
(312) 353-5688 FAX

Ms. Valerie Ross (B)
Business Development Specialist
Small Business Administration
511 West Capitol Street
Suite 302
Springfield, IL 62704
(217) 492-4416
(217) 492-4867 FAX | Women's Business Development
Center (WBDC)
Denise Miculski, Project Director
SBDC/Joliet Junior College
214 No. Ottawa, 3rd Floor
Joliet, IL 60431
(815) 727-6544 ext. 1312

Women's Business Development
Center (WBDC)
Joanne Seggebruch, Project Dir.
Kankakee Community College
4 Dearborn Square
Kankakee, IL 60901
(815) 933-0375

Women Business Owners
Advocacy Program (WBOAP)
Shirley DeBenedetto
Project Director
SBDC/Rock Valley College
1220 Rock Street
Rockford, IL 61101
(815) 968-4087

Women's Economic Venture
Enterprise (WEVE)
Lynn Spaight
Project Director
229 - 16th Street
Rock Island, IL 61201
(309) 788-9793
Serving Quad Cities of Moline
and Rock Island, IL and
Davenport and Bettendorf, IA | Greater Sterling Development Corp.
1741 Industrial Drive
Sterling, IL 61081
Contact: Reid Nolte
(815) 625-5255
Service Area: City of Sterling and
counties of Whiteside and Lee

The Economic Development
Council for the Peoria Area
124 S.W. Adams St, Suite 300
Peoria, IL 61602
Contact: Martin Mini
(309) 676-7500
Service Area: Counties of Peoria,
Tazwell and Woodford

Neighborhood Inst. and Women's
Self Employment Project
1750 East 71st Street
Chicago, IL 60649
Contact: Dorris J. Pickens
(312) 684-4610
Service Area: Parts of Chicago

Illinois Development Finance Auth.
2 North LaSalle St. Suite 980
Chicago, IL 60602
Contact: Joseph Derezinski
(312) 793-5586
Service Area: Statewide excepting
Peoria, Tazwell, Woodford, Lee
and Whiteside counties, the city
of Sterling, and parts of Chicago
served by WSEP. | Mollie Cole
Department of Commerce and
Community Affairs
State of Illinois Center
100 W. Randolph St.
Suite 3-400
Chicago, IL 60601
(312) 814-7176 |

State	SBA Representatives	Demonstration Projects	Microloan Program	State Offices
Indiana	Mr. Don Owen (D) Business Development Specialist Small Business Administration 429 North Pennsylvania Street Suite 100 Indianapolis, IN 46204 (317) 226-7272 (317) 226-7259 FAX	N/A	Eastside Comm. Investments Inc. 26 North Arsenal Avenue Indianapolis, IN 46201 Contact: Dennis J. West (317) 637-7300 Service Area: Indianapolis Metro Small Business Assistance Corp. 1 NW Martin Luther King, Jr. Blvd. Evansville, IN 47708-1869 Contact: Debra A. Lutz (812) 426-5857 Service Area: Vanderburgh, Posey, Gibson and Warrick counties	Ann Neal-Winston Small Business Development Corporation One N. Capitol Ave. Suite 1275 Indianapolis, IN 46204 (317) 264-2820
Iowa	Ms. Diane Reinerston (D) Loan Specialist Small Business Administration 373 Collins Road, NE Cedar Rapids, IA 52402 (319) 393-8630 (319) 393-7585 FAX Lori Walljasper (D) Business Development Specialist Small Business Administration 210 Walnut Street, Room 749 Des Moines, IA 50309 (515) 284-4761 (515) 284-4572 FAX	N/A	Siouxland Economic Dev. Corp. 400 Orpheum Electric Building P.O. Box 447 Sioux City, IA 51102 Contact: Kenneth A. Beekley (712) 279-6286 Service Area: Counties of Cherokee, Ida, Monona, Plymouth, Sioux and Woodbury Technical Assistance Only Inst. for Social and Econ. Dev. 1901 Broadway, Suite 313 Iowa City, IA 52240 Contact: John F. Else (319) 338-2331 Service Area: Statewide	Toni Hawley Iowa Department of Economic Development 200 E. Grand Ave. Des Moines, IA 50309 (515) 242-4758

Kansas	Mr. Dennis Larkin (D) Business Development Specialist Small Business Administration 100 East English, Suite 510 Wichita, KS 67202 (316) 269-6273 (316) 269-6499 FAX	N/A	South Central Kansas Economic Development District, Inc. 151 North Volutsia Wichita, KS 67214 Contact: Jack E. Alumbaugh (316) 683-4422 Service Areas: Butler, Cowley, Chautauqua, Elk, Greenwood, Harper, Harvey, Kingman, Marion, McPherson, Reno, Rice, Sedgwick and Sumner counties.	Antonio Augusto Office of Minority Business Kansas Dept. of Commerce 400 SW 8th St., 5th Floor Topeka, KS 66603-3957 (913) 296-3805
Kentucky	Ms. Verna (Carol) Hatfield (D) Business Development Specialist Small Business Administration 600 Dr. MLK, Jr. Place, Rm 188 Louisville, KY 40201 (502) 582-5971 (502) 582-5009 FAX	Ms. Charlotte Taylor, President CTA Management Group, Inc. Venture Concepts 900 Second St., N.E. Suite 205 Washington, DC 20002 (202) 289-0300 To establish a site in Kentucky	Kentucky Highlands Investment Corp. 362 Old Whitley Road London, KY 40741 Contact: Jerry A. Rickett (606) 864-5175 Service Area: Counties of Bell, Clay, Clinton, Harlan, Jackson, Knox, Laurel, McCreary, Pulaski, Rockcastle, Wayne and Whitley Purchase Area Development Dist. 1002 Medical Drive / Box 588 Mayfield, KY 42066 Contact: Henry A. Hodges (502) 247-7171 Service Area: Western Kentucky Technical Assistance Only: Community Ventures Corp. National City Plaza - 3rd Floor 301 East Main St. Lexington, KY 40507 Contact: Kevin R. Smith (606) 281-5475	Ann Ross Cabinet for Economic Development Capital Plaza Tower 23rd Floor Frankfort, KY 40601 (502) 564-7140

State	SBA Representatives	Demonstration Projects	Microloan Program	State Offices
Louisiana	Ms. Loretta Porse (D) Business Development Specialist Small Business Administration 1661 Canal St., 2nd Floor New Orleans, LA 70112 (504) 589-2354	N/A	Greater Jennings Chamber of Commerce 414 Cary Ave. PO Box 1209 Jennings, LA 70546 Contact: Jerry Arceneaux (318) 824-0933 Service Area: Jeff Davis Parish	Patricia Robinson Dept. of Economic Development State of Louisiana PO Box 94185 Baton Rouge, LA 70804-9185 (504) 342-5882
Maine	Ms. Bonnie Erickson (D) Business Development Assistant Small Business Administration 40 Western Avenue, Room 512 Augusta, ME 04330 (207) 622-6242 (207) 622-8277 FAX	N/A	Coastal Enterprises, Inc. P.O. Box 268 Water Street Wiscasset, ME 04578 Contact: Ronald L. Phillips (207) 882-7552 Service Area: Statewide Northern Maine Regional Planning Commission 2 South Main St. PO Box 779 Caribou, ME 04736 Contact: Robert P. Clark (207) 498-8736 Service Area: Arrostock, Piscata- quis and Washington counties. Community Concepts, Inc. 35 Market Sq. PO Box 278 South Paris, ME 04281 Contact: Charleen M. Chase (207) 743-7716 Service Area: Oxford county.	Joan Anderson-Cook Deputy Comm,Office of Business Dept. of Economic & Commercial Development State House, Station 59 Augusta, ME 04330 (207) 289-2656

State				
Maryland	Ms. Mindye Allentoff (D) Business Development Specialist Small Business Administration 10 North Calvert Street, 4th Fl. Baltimore, MD 21202 (410) 962-6149 ext. 338	N/A	Council for Equal Business Opportunity, Inc. The Park Plaza 800 North Charles St., Suite 300 Baltimore, MD 21201 Contact: Michael Gaines (410) 576-2326 Area: Counties Ann, Arundel, Baltimore, Carroll, Harford and Howard.	Janis Carmichael Executive Director Suburban Washington SBDC 9201 Basil Court, Suite 403 Landover, MD 20785 (301) 925-5032
Massachusetts	Ms. Mary Russell (R) WBO Coordinator Small Business Administration 155 Federal Street, 9th Floor Boston, MA 02110 (617) 451-2044 Ms. Lisa Gonzalez (D) WBO Representative Small Business Administration 10 Causeway Street, Room 265 Boston, MA 02222-1093 (617) 565-5595 (617) 565-5598 FAX Mr. Harry Webb (B) Branch Manager Small Business Administration 1550 Main Street, Room 212 Springfield, MA 01103 (413) 785-0268	N/A	Western Mass. Enterprise Fund 324 Wells Street Greenfield, MA 01301 Contact: Christopher Sikes (413) 774-7204 Service Area: W. Massachusetts Economic Development Industrial Corporation of Lynn One Market St., Suite 4 Lynn, MA 01901 Contact: Peter M. DeVeau (617) 592-2361 Service Area: City of Lynn Jobs for Fall River, Inc. One Government Center Fall River, MA 02722 Contact: Paul L. Vigeant (508) 324-2620 Service Area: City of Fall River Springfield Business Dev. Fund 36 Court St., Room 222 Springfield, MA 01103 Contact: James Asselin (413) 787-6050 Service Area: City of Springfield	Lynn Wachtel Office of Minority and Women's Business Assistance 100 Cambridge St., 13th Fl. Boston, MA 02202 (617) 727-8692

State	SBA Representatives	Demonstration Projects	Microloan Program	State Offices
Michigan	Ms. Catherine Gase (D) Business Development Specialist Small Business Administration 477 Michigan Avenue Detroit, MI 48226 (313) 226-6075 ext. 23 (313) 226-4769 FAX	EXCEL! Midwest Women Business Owners Development Team Chinyere Neale Project Director 200 Renaissance Ctr, Suite 1600 Detroit, MI 48243-1274 (313) 396-3576 Carol Lopucki Executive Director 200 Ottawa N.W., Suite 900 Grand Rapids, MI 49503-2465 (616) 458-4783 FAX: (616) 774-9081	Ann Arbor Comm. Dev. Corp. 2008 Hogback Rd., Suite 2A Ann Arbor, MI 48105 Contact: Michelle Richards Vasquez (313) 677-1400 Service Area: Washtenaw County Detroit Economic Growth Corp. 150 West Jefferson, Suite 1500 Detroit, MI 48226 Contact: Robert W. Spencer (313) 963-2940 Service Area: City of Detroit Flint Community Dev. Corp. 877 East Fifth Ave. Building C-1 Flint, MI 48503 Contact: Bobby J. Wells (313) 239-5847 Service Area: Genesee County Northern Econ. Initiatives Corp. 1009 West Ridge St. Marquette, MI 49855 Contact: Richard Anderson (906) 228-5571 Service Area: Upper Peninsula	Kathleen Mechem Manager - Women Business Owner Services Michigan Dept. of Commerce PO Box 30004 Lansing, MI 48909-7504 (517) 335-1835

Minnesota	Ms. Cynthia Collett (D) Business Development Specialist Small Business Administration 610 C Butler Square Minneapolis, MN 55403 (612) 370-2312 (612) 370-2324	BI-CAP, Inc. Women in New Development (WIND) Anne McGill, Project Director Cyndee Hoialmen, Economic Development Coordinator P.O. Box 579 Bemidji, MN 56601 (218) 751-4631 FAX (218) 751-8452 Ms. Mary Heisler Administrative Planner White Earth Reservation Tribal Council PO Box 418 White Earth, MN 56591 (218) 983-3285 To establish a site on the White Earth Tribal Reservation	Northeast Entrepreneur Fund Inc. Olcott Plaza, Suite 140 820 Ninth Street North Virginia, MN 55792 Contact Mary Mathews (218) 749-4191 Service Area: Northeastern area. Women Venture 2324 University Avenue St. Paul, MN 55114 Contact: Kay Gudmestad (612) 646- 3808 Service Area: Cities of Minneapolis and St. Paul and counties of An- dra, Carver, Chisago, Dakota, Hennepin, Isanti, Ramsey, Scott, Washington and Wright Minneapolis Consortium of Nonprofit Developers, Inc. 2600 East Franklin Avenue Minneapolis, MN 55406 Contact: Karen Reid (612) 338-8729 Service Area: Parts of Minneapolis Northwest Minn. Initiative Fund 922 Paul Bunyan Drive, NW Bemidji, MN 56601 Contact: Ruth Edevold (218) 759-2057 Service Area: Northwestern corner of the state	Tracy Troke Thompson Minnesota Small Business Development Center P.O. Box 5838 Winona, MN 55987-5838 (507) 457-5088

State	SBA Representatives	Demonstration Projects	Microloan Program	State Offices
Mississippi	Ms. Ora Rawls (D) ADD/MSB Small Business Administration 101 West Capitol St, Suite 400 Jackson, MS 39201 (601) 965-5323 (601) 965-4294 FAX Ms. Judith N. Adcock (B) Loan Officer Small Business Administration 1 Hancock Plaza, Suite 1001 Gulfport, MS 39501 (601) 863-4449 (601) 864-0179 FAX	N/A	Delta Foundation 819 Main Street Greenville, MS 38701 Contact: Harry J. Bowie (601) 335-5291 Service Area: Statewide Neighborhood Housing Services of Jackson, Inc. 1066 Pecan Park Circle Jackson, MS 39209 Contact: Carolyn Nelson (601) 353-6198 Service Area: City of Jackson	Motice Bruce Dept. of Economic Development P.O. Box 849 Jackson, MS 39205 (601) 359-3448
Missouri	Ms. Patricia Ingram (R) WBO Coordinator Small Business Administration 911 Walnut Street, 13th Floor Kansas City, MO 64106 (816) 426-5311 (816) 426-5559 FAX Ms. Ann Cason (D) Business Development Specialist Small Business Administration 323 West 8th, 5th Floor Kansas City, MO 64106 (816) 374-6762 (816) 374-6795 FAX	NAWBO of St. Louis Thelma Crawford Project Director 911 Washington Ave., Suite 140 St. Louis, MO 63101 (314) 621-6162	Center for Business Innovations, Inc 4747 Troost Ave. Kansas City, MO 64110 Contact: Robert J. Sherwood (816) 561-8567 Service Area: Statewide Technical Assistance Only: Community Development Corporation of Kansas City 2420 E. Linwood Blvd., Suite 400 Kansas City, MO 64109 Contact: Donald Maxwell (816) 924-5800 Service Area: Cass, Clay, Platte, Ray and Jackson counties	Dr. Sue McDaniel Council on Women's Economic Development P.O. Box 1684 Jefferson City, MO 65102 (314) 751-0810

| Missouri, *cont.* | Ms. LaVerne Johnson (D)
Public Affairs Specialist
Small Business Administration
815 Olive Street, Suite 242
St. Louis, MO 63101
(314) 539-6600
(314) 539-3785 FAX

Ms. LuAnn Wylie (B)
Business Development Specialist
Small Business Administration
620 South Glenstone, Suite 110
Springfield, MO 65802-3200
(417) 864-7670
(417) 864-4108 FAX | | |
| Montana | Ms. Michelle Johnston (D)
Business Development Specialist
Small Business Administration
301 S. Park Avenue, Room 528
Helena, MT 59626-0054
(406) 449-5381
(406) 449-5474 FAX | Ms. Kelly Rosenleaf
Women's Opportunity &
Resource Development Inc.
127 N. Higgins
Missoula, MT 59802
(406) 543-3550
To establish sites in five
counties in southwestern
Montana | Capital Opportunities
Human Resource Development
Council Inc.
321 East Main Street, Suite 300
Bozeman, MT 59715
Contact: Jeffery Rupp
(406) 587-4486
Service Area: Counties of
Gallatin, Park and Meagher

Women's Opportunity and
Resource Development, Inc.
127 North Higgins Avenue
Missoula, MT 59802
Contact: Kelly Rosenleaf
(406) 543-3500
Service Area: Counties of
Beverhead, Lake Mineral,
Missoula, Ravalli and Sanders | Misty Hammerbacker
Disadvantaged Business Center
Department of Transportation
Highway Building
2701 Prospect Ave.
Helena, MT 59620
(406) 444-6337 |

State	SBA Representatives	Demonstration Projects	Microloan Program	State Offices
Nebraska	Ms. Betty Gutheil (D) Business Development Specialist Small Business Administration 11145 Mill Valley Road Omaha, NB 68154 (402) 221-3604 (402) 221-3680 FAX	N/A	Rural Enterprise Assistance Project P.O. Box 406 Walthill, NE 68067 Contact: Don Ralston (402) 846-5428 Service Area: Northeast Nebraska West Central Nebraska Development District, Inc. 710 North Spruce St. PO Box 599 Ogailala, NE 69153 Contact: Ronald J. Radil (308) 284-6077 Service Area: West Central Neb.	Evan McKinney Small Business Division Nebraska Dept. of Economic Dev. 301 Centennial Mall S. Box 94666 Lincoln, NE 68509-4666 (406) 444-3494
Nevada	Ms. Donna Hopkins (D) ADD/Business Development Small Business Administration 301 East Stewart, Box 7527 Dowtown Station Las Vegas, NV 89125-2527 (702) 388-6611	N/A	N/A	Helen Myers Director, Office of Small Business Nevada Commission on Economic Dev. 3770 Howard Hughes Pkwy., Suite 295 Las Vegas, NV 89109 (702) 486-7282

New Hampshire	Ms. Sandra Sullivan (D) Business Development Assistant Small Business Administration Stewart Nelson Plaza, 2nd Floor 143 N. Main Street, PO Box 1257 Concord, NH 03302-1257 (603) 225-1400 (603) 225-1409 FAX	N/A	Institute for Cooperative Community Development, Inc. 2500 North River Road Manchester, NH 03106 Contact: Don Mason (603) 644-3103 Service Area: Statewide No. Community Investment Corp. 69 Willard St. Berlin, NH 03570 Contact: Robert V. Justis (802) 748-5101 Service Area: Grafton, Carol and Coos counties.	Michelle Sweet Small Business Dev. Center 108 McConnell Hall University of New Hampshire Durham, NH 03824 (603) 862-0710
New Jersey	Ms. Janis A. Wolfe Business Development Specialist Small Business Administration Military Park Building 60 Park Place, 4th Floor Newark, NJ 07102 (201) 645-3683 (201) 645-6265 FAX	New Jersey NAWBO EXCEL Harriet Nazareth, Project Director 120 Finderne Avenue P.O. Box 6336 Bridgewater, NJ 08807 (908) 707-0173	Trenton Business Assistance Corp. Div. of Economic Development 319 East State St. Trenton, NJ 08608-1866 Contact: James Harveson (609) 989-35090 Service Area: Portions of Trenton Greater Newark Business Development Consortium One Newark Center 22nd Floor Newark, NJ 07102-5265 Contact: Henry Hayman (201) 242-6237 Service Area: Bergen, Essex, Hudson, Middlesex, Monmouth, Morris, Passaic and Somerset counties with the exception of the city of Jersey City.	Cindy Conrad NJ Dept. of Commerce and Economic Development Division of Women and Minority Businesses 20 W. State St., CN 835 Trenton, NJ 08625-0835 (609) 292-3862

State	SBA Representatives	Demonstration Projects	Microloan Program	State Offices
New Jersey *cont.*	Union County Economic Development Corp. Liberty Hall Corporate Center 1085 Morris Ave., Suite 531 Union, NJ 07083 (908) 527-1166 Service Area: Union County. Jersey City Economic Development Corp. 601 Pavonia Ave. Jersey City, NJ 07306 Contact: Thomas D. Ahearn (201) 420-7755 Service Area: City of Jersey City.			
New Mexico	Ms. Susan Chavez (D) Business Development Specialist Small Business Administration 625 Silver SW, Room 320 Albuquerque, NM 87102 (505) 766-1879 (505) 766-1057 FAX	WESST Corp. Taos, NM Pamala Scalora Project Director Taos County Econ. Dev. Corp. P.O. Box 1389 Taos, NM 87571 (505) 758-1161 Women's Economic Self-Sufficiency Team (WESST Corp) Agnes Noonan Project Director 414 Silver Southwest Albuquerque, NM 87102 (505) 848-4760 To Serve Albuquerque, Sante Fe and Taos	Women's Economic Self-Sufficiency Team 414 Silver South West Albuquerque, NM 87102-3239 Contact: Agnes Noonan (505) 848-4760 Service Area: Statewide	Ernestine Florez Acting Director New Mexico Commission on Status of Women 4001 Indian School NE Santa Fe, NM 87110 (505) 841-4662

| New York | Mr. Thomas Agan (B)
Assistant Branch Manager
Small Business Administration
Elmira Savings Bank Building
333 East Water Street
Elmira, NY 14901
(607) 734-8142
(607) 733-4656 FAX

Ms. Carol Kruszona (B)
Business Development Technician
Small Business Administration
111 W. Huron St, Room 1311
Buffalo, NY 14202
(716) 846-4517
(716) 846-4418 FAX

Ms. Josephine Bermudez-Troy (B)
Business Development Specialist
Small Business Administration
35 Pinelawn Road, Room 102E
Melville, NY 11747
(516) 454-0753
(516) 454-0769 FAX

Ms. Sherry Kelleher (P)
Business Development Technician
Small Business Administration
Leo O'Brien Building, Room 815
Clinton & Pearl Streets
Albany, NY 12207
(518) 472-6300
(518) 472-7138 FAX | N/A | Adirondack Econ. Dev. Corp.
30 Main Street
Saranac Lake, NY 12983
Contact: Ernest Hohmeyer
(518) 891-5523
Service Area: Counties of Clinton, Essex, Franklin, Fulton, Hamilton, Herkimer, Jefferson, Lewis, Oneida, Oswego, St. Lawrence, Saratoga, Warren and Washington

Hudson Development Corp.
444 Warren Street
Hudson, NY 12534
Contact: Lynda S. Davidson
(518) 828-3373
Service Area: Columbia County

Rural Opportunities, Inc.
339 East Avenue
Rochester, NY 14604
Contact: W. Lee Beaulac
(716) 546-7180
Service Area: Counties of Allegheny, Cattaraugua, Cayuga, Chantanqua, Erie, Genessee, Livingston, Niagara, Ontario, Orleans, Seneca, Stephen, Wayne, Wyoming and Yates

Manhatten Borough Dev. Corp.
5 Beekman St., Suite 905
New York, NY 10038
Contact: Patricia Swann
(212) 791-3660
Service Area: the Borough of Manhattan | Celia A. Gonzales
Division of Minority and
Women's Business
Development
One Commerce Plaza
Albany, NY 12245
(518) 486-6688 |

State	SBA Representatives	Demonstration Projects	Microloan Program	State Offices
New York *cont.*	Ms. Stephanie Ubowski (D) Business Development Technician Small Business Administration 100 S. Clinton Street Room 1071 Syracuse, NY 13260 (315) 423-5375 (315) 423-5370 FAX Ms. Marcia Ketchum (P) Business Development Specialist Small Business Administration Federal Building 100 State Street Rochester, NY 14614 (716) 263-6700 (716) 263-3146 FAX Ms. Nita Whalen (D) Equal Employment Opp. Officer Small Business Administration 26 Federal Plaza, Room 3100 New York, NY 10278 (212) 264-1468 (212) 264-4963 FAX			
North Carolina	Ms. Eileen Joyce (D) Business Development Specialist Small Business Administration 200 No. College St., Sta. A2015 Charlotte, NC 28202-2173 (704) 344-6587 (704) 344-6769 FAX	N/A	Self-Help Ventures Fund 413 East Chapel Hill Street Durham, NC 27701 Contact: Robert Schall (919) 956-8526 Service Area: Statewide	Henry Payne Supervisor, Minority/Women Business Enterprise Program No. Carolina Dept. of Admin. 116 W. Jones St. Raleigh, NC 27603-8002 (919) 733-8965

State			
North Carolina *cont.*	Technical Assistance Only: NC Econ. Dev. Center, Inc. 4 North Blount St., 2nd Floor Raliegh, NC 27601 Contact: Billy Ray Hall (919) 821-1154 Service Area: Statewide		Pat Graff Director, Women's Business Development 1833 E. Bismark Expressway Bismarck, ND 58504 (701) 221-5342
North Dakota	Ms. Marlene Koenig (D) Business Development Specialist Small Business Administration 657 2nd Avenue North, Rm 218 P.O. Box 3088 Fargo, ND 58102 (701) 239-5131 (701) 239-5645 FAX	Ms. Penny R. Retzer Secretary/Tresurer Maldan Management Co., Inc. 901 Page Dr., PO Box 9064 Fargo, ND 68106-9064 (701) 235-6488 To serve women business owners in Fargo, ND.	Lake Agassiz Regional Council 417 Main Ave. Fargo, ND 58103 Contact: Irvin D. Rustad (701) 239-5373 Service Area: Statewide
Ohio	Ms. Rosemary Darling (D) Business Development Specialist Small Business Administration 1111 Superior Avenue, Suite 630 Cleveland, OH 44114-2507 (216) 522-4180 ext. 128 (216) 522-2038 FAX Ms. Janice Sonnenberg (D) Business Development Specialist Small Business Administration Two Nationwide Plaza, Sta. 1400 Columbus, OH 43215-2542 (614) 469-6860 ext. 274 (614) 469-2391 FAX	Ohio Coordinator Melody Borchers, (614) 466-4945 Cleveland Women's Business Development Center Kathy Velkoff or Neeta Chandra, Project Directors City Hall, Room 335 601 Lakeside Avenue Cleveland, OH 44114 (216) 664-4159 or 664-4162 FAX (216) 664-3870 Ms. Marianne Vermeer, Coordinator—Ohio Women's Business Resource Network 77 South High St., 28th Floor Columbus, OH 43266 (614) 593-1797 To establish a state program	Athens Small Business Center Inc. 900 East State Street Athens, OH 45701 Contact: Karen S. Patton (614) 592-1188 Service Area: Counties of Adams, Ashland, Athens, Belmont, Brown, Carrol, Columbiana, Coshocton, Gallia, Guernsey, Harrison, Highland, Holmes, Jackson, Jefferson, Knox, Lawrence, Meigs, Monroe, Morgan, Muskingum, Nocking, Noble, Perry, Pike, Ross, Scioto, Tuscarawas, Vinton and Washington	Melody Borchers Women's Business Resource Program 77 S. High St., 28th Fl. Columbus, OH 43215 (800) 848-1300

State	SBA Representatives	Demonstration Projects	Microloan Program	State Offices
Ohio, cont.	Mr. Gene O'Connell (B) Business Development Specialist Small Business Administration 525 Vine Street, Room 870 Cincinnati, OH 45202 (513) 684-6907 (513) 684-3251 FAX	Minority Female Entrepreneurship Program Linda Steward and Ann Martin Directors 37 North High Street Columbus, OH 43215-3065 (614) 225-6087 FAX (614) 469-8250 (614) 221-1321 Women's Economic Assistance Ventures (WEAV) Rosann Miller-Wethington Executive Director 105 West North College P.O. Box 512 Yellow Springs, OH 45387 (513) 767-2667 FAX (513) 767-1354 Women's Entrepreneurial Growth Organization (WEGO) Barbara Honthumb/Director 58 W. Center St. PO Box 544 Akron, OH 44309 (216) 535-9346 FAX (216) 535-4523 SBDC of Southeastern Ohio Marianne Vermeer, Director Mary Ann McClure, Project Director One President Street Athens, OH 45701 (614) 593-1797 FAX (614) 593-1795	Hamilton County Dev. Co. Inc. 1776 Mentor Avenue Cincinnati, OH 45212 Contact: David K. Main (513) 632-8292 Service Area: Southwestern Ohio including the city of Cincin- nati and the counties of Adams, Brown, Bugler, Clermont, Clinton, Highland, and Warren Columbus Countywide Dev. Corp. 941 Chatham Lane, Suite 207 Columbus, OH 43221 Contact: Mark Barbash (614) 645-6171 Service Area: Franklin County and the city of Columbus Women's Entrepreneurial Growth Organization of NE Ohio 58 West Center St., Suite 228 Akron, OH 44308 Contact: Barbara R. Honthumb (216) 535-4523 Service Area: Ashtabula, Cuya- hoga, Geaga, Lake, Lorain, Mah- oning, Medina, Portage, Stark, Summit, Trumbull, Wayne	

Oklahoma	Ms. Joyce Jones (D) Business Development Specialist Small Business Administration 200 NW 5th Street, Suite 670 Federal Building Oklahoma City, OK 73102 (405) 231-4494	N/A	Rural Enterprises, Inc. 422 Cessna St. Durant, OK 74701 Contact: Tom S. Smith (405) 924-5094 Service Area: Statewide Tulsa Economic Dev. Corp. 130 North Greenwood Ave., Suite G Tulsa, OK 74120 Contact: Frank F. McCrady III (918) 585-8332 Service Area: NE Oklahoma	Marketia Head Office of Women-Owned Business Assistance 6601 Broadway Ext. Oklahoma City, OK 73116 (405) 843-9770
Oregon	Ms. Inga McNeese (D) Business Development Specialist Small Business Administration 222 SW Columbia Av., Rm. 500 Portland, OR 97201-6605 (503) 326-5202 (503) 326-2808 FAX	N/A	Cascades West Financial Ser- vices, Inc. 408 SW Monroe St. Corvallis, OR 97333 Contact: Deborah L. Wright (503) 757-6854 Service Area: Benton, Clacka- mas, Hood River, Jefferson, Lane, Lincoln, Linn, Marion, Multnomah, Polk, Tillamook, Wasco, Washington, Yamhill	Clifford Freeman Office of Minority, Women and Emerging Small Business 155 Cottage St., NE Third Floor Salem, OR 97310 (503) 378-5651
Pennsylvania	Ms. Diane Heal (D) WBO Coordinator Small Business Administration 475 Allendale Square Road Suite 201 King of Prussia, PA 19406 (215) 962-3712 (215) 962-3795 FAX	Ms. Bridget M. Canedy, President National Association of Women Business Owners Pittsburgh 312 Boulevard of the Allies Pittsburgh, PA 15222 (412) 261-1235 To serve women business owners in Pittsburgh, PA	The Ben Franklin Technology Center of SE Pennsylvania 3624 Market St. Philadelphia, PA 19104-2615 Contact: Phillip A. Singerman (215) 382-0380 Service Area: Bucks, Chester, Delaware, Montgomery and Philadelphia counties	Lenore Cameron Dept. of Commerce Bureau of Women's Business Development 462 Forum Building Harrisburg, PA 17120 (717) 787-3339

State	SBA Representatives	Demonstration Projects	Microloan Program	State Offices
Pennsylvania, cont.	Ms. Giovanna Capace (D) Business Development Specialist Small Business Administration 475 Allendale Road Suite 201 King of Prussia, PA 19406 (215) 962-3818 Ms. Mary Merman District Counsel Small Business Administration 960 Penn Avenue, 5th Floor Pittsburgh, PA 15222 (412) 644-2785		The Washington County Council on Econ. Dev. 703 Courthouse Sq. Washington, PA 15301 Contact: Malcolm L. Morgan (412) 228-6816 Service Area: Southwestern PA York County Industrial Development Corp. One Market Way East York, PA 17401 Contact: David B. Carver (717) 846-8879 Service Area: York county.	
Rhode Island	Ms. Fran de Sousa (D) WBO Representative Small Business Administration 380 Westminister Mall Providence, RI 02903 (401) 528-4598 (410) 528-4539 FAX	N/A	Elmwood Neighborhood Housing Services, Inc. 9 Atlantic Avenue Providence, RI 02907 Contact: Irwin Becker (401) 461-4111 Service Area: Elmwood neighborhood of the city of Providence	Issac Wallace Department of Economic Development Office of Minority Assistance 7 Jackson Walkway Providence, RI 02903 (401) 277-2601
South Carolina	Ms. Kim Hite (D) Business Development Specialist Small Business Administration 1835 Assembly Street, Room 358 Columbia, SC 29202 (803) 253-3360 (803) 765-5962 FAX	N/A	Charleston Citywide Local Development Corporation 496 King Street Charleston, SC 29403 Contact: Sharon Brennan (803) 724-3796 Service Area: City of Charleston	Adriene Wright Office of Small and Minority Business Assistance 1205 Pendleton St. Room 441 Columbia, SC 29201 (803) 734-0657

South Carolina, cont.			Santee Lynches Regional Development Corp. 115 North Harvin St., 4th Floor Sumter, SC 29151-1837 Contact: James T. Darby, Jr. (803) 775-7381 Service Area: Clarendon, Lee, Kershaw and Sumter counties.	
South Dakota	Ms. Darlene Michael (D) Business Development Specialist Small Business Administration 110 S. Phillips Ave., Suite 200 Sioux Falls, SD 57102 (605) 330-4231 (605) 330-4215 FAX	N/A	Northeast South Dakota Energy Conservation Corporation 414 Third Avenue, East Sisseton, SD 57262 Contact: Arnold Petersen (605) 698-7654 Service Area: Beadle, Brown, Buffalo, Campbell, Clark, Codington, Day, Edmunds, Faulk, Grant, Hand, Hyde, Jerauld, Kingsbury, McPherson, Marshall, Miner, Potter, Roberts, Sanborn, Spink and Walworth counties.	Steve Withorn Director, Minority Business Office Governor's Office of Econ. Dev. 711 Wells Ave. Capital Lake Plaza Pierre, SD 57501 (605) 773-5032
Tennesee	Ms. Saundra Jackson (D) ADD/MSB Small Business Administration 50 Vantage Way, Suite 201 Nashville, TN 37228 (615) 736-7176 (615) 736-7232 FAX	N/A	N/A	Brenda Logan Dept. of Economic and Community Development Small Business Office 7th Floor 320 Sixth Ave. North Nashville, TN 37243-0405 (615) 741-2545

State	SBA Representatives	Demonstration Projects	Microloan Program	State Offices
Texas	Ms. Willianne Lewis (D) Executive Secretary for DD Small Business Administration 9301 SW Freeway, Suite 550 Houston, TX 77074 (713) 773-6528 (713) 773-6550 FAX	CWBE Austin Site Susan Spencer, Austin Site Coordinator Center for Women's Business Enterprise 2020 E. St. Elmo, Suite 130 Austin, TX 78744 (512) 462-9705 FAX (512) 462-9470	Southern Dallas Development Corporation 1501 Beaumont Street Dallas, TX 75215 Contact: Jim Reid (214) 428-7332 Service Area: Portions of the city of Dallas	Shawn Holt Certification Coordinator, Small Business Division Dept. of Commerce PO Box 12728 Austin, TX 78701 (512) 320-9549
	Ms. Diane Cheshier (D) ADD/Business Development Small Business Administration 4300 Amon Carter Blvd., Sta. 114 Fort Worth, TX 76155 (817) 885-6504 (817) 885-6516 FAX	CWBE Dallas Site Vacant Dallas Site Coordinator 2734 West Kingsley Rd, Suite 54 Garland, TX 75041 (214) 205-2791 or (214) 241-0675	Business Resource Center Incubator 4601 N. 19th St. Waco, TX 7670-8 Contact: Curtis Cleveland (817) 754-8898 Service Area: Bell, Bosque, Cory- ell, Falls, Hill and McLennan counties	
	Ms. Gracie Guillen (D) Business Development Specialist Small Business Administration 222 E. Van Buren St., Suite 500 Harlingan, TX 78550 (512) 427-8533 (512) 427-8537 FAX	Center for Women's Business Enterprise (CWBE) Linda Schneider, State Coordinator 1300 Main Street, Houston, TX 77002 (713) 650-3833 (voice mail) FAX: (713) 658-0105 (713) 578-7061	San Antonio Local Dev. Corp. 100 Military Plaza 4th Floor City Hall San Antonio, TX 78205 Contact: Robert Nance (210) 299-8192 Service Area: Atascosa, Bandera, Bexar, Comal, Friom, Gillespie, Guadalupe, Karnes, Kendall, Kerr, Medina and Wilson counties	
	Ms. Gwen Syers (D) Officer Services / SBA 10737 Gateway West, Suite 320 El Paso, TX 79902 (915) 540-5564	Southwest Resource Development Joyce Hipp Project Director 8700 Crownhill, Suite 700 San Antonio, TX 78209 (512) 828-9034 Marilyn Cooper, Site Director		
	Ms. Ruby Abarca (D) Business Development Technician Small Business Administration 1611 10th Street, Suite 200 Lubbock, TX 79401 (806) 743-7462			

Texas, *cont.*	Ms. Geraldine Cook (D) Contact Representative Small Business Administration 7400 Blanco Road, Suite 200 North Star Executive Center San Antonio, TX 78216 (512) 229-4535 VACANT (B) WBOR Small Business Administration 606 N. Caranchua Corpus Christi, TX 78476 (512) 888-3301		
Utah	Ms. Jean Fox (D) Business Development Specialist Small Business Administration Federal Building 125 South State Street Salt Lake City, UT 84138-1195 (801) 524-6831 (801) 524-4160 FAX	N/A Utah Technology Finance Corp. 185 South State St., Suite 208 Salt Lake City, UT 84111 Contact: Karl N. Snow (801) 364-4346 Service Area: Carbon, Emery, Grand, Iron, Juab, Milard, San Juan, Sanpete, Sevier, Tooele, Washington and parts of Utah and Weber counties	Kathy Ricci Utah Small Business Develop- ment Center 102 W. 500 South, Suite 315 Salt Lake City, UT 84101 (801) 581-7905
Vermont	Ms. Brenda Fortier (D) Loan Specialist Small Business Administration 87 State Street, Room 204 P.O. Box 605 Montpelier, VT 05602 (802) 828-4422 (802) 828-4485 FAX	N/A Northern Community Invest- ment Corporation 20 Main Street Saint Johnsbury, VT 05819 Contact: Robert B. Justis (802) 748-5101 Service Area: Counties of Caledonia, Essex and Orleans	Curt Carter Economic Development Dept. 109 State St. Montpelier, VT 06602 (802) 828-3221

State	SBA Representatives	Demonstration Projects	Microloan Program	State Offices
Vermont, cont.			Economic Development Council of No. Vermont, Inc 155 Lake St. St. Albans, VT 05478 (802) 524-4546 Service Area: Franklin, Grand Isle and Lamoille counties	
Virginia	Ms. Fannie Gargoudis (D) Business Development Technician Small Business Administration 400 North 8th St, Room 3015 P.O. Box 10126 Richmond, VA 23240 (804) 771-2765 ext. 112	N/A	N/A	Ann Parker Maust Women's Business Enterprise Program Virginia Small Business Dev. Ctr. Commonwealth of Virginia - Dept. of Commerce PO Box 798 1021 E. Cary St. Richmond, VA 23206-0798 (804) 371-8208
Washington	Ms. Gwen Elliott (R) Business Dev. Project Officer Small Business Administration 2615 4th Street, Room 440 Seattle, WA 98121-1233 (206) 553-8547 (206) 553-4155 FAX Ms. Connie Alvarado (D) Business Development Specialist Small Business Administration 915 2nd Avenue, Room 1792 Seattle, WA 98174-1088 (206) 220-6523 (206) 553-8635 FAX	N/A	Snohomish County Private Industry Council 917 134th St., SW Suite A-10 Everett, WA 98204 Contact: Emily Duncan (206) 743-9669 Service Area: Snohomish, Skagit, Yakima and Chelan counties and the city of Wenatchee	James Hedina Office of Minority and Women's Business Enterprises 406 S. Water, MS:FK-11 Olympia, WA 98504-4611 (206) 753-9693

Washington, cont.	Ms. Coralie Myers (D) Laon Officer Small Business Administration West 601 First Avenue 10th Floor East Spokane, WA 99204-0317 (509) 353-2815 (509) 353-2829 FAX	Tri-Cities Enterprise Association 2000 Logston Blvd. Richland, WA 99352 Contact: Dallas E. Breamer (509) 375-3268 Service Area: Benton and Franklin counties	
West Virginia	Ms. Sharon Weaver (D) Business Development Technician Small Business Administration 168 West Main Street P.O. Box 1608 Clarksburg, WV 26302 (304) 623-5631	N/A	Ohio Valley Industrial and Business Development Corp. 12th and Chapline St. Wheeling, WV 26003 Contact : Terry Burkhart (304) 232-7722 Service Area: Belmont, Marshall, Ohio and Wetzel counties.	Elizabeth Older Rural Business Dev. Specialist Governor's Office of Community and Industrial Dev. 1115 Virginia St. East Charleston, WV 25305 (304) 348-2960
Wisconsin	Ms. Rebecca Jorgensen (D) Business Development Specialist Small Business Administration 212 E. Washington Ave., Rm. 213 Madison, WI 53703 (608) 264-5516 (608) 264-5516 FAX Mr. John Lonsdale (B) Business Development Specialist Small Business Administration 310 West Wisconsin Avenue Milwaukee, WI 53202 (414) 297-3941 (414) 297-4267	Women's Business Initiative Corporation (WBIC) Lidia Paz-Beckett Project Director 1020 North Broadway Milwaukee, WI 53202 (414) 277-7004	Advocap, Inc. 19 West First Street P.O. Box 1108 Fond du Lac, WI 54936-1108 Contact: Richard Schlimm (414) 922-7760 Service Area: Counties of Fond du Lac and Winnebago Impact Seven, Inc. 100 Digital Drive Clear Lake, WI 54005 Contact: William Bay (715) 263-2532 Service Area: Statewide except- ing counties of Milwaukee, Dane, Brown and Waukesha	Mary Strickland Dept. of Development 123 W. Washington Ave. P.O. Box 7970 Madison, WI 53707 (608) 266-0593

State	SBA Representatives	Demonstration Projects	Microloan Program	State Offices
Wisconsin *continued*			Northwest Side Community Development Corp. 5174 North Hopkins Avenue Milwaukee, WI 53209 Contact: Howard Snyder (414) 462-5509 Service Area: Inner City Milwaukee Women's Business Initiative Corp. 1020 North Broadway, Suite G-9 Milwaukee, WI 53202 Contact: Lidia Paz-Beckett (414) 277-7004 Service Area: Counties of Kenosha, Milwaukee, Ozaukee, Racine, Walworth, Washington and Waukesha	
Wyoming	Ms. Kay Stucker (D) Business Dev. Specialist SBA 100 East B Street, Room 4001 P.O. Box 2839 Casper, WY 82602 (307) 261-5761 (307) 261-5499 FAX	N/A	N/A	Paula Horton Wyoming Commission for Women Herschler Building Second Floor—East Cheyenne, WY 82002 (307) 777-7349
Puerto Rico	Ms. Zulma Kinard (D) Business Dev. Specialist/SBA Carlos Chardon Avenue Hato Ray, PR 00918 (809) 766-5001 (809) 766-5309 FAX	N/A	Corporation for the Economic Dev. of the City of San Juan Avenue Munos Rivera, #1127 Rio Piedras, PR 00919-1791 Contact: Jesus M. Rivera Viera (809) 756-5080 Service Area: Specific communities in the city of San Juan	N/A

Virgin Islands	Mr. Lionel Baptiste (P) Business Industry Specialist Small Business Administration Federal Office Building, Rm 283 Veterans Drive St. Thomas, Virgin Islands 00801 (809) 774-8530 (809) 774-2312 Mr. Carl Christianson (P) Loan Specialist F&I Small Business Administration United Shopping Plaza, Room 7 4 C/D State Sion Farm Christiansted, St. Croix Virgin Islands, 00801 (809) 778-5380 (809) 778-1102 FAX	N/A	N/A	N/A

ADDITIONAL RESOURCES

National Association of Women Business Owners
1377 K St., NW
Suite 637
Washington, DC 20005

American Women's Economic Development Corporation
60 East 42nd St.
Room 405
New York, NY 10165

National Association for Female Executives
127 West 24th St.
New York, NY 10011

American Business Women's Association
9100 Ward Parkway
Box 8728
Kansas City, MO 64114

National Women's Economic Alliance
1440 New York Avenue, NW
Suite 300
Washington, DC 20005

Zonta International
557 W. Randolph
Chicago, IL 60606

For a directory of micro-enterprise programs, write to:

Self-Employment Learning Project
Aspen Institute
Publications Office
P.O. Box 222
Queenstown, MD 21658

You can also call them at (410) 820-5326,
Cost of the directory is $10.

Personal Financial
Statement Worksheets

Personal Balance Sheet

ASSETS
Liquid assets
Cash and checking accounts .... _____

Savings accounts .... _____

Money market funds .... _____

Life insurance cash values .... _____

United States savings bonds .... _____

Brokerage accounts .... _____

Other liquid assets .... _____

Total Liquid Assets .... _____

Investments
Common stocks .... _____

Mutual funds .... _____

Corporate and municipal bonds .... _____

Certificates of deposit .... _____

Business interests .... _____

Investments in real estate .... _____

Pension accounts .... _____

IRA and retirement plan accounts .... _____

Other investments .... _____

Total Investments .... _____

Personal Assets
Residence .... _____

Vacation home .... _____

Autos, boats, and rec. vehicles .... _____

Furs and jewelry .... _____

Collections, hobbies, etc. .... _____

Furniture and appliances .... _____

Other personal assets .... _____

Total Personal Assets .... _____

Total Assets .... _____

LIABILITIES AND NET WORTH
Current Liabilities
Charge accounts .... _____

Short-term loans .... _____

Total Current Liabilities .... _____

Long-term Liabilities
Mortgages on real estate .... _____

Bank loans .... _____

Other long-term liabilities .... _____

Total Long-term Liabilities .... _____

Total Liabilities .... _____

NET WORTH OR EQUITY .... _____
(Total Assets minus Total Liabilities)

Personal Income Statement

Savings
Short-term goals .... _____
Long-term goals .... _____

Housing
Rent/mortgage .... _____
Electricity .... _____
Fuel: Gas/oil .... _____
Water/garbage .... _____
Telephone .... _____
Snow removal/lawn care .... _____

Food
Home (groceries) .... _____
Lunches (school, work, out) .... _____
Beverages (coffee breaks) .... _____
Household supplies .... _____

Transportation
Car Payment .... _____
Gasoline .... _____
Parking .... _____
Repairs .... _____
Insurance .... _____
License plates .... _____
Bus pass .... _____

Clothing
Children .... _____
Self / Spouse .... _____
Cleaning/laundry .... _____

Medical
Doctor .... _____
Dentist .... _____
Medication/presecription .... _____
Insurance .... _____

Entertainment
Children .... _____
Self / Spouse .... _____
Dining out .... _____
Alcoholic beverages .... _____
Babysitting .... _____
Hobbies .... _____
Cable .... _____
Entertainment clubs .... _____

Subtotal .... _____

Subtotal (from page 1) .... _____

Education
    Tuition .... _____
    Books/newspapers/magazines .... _____

Personal
    Hair care .... _____
    Cigarettes .... _____
    Toiletries .... _____

Credit Payments
    Loans .... _____
    Charges .... _____

Miscellaneous
    Bank charges .... _____
    Taxes .... _____
    Life insurance .... _____
    Household insurance .... _____
    Household repair .... _____
    Alimony/child support .... _____
    Child care for work .... _____
    Pet care .... _____
    Donations/church .... _____
    Holidays/birthdays .... _____
    Allowances (children/personal) .... _____
    Vacations .... _____
    Other .... _____

Total Expenses .... _____

Income
    Salary and wages .... _____
    Interest and dividends .... _____
    Rental property income .... _____
    Income from business or profession .... _____
    Child support/alimony .... _____
    Other .... _____

Total Income .... _____

NET INCOME .... _____
(Total Income minus Total Expenses)

Credit Report

Name	Date of birth

Address

Telephone number	Years there

Former address

Years there	Marital status	Name of spouse

No. of deps. (inc. spouse)	Employer	Years there

Address

Phone	Kind of business	Position	Net income $/

Former employer and address	Years there

Spouse's employer and address

Net income $/	Other income sources—$/month

Account	Bank	Acct. No.	Balance
Checking			
Savings			

Auto owned (year and make)	Purchased from

Financed by	Balance owed $	Monthly

Rent or mortgage payment/mo. $	Paid to

Real estate owned in name of	Purchase price	Mtge bal.

Credit references and all debts owing—other than above
(Bank, loan or finance cos., credit unions, budget)

Name	Address	Orig. Amt.	Bal.	Mo. payment

Life insurance amount	Company

If co-maker for others, state where and for whom

Nearest relative or friend not living with you/relationship

Address

Business Financial Statement Worksheets

Sources and Uses of Cash

USES OF CASH

Pre-opening (or expanding)

Opening inventory .... _____

Capital equipment .... _____

Property .... _____

Renovations .... _____

Pre-opening marketing and promotions .... _____

Deposits .... _____

Other pre-opening expenses .... _____

Total .... _____

Operating

Working capital .... _____

Contingency funds .... _____

Total .... _____

Capital Equipment

(post-opening or expanding) .... _____

Total Uses of Cash .... _____

SOURCES OF CASH

Savings .... _____

Loans from relatives/friends

1. .... _____

2. .... _____

3. .... _____

Loan from bank .... _____

Other .... _____

Total Sources of Cash .... _____

Captial Equipment List

Office Equipment/Business Machines	Model	Purchase Date	Cost
_____			
_____			
_____			

Total .... _____

Store Fixtures	Model	Purchase Date	Cost
_____			
_____			
_____			

Total .... _____

Machinery Used to Make Product	Model	Purchase Date	Cost
_____			
_____			
_____			

Total .... _____

Vehicles	Model	Purchase Date	Cost
_____			
_____			
_____			

Total .... _____

Income Statement, 12-Month, Year 1

	JAN	FEB	MAR	APR	MAY
1. SALES					
2. Total Sales					
3. COST OF GOODS SOLD					
4. Materials					
5. Labor					
6. Other					
7. Total Cost of Goods Sold					
8. GROSS PROFIT					
(Sales – Cost of Goods Sold)					
9. OPERATING EXPENSES					
10. Salaries and Wages					
11. Payroll Taxes and Benefits					
12. Rent					
13. Utilities					
14. Advertising and Promotion					
15. Office Supplies					
16. Postage					
17. Telephone					
18. Professional Fees					
(Legal, Accounting, et al)					
19. Repairs and Maintenance					
20. Car/Travel					
21. Depreciation					
22. Others:					
23. TOTAL OPERATING EXPENSES					
24. OTHER EXPENSES					
25. Interest					
26. TOTAL EXPENSES					
27. PROFIT (LOSS) PRE-TAX					
28. TAXES					
29. NET PROFIT (LOSS)					
Explanation of Income Statement Projections					

Income Statement, 12-Month, Year 1

JUN	JUL	AUG	SEP	OCT	NOV	DEC	TOTAL

Income Statement Quarterly, Year 2

	1st Quarter	2nd Quarter	3rd Quarter	4th Quarter	TOTAL
1. SALES					
2. Total Sales					
3. COST OF GOODS SOLD					
4. Materials					
5. Labor					
6. Other					
7. Total Cost of Goods Sold					
8. GROSS PROFIT					
(Sales – Cost of Goods Sold)					
9. OPERATING EXPENSES					
10. Salaries and Wages					
11. Payroll Taxes and Benefits					
12. Rent					
13. Utilities					
14. Advertising and Promotion					
15. Office Supplies					
16. Postage					
17. Telephone					
18. Professional Fees					
(Legal, Accounting, et al)					
19. Repairs and Maintenance					
20. Car/Travel					
21. Depreciation					
22. Others:					
23. TOTAL OPERATING EXPENSES					
24. OTHER EXPENSES					
25. Interest					
26. TOTAL EXPENSES					
27. PROFIT (LOSS) PRE-TAX					
28. TAXES					
29. NET PROFIT (LOSS)					

Explanation of Income
Statement Projections

Income Statement Quarterly, Year 3

	1st Quarter	2nd Quarter	3rd Quarter	4th Quarter	**TOTAL**
1. SALES					
2. Total Sales					
3. COST OF GOODS SOLD					
4. Materials					
5. Labor					
6. Other					
7. Total Cost of Goods Sold					
8. GROSS PROFIT					
(Sales – Cost of Goods Sold)					
9. OPERATING EXPENSES					
10. Salaries and Wages					
11. Payroll Taxes and Benefits					
12. Rent					
13. Utilities					
14. Advertising and Promotion					
15. Office Supplies					
16. Postage					
17. Telephone					
18. Professional Fees					
(Legal, Accounting, et al)					
19. Repairs and Maintenance					
20. Car/Travel					
21. Depreciation					
22. Others:					
23. TOTAL OPERATING EXPENSES					
24. OTHER EXPENSES					
25. Interest					
26. TOTAL EXPENSES					
27. PROFIT (LOSS) PRE-TAX					
28. TAXES					
29. NET PROFIT (LOSS)					

Explanation of Income
Statement Projections

Cash Flow Statement—12-Month, Year 1

		Pre-Opening	JAN	FEB	MAR
CASH INFLOW	**1. CASH FROM SALES**				
	2.　　　Cash Sales				
	3.　　Cash from Receivables				
	4.　　　　**TOTAL**				
	5. CASH FROM FUNDING SOURCES				
	6.　　　Cash from Owners				
	7.　　　Cash from Loans				
	8.　　Cash from Other Investors				
	9.　　　　**TOTAL**				
	10. TOTAL CASH INFLOW				
CASH OUTFLOW	**11. PRE-OPENING (OR EXPANSION) EXPENSES**				
	12.　　　Opening Inventory				
	13.　　　Capital Equipment				
	14.　　　Property				
	15.　　　Renovations				
	16.　Marketing & Promotions				
	17.　　　Deposits				
	18.　　　Other				
	19.　　　**TOTAL**				
	20. Cost of Goods Sold				
	21. OPERATING EXPENSES				
	22.　　　Owner's Salary				
	23.　Other Salaries & Wages				
	24.　Payroll Taxes & Benefits				
	25.　　　Rent				
	26.　　　Utilities				
	27.　Advertising and Promotion				
	28.　　　Office Supplies				
	29.　　　Postage				
	30.　　　Telephone				
	31.　　Professional Fees				
	32.　　　Insurance				
	33.　Repairs and Maintenance				
	34.　　　Car/Travel				
	35.				
	36.				
	37.				
	38.				
	39.　　　**TOTAL**				
	40. LOANS				
	41.　　　Interest Payment				
	42.　　Principal Payment				
	43. OTHER CAPITAL EQUIPMENT				
	44. TAXES				
	45. TOTAL CASH OUTFLOW				
CASH FLOW NEEDS	**46. NET CASH FLOW**				
	47. CUMULATIVE CASH FLOW				
CHECKING ACCOUNT RECONCIL-IATION	**48. OPENING BALANCE**				
	49.　　　+ Cash Inflow				
	50.　　　- Cash Outflow				
	51. CLOSING BALANCE				

Cash Flow Statement—12-Month, Year 1

APR	MAY	JUN	JUL	AUG	SEP	OCT	NOV	DEC	TOTAL

Cash Flow Statement—Quarterly, Year 2

		1st Qtr	2nd Qtr	3rd Qtr	4th Qtr	TOTAL
CASH INFLOW	1. CASH FROM SALES					
	2. Cash Sales					
	3. Cash from Receivables					
	4. TOTAL					
	5. CASH FROM FUNDING SOURCES					
	6. Cash from Owners					
	7. Cash from Loans					
	8. Cash from Other Investors					
	9. TOTAL					
	10. TOTAL CASH INFLOW					
CASH OUTFLOW	11. PRE-OPENING (or expansion) EXPENSES					
	12. Opening Inventory					
	13. Capital Equipment					
	14. Property					
	15. Renovations					
	16. Marketing & Promotions					
	17. Deposits					
	18. Other					
	19. TOTAL					
	20. COST OF GOODS SOLD					
	21. OPERATING EXPENSES					
	22. Owner's Salary					
	23. Other Salaries & Wages					
	24. Payroll Taxes & Benefits					
	25. Rent					
	26. Utilities					
	27. Advertising and Promotion					
	28. Office Supplies					
	29. Postage					
	30. Telephone					
	31. Professional Fees					
	32. Insurance					
	33. Repairs and Maintenance					
	34. Car/Travel					
	35.					
	36.					
	37.					
	38.					
	39. TOTAL					
	40. LOANS					
	41. Interest Payment					
	42. Principal Payment					
	43. OTHER CAPITAL EQUIPMENT					
	44. TAXES					
	45. TOTAL CASH OUTFLOW					
CASH FLOW NEEDS	46. NET CASH FLOW					
	47. CUMULATIVE CASH FLOW					
CHECKING ACCOUNT RECONCILIATION	48. OPENING BALANCE					
	49. + Cash Inflow					
	50. - Cash Outflow					
	51. CLOSING BALANCE					

Cash Flow Statement—Quarterly, Year 3

		1st Qtr	2nd Qtr	3rd Qtr	4th Qtr	TOTAL
CASH INFLOW	1. **CASH FROM SALES**					
	2. Cash Sales					
	3. Cash from Receivables					
	4. **TOTAL**					
	5. **CASH FROM FUNDING SOURCES**					
	6. Cash from Owners					
	7. Cash from Loans					
	8. Cash from Other Investors					
	9. **TOTAL**					
	10. **TOTAL CASH INFLOW**					
CASH OUTFLOW	11. **PRE-OPENING (or expansion) EXPENSES**					
	12. Opening Inventory					
	13. Capital Equipment					
	14. Property					
	15. Renovations					
	16. Marketing & Promotions					
	17. Deposits					
	18. Other					
	19. **TOTAL**					
	20. COST OF GOODS SOLD					
	21. **OPERATING EXPENSES**					
	22. Owner's Salary					
	23. Other Salaries & Wages					
	24. Payroll Taxes & Benefits					
	25. Rent					
	26. Utilities					
	27. Advertising and Promotion					
	28. Office Supplies					
	29. Postage					
	30. Telephone					
	31. Professional Fees					
	32. Insurance					
	33. Repairs and Maintenance					
	34. Car/Travel					
	35.					
	36.					
	37.					
	38.					
	39. **TOTAL**					
	40. **LOANS**					
	41. Interest Payment					
	42. Principal Payment					
	43. **OTHER CAPITAL EQUIPMENT**					
	44. **TAXES**					
	45. **TOTAL CASH OUTFLOW**					
CASH FLOW NEEDS	46. **NET CASH FLOW**					
	47. **CUMULATIVE CASH FLOW**					
CHECKING ACCOUNT RECONCIL-IATION	48. **OPENING BALANCE**					
	49. + Cash Inflow					
	50. - Cash Outflow					
	51. **CLOSING BALANCE**					

Sample Balance Sheet

ASSETS (What your business owns)	LIABILITIES (What your business owes) Plus NET WORTH (the value of your business)
Current Assets	**Current Liabilities**
Cash _____	Accounts Payable _____
Accounts Receivable _____	Accrued Expenses _____
Inventory _____	Taxes Payable _____
Prepaid Expenses _____	Short-Term Notes Payable _____
TOTAL _____	TOTAL _____
Fixed Assets	**Long-Term Liabilities**
Fixtures and Equipment _____	Mortgages _____
Minus Accumulated Depreciation _____	Long-Term Notes Payable _____
	TOTAL _____
TOTAL _____	
	TOTAL LIABILITIES _____
	NET WORTH _____ (what your business owes you)
TOTAL ASSETS _____	TOTAL LIABILITIES PLUS NET WORTH _____

Budget Deviation Analysis Income Statement, Monthly

From the Income Statement for year-to-date	A. Actual for Month	B. Budget for Month	C. Deviation (B-A)	D. % Deviation (C/B x 100)
1. SALES				
2. Total Sales				
3. COST OF GOODS SOLD				
4. Materials				
5. Labor				
6. Other				
7. Total Cost of Goods Sold				
8. GROSS PROFIT (Sales – Cost of Goods Sold)				
9. OPERATING EXPENSES				
10. Salaries and Wages				
11. Payroll Taxes and Benefits				
12. Rent				
13. Utilities				
14. Advertising and Promotion				
15. Office Supplies				
16. Postage				
17. Telephone				
18. Professional Fees (Legal, Accounting, et al)				
19. Repairs and Maintenance				
20. Car/Travel				
21. Depreciation				
22. Others:				
23. TOTAL OPERATING EXPENSES				
24. OTHER EXPENSES				
25. Interest				
26. TOTAL EXPENSES				
27. PROFIT (LOSS) PRE-TAX				
28. TAXES				
29. NET PROFIT (LOSS)				

Budget Deviation Analysis Income Statement, Year-to-Date

From the Income Statement for year-to-date	A. Actual for Year-to-Date	B. Budget for Year-to-Date	C. Deviation (B-A)	D. % Deviation (C/B x 100)
1. SALES				
2. Total Sales				
3. COST OF GOODS SOLD				
4. Materials				
5. Labor				
6. Other				
7. Total Cost of Goods Sold				
8. GROSS PROFIT (Sales – Cost of Goods Sold)				
9. OPERATING EXPENSES				
10. Salaries and Wages				
11. Payroll Taxes and Benefits				
12. Rent				
13. Utilities				
14. Advertising and Promotion				
15. Office Supplies				
16. Postage				
17. Telephone				
18. Professional Fees (Legal, Accounting, et al)				
19. Repairs and Maintenance				
20. Car/Travel				
21. Depreciation				
22. Others:				
23. TOTAL OPERATING EXPENSES				
24. OTHER EXPENSES				
25. Interest				
26. TOTAL EXPENSES				
27. PROFIT (LOSS) PRE-TAX				
28. TAXES				
29. NET PROFIT (LOSS)				

Budget Deviation Analysis Cash Flow, Monthly

From the Income Statement for year-to-date	A. Actual for Month	B. Budget for Month	C. Deviation (B-A)	D. % Deviation (C/B x 100)
1. CASH FROM SALES				
2. Cash Sales				
3. Cash from Receivables				
4. TOTAL				
5. CASH FROM FUNDING SOURCES				
6. Cash from Owners				
7. Cash from Loans				
8. Cash from Other Investors				
9. TOTAL				
10. TOTAL CASH INFLOW (9 + 4)				
11. PRE-OPENING (or expansion) EXPENSES				
12. Opening Inventory				
13. Capital Equipment				
14. Property				
15. Renovations				
16. Marketing & Promotions				
17. Deposits				
18. Other				
19. TOTAL				
20. COST OF GOODS SOLD				
21. OPERATING EXPENSES				
22. Owner's Salary				
23. Other Salaries & Wages				
24. Payroll Taxes & Benefits				
25. Rent				
26. Utilities				
27. Advertising and Promotion				
28. Office Supplies				
29. Postage				
30. Telephone				
31. Professional Fees				
32. Insurance				
33. Repairs and Maintenance				
34. Car/Travel				
35. Others				
36.				
37.				
38.				
39. TOTAL				
40. LOANS				
41. Interest Payment				
42. Principal Payment				
43. OTHER CAPITAL EQUIPMENT				
44. TAXES				
45. TOTAL CASH OUTFLOW				
46. NET CASH FLOW				
47. CUMULATIVE CASH FLOW				
48. OPENING BALANCE				
49. + Cash Inflow				
50. - Cash Outflow				
51. CLOSING BALANCE				

BDA—Cash Flow, Year-to-Date

From the Income Statement for year-to-date	A. Actual for Year-to-Date	B. Budget for Year-to-Date	C. Deviation (B-A)	D. % Deviation (C/B x 100)
1. CASH FROM SALES				
2. Cash Sales				
3. Cash from Receivables				
4. TOTAL				
5. CASH FROM FUNDING SOURCES				
6. Cash from Owners				
7. Cash from Loans				
8. Cash from Other Investors				
9. TOTAL				
10. TOTAL CASH INFLOW (9 + 4)				
11. PRE-OPENING (or expansion) EXPENSES				
12. Opening Inventory				
13. Capital Equipment				
14. Property				
15. Renovations				
16. Marketing & Promotions				
17. Deposits				
18. Other				
19. TOTAL				
20. COST OF GOODS SOLD				
21. OPERATING EXPENSES				
22. Owner's Salary				
23. Other Salaries & Wages				
24. Payroll Taxes & Benefits				
25. Rent				
26. Utilities				
27. Advertising and Promotion				
28. Office Supplies				
29. Postage				
30. Telephone				
31. Professional Fees				
32. Insurance				
33. Repairs and Maintenance				
34. Car/Travel				
35. Others				
36.				
37.				
38.				
39. TOTAL				
40. LOANS				
41. Interest Payment				
42. Principal Payment				
43. OTHER CAPITAL EQUIPMENT				
44. TAXES				
45. TOTAL CASH OUTFLOW				
46. NET CASH FLOW				
47. CUMULATIVE CASH FLOW				
48. OPENING BALANCE				
49. + Cash Inflow				
50. Cash Outflow				
51. CLOSING BALANCE				

Sales Forecast—Year 1

Total Annual Sales (Units): _____

Based on the following assumptions:
1. _____
2. _____
3. _____
4. _____
5. _____

Total Annual Sales ($): _____

Based on the following assumptions:
1. _____
2. _____
3. _____
4. _____
5. _____

	JAN	FEB	MAR	1st QTR TOTAL	APR	MAY	JUN	2nd QTR TOTAL
# of Units								
Sales $								

	JUL	AUG	SEP	3rd QTR TOTAL	OCT	NOV	DEC	4th QTR TOTAL
# of Units								
Sales $								

Assumptions for distributing sales by month:

1. _____
2. _____
3. _____
4. _____
5. _____

_____

Sales Forecasts—Years 2 & 3

Total Annual Sales (Units) Year 2:

Based on the following assumptions:

1. _____

2. _____

3. _____

4. _____

5. _____

	1st Quarter	2nd Quarter	3rd Quarter	4th Quarter	TOTAL
# of Units					
Sales $					

Total Annual Sales (Units) Year 3:

Based on the following assumptions:

1. _____

2. _____

3. _____

4. _____

5. _____

	1st Quarter	2nd Quarter	3rd Quarter	4th Quarter	TOTAL
# of Units					
Sales $					

Legal Forms of Business

One of the decisions you have to make about your business is which legal structure is best for you. There are four basic forms of business: sole proprietorship, partnership, corporation and cooperative.

There are four main issues to consider as you make your decision:

- Control: Who gets to make the decisions that affect the business?

- Taxes: How are taxes assessed, who is responsible for paying them and how much must be paid?

- Liability: Who is liable (i.e., responsible) if the company loses money or, even worse, goes bankrupt?

- Complexity: How difficult and expensive is it to set up the business?

No one form is ideal in all four of these areas—each form has its advantages and disadvantages, and you must consider the trade-offs as you decide which form of business is right for you. You may want to consult with your attorney and/or business advisors as you make your choice.

While you must choose one form to get started, you can change to a different one as your business grows and changes. This is not a decision to be taken lightly, but it's reassuring to know your business structure is not cast in concrete for the life of your business.

SOLE PROPRIETORSHIP

A sole proprietorship is a business organization in which one individual owns the business. This is by far the easiest, least expensive and least complicated way to start and run a business, and about 90% of all American small businesses fit in this category. Here is how this business form stacks up on the four key issues.

Control: As a sole proprietor, you will have complete control over all the decisions made for your business. This gives you the greatest freedom of action to run your business the way you want to.

Taxes: You are personally taxed on total business income whether or not you draw it out for personal use. In some ways, you get more income tax benefits than if you were in a traditional nine-to-five job because you can often write off

321

some of your day-to-day expenses. However, you are liable for the 15 % self-employment tax.

Liability: You are completely liable for all business debts. If the business loses money and can't repay its debts, your home and possessions are at stake. If a customer sues you and wins, your personal property could be sold for repayment. Of course, some of this risk can be mitigated with an appropriate insurance policy.

Complexity: Sole proprietorships are very easy to start. While the laws vary from state to state, you often need to do no more than register your firm's name with the state (if you use a fictitious name) and obtain a business license. For some businesses, you don't even need to do this much; you just decide to get started and you're in business. The one requirement is to include your business on Schedule C of the tax forms when you file your income taxes. For this reason, sole proprietorships are often referred to as "Schedule C Businesses."

PARTNERSHIPS

A partnership is a business organization in which two or more people own the business. Here is how this business form stacks up on the four key issues.

Control: The partners share control and management of the business. This allows you to divide the business responsibilities between two or more people, plus you have ready access to the talents and expertise of more than one person. The downside is the conflict that can result when two or more people try to make decisions for one business. Also, it is difficult to take quick, decisive actions when you have to get the OK of more than one person.

Taxes: Like sole proprietors, partners show their business income on their personal tax returns. Occasionally income and expense items can be apportioned among the partners in a way that gives each of them better tax results. Each partner must also pay her portion of the 15 percent self-employment tax.

Liability: All partners are liable for the obligations (including all debts) of the partnership. In addition, since each partner is an "agent" of the partnership, each can make binding contracts for it or incur debts or other obligations. In other words, you can be liable for the acts of your partners. As with sole proprietorships, some of this risk can be minimized with an appropriate insurance policy.

Complexity: From a regulation standpoint, partnerships are very easy to set up. Just register your firm's name with the state and obtain a license if you need one for your type of business. However, *you should never set up a partnership without a written, signed agreement documenting the terms of the association.* This agreement should include: Duties and responsibilities of each partner, the capital contribution of each partner, whether the partners may make any additional contributions, the participation of each partner in profits and losses, and how you will liquidate if the partnership is dissolved. It may take you a while to put this agreement together to everyone's satisfaction and you may be eager to get started before you have the details ironed out, but you are putting yourself, your business and your relationship with your partner at great risk if you don't develop this agreement ahead of time.

One more note: What I have described above is called a "general partnership." There are also limited partnerships in which the limited partner is only liable up to the amount of money she or he contributes to the business and has no say in the day-to-day management of the business. This business structure is used as a way of raising capital to run the business.

CORPORATION

A corporation is a legal entity which is separate and distinct from its owners. It can sue and be sued, it can incur debt and tax liabilities, and it has a continuous life of its own, i.e., it is not dissolved when a partner leaves or when the owner decides to discontinue the business. A corporation is owned by the stockholders who purchase little "chunks" of the business called stock. Here is how this business form stacks up on the four key issues.

Control: Corporate decisions are made by a voting process. As a general rule, one share of stock is worth one vote. Therefore, corporations are controlled by whoever has more than 50% of the voting stock. In some cases, no single person owns 51% of the voting stock, but two or more people together do, and they can form a coalition which makes the decisions for the business.

Realistically it is impractical to make day-to-day decisions for the business in this manner. Typically the stockholders elect a Board of Directors to set policy for the corporation, and the Board elects the officers to manage the daily business operations.

For most small corporations, the person with the original business idea has the majority of the stock, is on the Board of Directors and is the president of the company. In some cases, that person is also the vice president, secretary and treasurer. As owner, if you do not retain the majority of the stock and if the business has short-term problems, it is not unheard of for you to be voted out of your company.

Taxes: There are two types of corporations, C-Corps and S-Corps. In a C-Corp, the corporation files its own tax returns and all corporate income is taxed at the corporate tax rate (which is different from the individual tax rate). As president of the corporation, you are a company employee, and you are personally taxed on whatever income you take home as salary. In addition, if the company declares dividends as a way of distributing profit back to the owners, anyone receiving dividends (including you) is personally taxed on that money. If this sounds like double taxation, it is.

In an S-Corp, there is no separate corporate income tax, thus eliminating the burden of double taxation. Instead the stockholders pay taxes on the corporate income, even if it is not distributed to them in the form of salary or dividends. In addition, stockholders can deduct any net operating loss sustained by the corporation on their individual tax returns, thus minimizing their personal tax burden. There are some additional accounting costs involved in setting up an S-Corp (over a sole proprietorship), but there are generally some tax and liability benefits.

In addition, for both types of corporations there are some fringe benefits of setting up a corporation. Things like group insurance, worker's compensation and tax-free reimbursement of medical expenses can be set up as deductible expenses of the business and written off on the corporate income taxes.

Liability: One of the biggest benefits of incorporation is that it shields you from personal liability and loss for business debts and obligations. The corporation is liable, but your home and belongings are relatively safe.

Complexity: Corporations are expensive to form than sole proprietorships or partnerships, and there are also a few additional legal formalities. Most people hire an attorney to set up their corporatoin (fees typically range from $250 to $1,000), but you can buy a book and incorporate yourself. The primary formality is that you must hold an annual meeting every year and maintain a record of the minutes. For many small businesses, this annual meeting (including writing up the minutes) takes all of a half hour meeting with an attorney.

COOPERATIVE

Cooperatives are unusual business structures and are not often described in business literature. I describe them here because they can be an excellent form of business for very small, labor-intensive businesses in which the owners do not have a lot of money to invest and/or are ideologically committed to running a democratically controlled business.

A cooperative is a business structure, usually a corporation, in which the employees own and manage the business. The characteristics of cooperatives include: democratic control of the business in which each worker has one vote; all members have the right to work in the cooperative; and return of profits to owner-members is based on investment of labor rather than of capital (i.e., profits are allocated based on how much time you put into the business rather than how much money you invest in the business).

Most cooperatives are small businesses (fewer than ten employees) in which the workers desire to own part of the business and be part of a democratically run organization. Many cooperatives are formed when the original business owner wants to sell the business and the employees elect to buy it. Here is how this business form stacks up on the four key issues.

Control: Corporate decisions are made by a voting process in which each employee has one vote, and major decisions are often made by consensus (i.e., no group action is taken if at least one member maintains strong opposition to the decision). While this can be a very time-consuming and cumbersome process, it generally assures that decisions have the full support of all the employees and are rapidly and carefully implemented.

As with other partnerships, it is absolutely necessary that an agreement be written and signed by all parties designating how the group process will work, what each person's responsibilities are, how members can enter and leave the group, and so on.

Taxes: In a cooperative, employee-owners pay personal income taxes on profits which are distributed to them. (Typically they vote on how much of the profit to pay out and how much to retain in the business.) The cooperative itself pays corporate taxes *after* the profits are distributed. Thus cooperatives avoid the double taxation incurred by a corporation.

Liability: If the cooperative is incorporated, it bears the liability for the debts of the business, and the owners are removed from this liability. If the cooperative is formed as a partnership, the owner-employees are liable for the business obligations.

Complexity: From a regulatory perspective, a cooperative can be as simple or as difficult to set up and run as the business form it's patterned after. If it is a partnership, it's easy. If it is a corporation, it's expensive and complex.

Regardless of the basic business structure, all cooperatives require a very detailed, very complex owner-employee agreement which spells out voting requirements, working relationships, restrictions and control, and so on. This agreement must be completely accepted and adhered to by everyone involved in order for the cooperative to work. It is not a document to be taken lightly as it will guide the activities, successes and failures of your business. If you elect to use the cooperative structure for your business, I strongly recommend you get support from organizations that have done this in the past.

Federal Enforcement Agencies for Regulation of Savings Institutions

All creditors are subject to the Equal Credit Opportunity Act and Regulation B. The following is a list of the federal agencies that enforce the ECOA and Regulation B for particular classes of financial institutions. Any questions concerning a particular financial institution should be directed to its enforcement agency.

State Member Banks of the Federal Reserve System
Division of Consumer and Community Affairs
Board of Governors of the Federal Reserve Board
20th and Constitution Ave., NW
Washington, DC 20551
(202) 452-3000

Non-Member Federally Insured Banks
Office of Consumer Programs
Federal Deposit Insurance Corporation
550 Seventeenth Street, NW
Washington, DC 20429
(800) 934-3342
(202) 898-3536

National Banks
Consumer Examinations Division
Office of the Comptroller of the Currency
Washington, DC 20219
(202) 874-4428

Federal Savings and Loans
Office of Thrift Supervision
1700 G Street, NW
Washington, DC 20552
(202) 906-6000

Federal Credit Unions
National Credit Union Administration
1776 G Street, NW
Washington, DC 20456
(202) 682-9600

FINANCE COMPANIES AND OTHER CREDITORS NOT LISTED ABOVE:

Office of Credit Practices
Bureau of Consumer Protection
Federal Trade Commission
Washington, DC 20580
(202) 326-3224

Index